Equestrian Art:
The Collected Later Works

by
Master Nuno Oliveira

Copyright 2023

Title:
Equestrian Art: The Collected Later Works

Author: Master Nuno Oliveira
ISBN: 9781948717526
Copyright © 2023 Xenophon Press LLC

Hardback Collector's Color Edition ISBN: 9781948717335
Copyright © 2022 Xenophon Press LLC

All rights reserved. No part of this book may be reproduced, stored in a retrieval system, or transmitted in any form or by any means, electronic, mechanical, photocopying, recording, or otherwise, without the prior written permission of the publisher, except
as provided by United States of America copyright law.

Published by Xenophon Press LLC
10237 Rogers Drive
Nassawadox Va 23413 USA
XenophonPress@gmail.com
1-757-442-1060

Translations by Desirée du Pisanie, Léa Forge, Pureza Oliveira, Susan Cromarty Oliveira
Edited by Catherine Laurenty, Geneviève Hulin, Stephanie Millham, Richard Williams

Design and layout by Robert Ashbaugh Digital Design and Imaging. Tucson, AZ

Original edition:
Die Kunst des Reitens. Gesammelte Schriften.
Copyright © Georg Olms AG Publishers, Hildesheim/Germany 2016
ISBN 9783487085586
www.olms.de

Front Cover image: Invencível, preparing the pirouette, at the manège of Mr. Haverland, Belgium 1974. *Photo by Francine Halkin.*
Back Cover image: Patience and affection... understanding how to use such valuable tools is a testament to a rider's common sense.

Publisher's Introduction

This project has been the vision of Xenophon Press for over eleven years. Ever since we published the first book in the series authored by the students of Master Nuno Oliveira: *30 Years with Master Nuno Oliveira* by Michel Henriquet, we noticed the scarcity of copies of Nuno Oliveira's original works. Nuno Oliveira was truly unique and a worldwide living treasure to the equestrian arts. His wisdom, passion, dedication to the art, and enthusiasm for teaching inspired countless horsemen and horsewomen to become good, and even great. They, in turn, are spreading correct knowledge of horsemanship around the globe. Nuno Oliveira lives on through the work of his students and their students. And now for the first time in the English language, we have collected all of his later works into one volume so that his words can be absorbed by today's equestrians and future generations of riders.

A full list of other titles by followers of Nuno Oliveira's teaching is available in the Xenophon Press Library at the back of this book. Also included in the Library are many of the works that Master Oliveira refers to throughout this book. We encourage you to study them further. The concept of the Xenophon Press Library is to build a worthwhile collection of written works where each contributes to the knowledge base of its readers. With this particular work published, we have achieved a major cornerstone in the Library.

On a personal note, I did not ride with Nuno Oliveira, but I have ridden with and become friends with a great many of his students who went on to become great teachers, trainers, riders, and some, authors. Each of these disciples shows loving care for the well-being of the horses they come in contact with. In particular, I want to thank author, Stephanie Millham for her invaluable editorial help. Her familiarity with Master Oliveira's teaching enabled us to ensure the accuracy of the translation and her assistance in selecting the photographic material enriches this historic collection. In reading and editing this manuscript, and all of the other works in our library, I feel steeped in classical equestrian culture. It has been a huge gift to be in close contact with these works and, Nuno Oliveira's life's writings represent incredible documentation of method and insight gained over a lifetime. Knowledge is shared with love for the horse and care for the rider; this comes through on every page. We are pleased to announce the publication of the companion volume to this text: *Equestrian Art: The Early Writings (1951-1956)* by Master Nuno Oliveira.

Read, re-read, practice, repeat, and enjoy your horsemanship new with a fresh insight from the Master.

Richard F. Williams
Editor-in-Chief
Xenophon Press

Acknowledgements

First, my many thanks go to Danielle Merzbach, who, in the name of Georg Olms AG publishing house, accepted my original proposal to undertake the translation of my father's most important writings into English. Through the years, she has been unwaveringly supportive and patient with me.

In her effort to be as faithful and accurate as possible to the original, my thanks go to Desirée du Pisanie, who spent countless patient hours with me translating the *Classical Principles* manuscript, which I preferred to take up again, despite the existence of other translations.

I owe thanks to Catherine Laurenty who carefully revised the *Classical Principles* translation and assisted greatly in the technical interpretation of particular points.

Horses and Their Riders was kept in its original translation by Susan Cromarty Oliveira.

Léa Forge was the translator of *From an Old Écuyer to Young Riders* and *Notes on the Teaching of Nuno Oliveira* (compiled by Jeanne Boisseau[1]); I am very grateful not only for her work but also her understanding of my continuous revisions.

I would also like to thank our publisher Richard Williams of Xenophon Press who patiently waited for this work and worked cooperatively with Olms to realize the English edition in print in all of its versions both color and black and white. Xenophon added editing and important, seamless world-wide distribution making this volume available to readers around the globe.

My many big thanks to the generous help of my friend Geneviève Hulin, an English teacher and also a rider, who so kindly revised and corrected the English syntax in the books translated by Léa Forge and myself (with the exception of *Classical Principles*).

And finally, I wish to also mention the invaluable work of Stephanie Millham and thank her for combing through the entire manuscript and making many judicious corrections.

Pureza Oliveira

---

[1] 1979, Crépin-Leblond editions: Notes collected by Jeanne Boisseau. Set of sentences and short texts taken by some students during different lessons through the years. The book, *Notes sur l'enseignement*, is also included in the *Oeuvres complètes* published by Editions Belin. - Translator's note.

Summary

Publisher's Introduction..3

Acknowledgements..4

Foreword by Stephanie Grant Millham..6

Book 1 Classical Principles of the Art of Training Horses.......................9

Book 2 Horses and Their Riders..57

Book 3a Notes on the Teaching of Nuno Oliveira..................................81

Book 3b Notes on Elementary Equitation...115

Book 4 From an Old *Écuyer* to Young Riders.......................................127

Book 5 Reminiscences of a Portuguese Rider.......................................167

Appendix: Conference on *Descente de Main*...214

Foreword

Nuno Oliveira: The Twentieth Century's Great Master

In most of the world's fine arts, every generation produces its own icons who amass a huge following, though often posthumously. Few such luminaries go on to define a century. Only great masters achieve such stature, and their works are passed down as the arbiters of something grand, something pure, noble and timeless, the intellectual and artistic giants of their age.

In the world of classical dressage, a living art that seems fleeting, as the artist's canvas is a sentient being that rarely outlives its master, Nuno Oliveira is renowned as such an icon. It is with a sense of honor and responsibility I write this some forty-five years after meeting the man from Portugal who would become my own master, knowing this is destined to become the seminal work on classical equitation.

Though this may seem hyperbolic, it is not. Few riders have been so revered and so controversial, all for promoting a type of equitation held up as the ideal, yet seemingly impractical today when many riders, trainers and judges seem to give mere lip service to the concept of lightness rather than its actual application. Therein is where Oliveira shone.

He is almost universally acknowledged as a genius. Through his synthesis of what was best in the work of earlier masters he brought classical equitation to new heights of artistic expression that inspired beginners and connoisseurs alike. While his artistry may have seemed puzzling and unattainable, the answers are in his very words. Deceptively simple, they unlock the secrets to what he was able to achieve, transforming even mediocre horses into living works of art. But while the technique of what he practiced is all there in his writings, it is truly his heart and soul which shine through and give that added dimension to his artistry which has touched and moved so many.

Far from being an unreachable ideal, the methods of the master unfold logically and simply. Each small book is a classic. Together they form a library, the alpha and omega of thoughtful, compassionate training. Riders at any level can pick up his books and find the answer to the riding dilemma of the day. The more one advances, the more one discovers with each rereading. This goes on for a lifetime. There is a depth that only becomes truly apparent as the reader gains more experience, leading to new feelings once only imagined. As one develops, so does a deeper appreciation for Oliveira's mastery.

We are now fortunate to have access to the books long out of print in English in this important edition, which promises to inspire a new generation seeking a more enlightened form of equitation. Although many of those closest to his teachings have now passed, some have left works and students of their own who carry the unmistakable Oliveira stamp. His reach in France was vast, from the work of his great friend Michel Henriquet to his influence at the famed Cadre Noir. The great Portuguese School of Equestrian Art owes its existence to his Portuguese students, as do a few less publicized schools throughout the world.

I have often remarked that I know of no other trainer who produced so many Grand Prix riders and trainers. Nuno Oliveira may be unique in this regard. While many of his dedicated students chose not to compete, some did and became known on the international scene. There is an anecdote about an Olympic medalist who, when asked what to do in the case of a horse that had difficulty with piaffe, replied: "Put him on a train to Nuno." Though humorous, this represents the esteem and respect he garnered in the highest echelons.

As we grow farther distant from the days he knew, it becomes incumbent on those who remember him to keep his core message of lightness and kindness alive so that future generations will have access to the light that was Nuno Oliveira. Here is where this book is so important, perhaps the most pivotal work penned by a modern master, one who straddled the old classical world and the new era of many methods and contradictions. In the vast confusion today's multiplicity of advice can bring, Nuno Oliveira is a sound and immensely valuable landing point and a springboard to equestrian art. His suggestions are a treasure trove and will bring a new dimension to your horsemanship.

The spiritual component to his work, though deeply personal, was not lost on his admirers. "It is important to love horses," he once told a group of trainers questioning him on technique. This love for his horses was a strong thread weaving a tapestry of the most profound moments of equestrian brilliance for delighted onlookers, as well as those quiet, almost meditative moments he worked alone, with only the sound of his chosen operatic music accompanying the footfalls of his equine companion. To observe such a moment was a priceless, unforgettable lesson in itself.

Nuno Oliveira was the benchmark of our times, and he came at a watershed moment in equestrian history. As his artistry has become legendary, so too I predict the influence of this important work will be far-reaching and unique.

For those of you reading Oliveira for the first time, I envy you. Read this book with an open mind and an open heart. Let the images of the master and his horses fill your mind's eye. Read it and be inspired to do better every day for your horses. Let Oliveira's wisdom and pursuit of equestrian art be your inspiration, and you too may claim his life's work as one of the most important mentors to your own horsemanship. For all those with such abiding respect, the master still lives.

Stephanie Grant Millham
Rixeyville, Virginia

Book 1
Classical Principles of the Art of Training Horses

The French-born Thoroughbred, Talar, in piaffe in *descente de main* (release of the hand). *Oliveira Archives*.

*"I may lack the strength to arrive where I wish to arrive,
but I know perfectly well what I want."*
- Extract from a letter of Giuseppe Verdi to Arrivabene in 1874

Contents

Chapter 1: View of dressage today..11

Chapter 2: About the shoulder-in...14

Chapter 3: About half-pass..18

Chapter 4: About halt, rein back, half pirouette at walk.........................23

Chapter 5: Cadence and Extensions...25

Chapter 6: Canter, departure to canter...28

Chapter 7: Flying Changes..32

Chapter 8: The Pirouette..35

Chapter 9: Piaffe..37

Chapter 10: Passage..40

Chapter 11: A rider's main endeavor, to always keep his horse correct............42

Chapter 12: Work in hand...44

Chapter 13: About the lightness in the action of the rider's legs...........49

Chapter 14: *Descente de Main et de Jambes* (Lowering of hand and legs).........51

Chapter 15: The *Écuyer* as Teacher..52

In Closing..55

Chapter 1:
View of dressage today

One often tends to speak of different schools of riding: the French school, the German school, Swedish school, et cetera. It is understood that there are different types of horses, and one should be more attentive to certain details with one type of horse, and more attentive to different details with another type of horse. However, nowadays in Europe, there is a tendency to use a type of horse that is more or less similar everywhere. The reign of the English Thoroughbred and Anglo-Arab is somewhat outdated in the current dressage competitions.

The Germans, through their character, their spirit of organization and discipline, ended up using strong horses with good backs, with really correct and big movements and above all, the right temperament for dressage competitions; horses more stable and less emotional, unlike the Thoroughbreds and Anglo-Arabs that were fashionable in France in the 20s, 30s, 40s, and even 50s and 60s. While not saying that one method, let us say the German method, is superior, it has to be recognized that dressage is popular in Germany, where there are around 45 juniors with the capacity to compete in the Prix St. Georges.

Of course, all this riding in the German tradition, marked by its discipline and severity, made more noticeable by its successes, is at the front of the equestrian scene. There was a time when it happened that at the highest level one saw performances during which one could notice the execution of *descentes de main*. One could notice the recording of this at the World Championships in Lausanne, with Reiner Klimke. Unfortunately, these are fleeting moments and do not seem to be part of a methodology.

What is surprising nowadays, when you see the great show jumpers like [Paul] Schockemöhle, [Nelson] Pessoa, and [Raimondo] d'Inzeo, you see how they need true collection for their horses to be able to turn on their haunches and get over the mighty jumps: their horses are light, with very soft contact on the reins.

Without the horse being truly light, exercises such as the pirouette, passage and piaffe, not to mention the passage-piaffe transitions, are not really correct or brilliant. One should look closer at history in order to return to our days and to understand a little bit of the foundation of the equestrian art and its development.

Spain was once powerful and conquered a great part of the world, thanks to their horses and their mobility. When the riders came from the north of Europe, riding on their big, heavy horses, with heavy armor, they were easily conquered by the Spanish horsemen because of the lighter and more agile Iberian horses, who were much more capable of lateral attacks and could be turned in all directions. Thanks to this, people wanted to give other types of horses in Europe the same maneuverability as

Invencível, 1970, high levade (pesade) with the lightest contact.
Courtesy of Pedro Villalva.

Invencível, levade, 1974. The levade is a strengthening exercise to prepare the school jumps. *Photo by Francine Halkin.*

[Notice the improvement in strength from the pesade four years earlier. - Editor's note.]

the horses of Spain and founded the riding academy of Naples in Italy. [Federico] Grisone [*The Rules of Riding*, Grisone/Tobey Xenophon Press 2023] and [Cesar] Fiaschi were the great masters of this academy, and this was the start in the Renaissance of the *Haute Équitation*.

The Frenchman Antoine de Pluvinel [*The Maneige Royal*, de Pluvinel/Nelson 2010 Xenophon Press] went to this academy and brought the teachings of the Italian masters back to France. He was the first Frenchman with the title of *Écuyer* and was the teacher of King Louis XIII. With Louis XIV, the rise of the most famous equestrian academy in the world, the school of Versailles, took place. The horses that the Masters used most readily were Spanish. One can see, on a famous engraving of that time, Monsieur de Nestier, *Écuyer*

Monsieur de Nestier *Écuyer Ordinaire de la Grande Écurie du Roy*, 1753, Jean Daullé, French, 1703–1763, Etching and engraving on paper after Philibert Benoît Delarue, (French, 1718–1780).

Cavalcadour du Roy, riding El Florido, who has on his right hindquarter a brand RE, meaning Reyno d'Espagna.

From Versailles, we proceed to the academy of Tuileries, where Monsieur

François Robichon de la Guérinière wrote his book *École de Cavalerie* [Xenophon Press 2015] which today is acknowledged as the Equestrian Bible by all schools (Viennese school, German school) and where he defined the shoulder-in and spoke of the *descente de main* as soon as the horse bends his haunches. The Germans and all other countries in Europe were following this teaching.

Enter the English Thoroughbred and you see that riding starts to change and so do the horses. In France, people start to breed, with the use of these Thoroughbreds, a lighter horse, like the Anglo-Arab.

François Baucher wisely adapted the teachings of the old masters from Versailles and could make use of this new type of horse by creating new movements, for example flying changes every stride, to substitute the airs used by the old masters that were less suitable for longer and less round horses. His riding is based on lightness, which is a crucial requirement for excitable and sensitive horses such as the English Thoroughbred or Anglo-Arab types.

The Germans continued consistently to ride their horses used in the cavalry for riding as well as driving.

A German master and contemporary of Baucher, Gustav Steinbrecht [*Gymnasium of the Horse*, Xenophon Press 1994], viewed by many present-day German riders as one of the great classical masters, attempts at the end of each chapter in his book to criticize Baucher and his method. However, any real expert can see that the two masters say, in their different ways, more or less the same thing. Depending on which side of the Rhine River you were, it was a question of nationalism, a consequence of the time.

The Germans later introduced English blood in their horses, but they stayed more powerful, more solid than the French horses, more suitable for the kind of dressage that is practiced today.

Now, this kind of horse has turned into the prototype of the dressage horse of today. This was thanks to the sheer numbers of the German riders and their organization. This does not mean that horses of different types and breeds cannot do competition. What I want to explain is that only through tactful equitation, practiced with light horses, can one obtain truly sound results and aspire to reach Grand Prix. The finer and more sensitive a horse is, the finer his training should be.

If you want to reach the top you must watch the big riders that all work with the same target in mind (the submission and perfect relaxation of the whole body of the horse).

If one wants to remain within the limits of mediocrity one can win the local tests but the horse will never be happy, will be worn out prematurely, and nothing will ever be good or genuine.

Nevertheless, despite all of the currently fashionable tendencies, Dressage claims to come from La Guérinière who was French and, amongst other fundamental things, wrote in his *École de Cavalerie* [Xenophon Press 2015]: *"La grâce est un si bel ornement de l'Art."*[2] Without grace, one cannot practice refined equitation, and without finesse, one cannot aspire to art. Despite this, harshness and force is the prerogative of the mediocre, who never want to be true.

Chapter 2: About the shoulder-in

"Shoulder-in is the first and the last lesson to give to a horse."
- François Robichon de la Guérinière

Shoulder-in is an exercise that is fundamental for suppleness. It is important that it is executed and asked for correctly. If not, it is as we often see a movement that is twisted sideways, that instead of suppling the horse sends the weight to the outside shoulder. One should say, shoulders-in and not shoulder-in, because both shoulders are to the inside and it goes without saying that one is more than the other.

For a young horse that does not know shoulder-in here is how you start:

In a corner of the school start by doing a correct circle at the walk.

What is a circle?

Most times the riders are not attentive enough to do a geometrical circle. A circle is a line of even curvature and to ask for it, it is shaped by the rider putting his outside shoulder more forwards while paying attention to keep a contact on the outside rein and not the pulling back of the inside rein. This circle has to be made on half of the short side and should include the corner and the beginning of the long side.

As soon as we have obtained a well-ridden circle in an even rhythm, when we reach the corner (the end of the short side) we will move both hands,

Vizir, a son of Euclides, left shoulder-in at Quinta do Brejo. *Photo: Private collection.*

but without pulling, to the outside. The hands that have very light contact on the reins move to the outside and return to the inside, at the same time that the inside leg touches at every step (the leg touches lightly and then releases). The inside rein must act in the direction of the outside shoulder of the rider. When the horse makes one or two small steps of a hint of shoulder-in, we release the reins and praise him. Then we start again until little by little the horse can do more steps.

Ask little every time and praise a lot.

The horse progressively does more steps on the long side and this is the moment that the rider should take care that the weight of the horse remains on the inside hind leg and not on the outside shoulder. For this reason, it is very good from time to time to make a little circle the size of the horse's body, using the outside rein more, and the moment when the horse arrives at the wall, start once again. The inside leg must act near the girth and the outside leg a little more to the back. The body of the rider must remain in the center of the horse and not on the inside, which will prematurely overload the inside hind leg. A very important point is to feel the degree of yield of the horse in the exercise and depending on the degree of the yield, give a release of the aids.

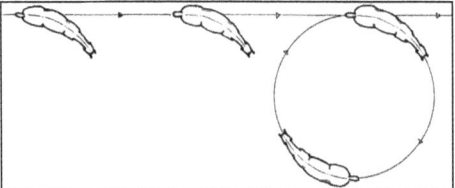

It is good to ride shoulder-in along the wall of the arena and then return to ride a small circle. *Courtesy of Colonel Fernando de Abreu.*

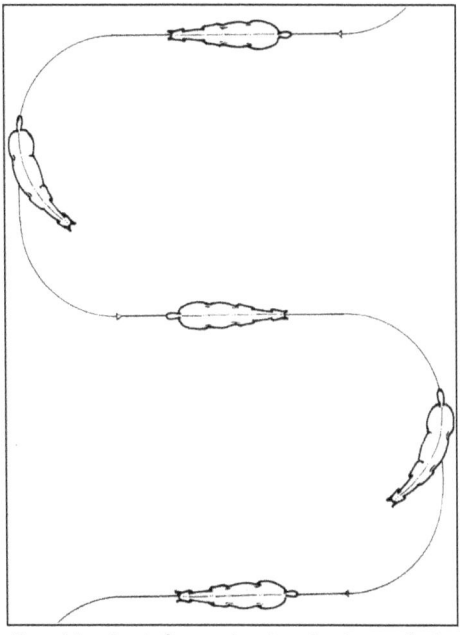

Shoulder-in left at the beginning of the long wall of the arena, change hand through the middle of the arena using the outside rein, then ask for shoulder-in to the right. *Courtesy of Colonel Fernando de Abreu.*

Later on, when the young horse already knows the shoulder-in a little, it is necessary to pay attention to the beginning of the exercise, that it is the

In lateral bending it is necessary for the horse to remain balanced in the vertical axis and not shift any weight to the inside or outside. *Oliveira Archives.*

use of the outside rein that first puts the shoulder of the horse to the inside and afterwards the inside rein, which should not go further than a vertical line through the middle of the forelegs, gives the bend.

An exercise that is also very good to do with a young horse is, for example, to ask for left shoulder-in at the beginning of the long side and when the horse gives some good steps in balance, cut straight across the school with the use of the outside rein, and upon arriving at the other side do a shoulder-in to the right. When the horse does some good steps again, cross the school once more with the horse really going straight, to the other side, then do the left shoulder-in again.

In the work at walk always pay attention that the horse does the shoulder-in in a slow, not running, walk. The stride should not be too big because, due to the mechanics of walk (which is a four-beat movement that starts with the forelegs and in which the diagonals are not simultaneous), if the stride is too big, the back will hollow.

Later on, when the horse performs the shoulder-in well at the walk on the long sides, start to ask for it in a large circle, or half a circle, always using the outside rein that enables to put the horse straight on the center line again.

Now and again, when working the shoulder-in at walk, reward by releasing the reins at times and at other times straighten the horse at a trot. The angle of a good shoulder-in should be more or less forty-five degrees. All the action of the inside rein should have a repercussion on the outside rein. The contact on the reins should be the same and the soft tension (resulting from having done the exercise correctly) should be the same as well.

When the horse does this exercise well at the walk, without difficulty, it is the moment to start it at the trot. Before asking the shoulder-in at the trot, it is a very important point that the rider is sure of the rhythm in the trot, that the horse can maintain that rhythm so that when he asks the shoulder-in, the horse is already in the rhythm in which he is going to do the shoulder-in.

At the walk, it is also very good to ask the horse to do a halt (completely still) in the shoulder-in position and after a few seconds to continue in the same shoulder-in, or change the horse around into the other shoulder-in and continue on that side. The hindquarters must always remain near the wall.

When the horse can do all of this without difficulty, one can ask for the following exercise first at the walk and then at the trot:

Start the shoulder-in on the long side, continue in shoulder-in on the short side (when passing the corner, support the shoulder slightly and activate the hindquarters more to arrive on the short side in the same angle) and

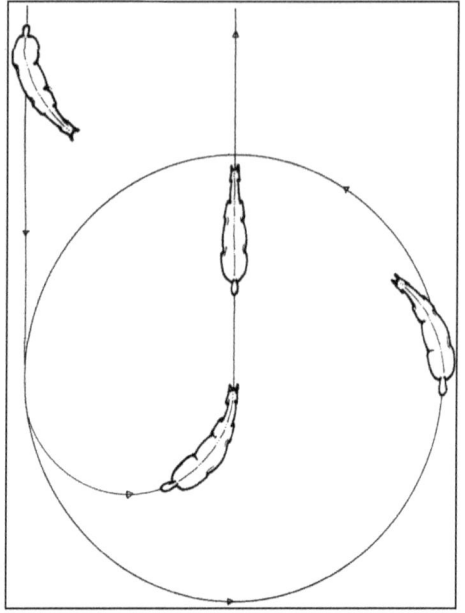

Ask for shoulder-in on the circle, always with the outside rein, and then guide the horse back to the center line well-straightened.

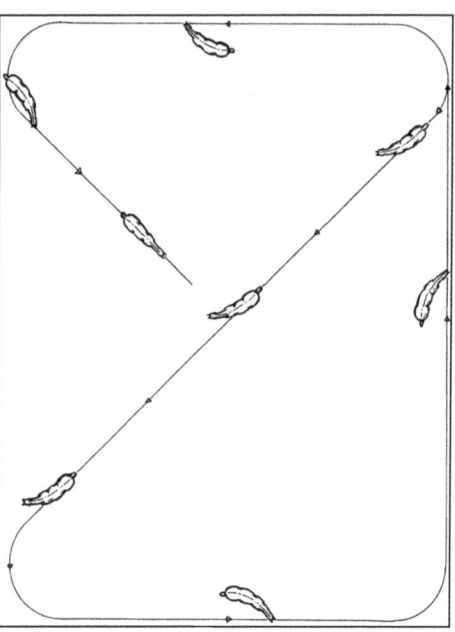

Courtesy of Colonel Fernando de Abreu.
Shoulder-in along the wall. Through the corners hold back the shoulders and activate the haunches, change rein in shoulder-in across the diagonal, when you reach the opposite wall continue in counter-shoulder-in [shoulder-out].
Courtesy of Colonel Fernando de Abreu.

then change the rein across the diagonal in the same shoulder-in, arrive at the wall and continue in counter shoulder-in; continue along the short side in counter shoulder-in, when you arrive at the beginning of the long side, cross the diagonal in shoulder-in, with the horse always bent in the same direction, and as you gradually release the reins on this diagonal, always maintaining the bend in the same direction, the horse will also stretch his body and put his neck down softly, and little by little lengthen his stride and progressively change from the bend to a straight position of his neck.

I want to finish by saying that when you go straight in a riding school, every corner is a little moment of shoulder-in and one cannot forget that the school has four corners.

Chapter 3: About half-pass

When the horse already understands the shoulder-in well and he knows how to maintain, through the training of this exercise, a certain degree of roundness, he is then able to start to learn the half-pass. Through shoulder-in he also learned (if his rider took care to keep his legs relaxed) to move away from one leg and to be positioned by the other leg.

This is how we will act in order to begin the half-pass: Start shoulder-in in the middle of the long side of the arena, continue until the middle of the short side, in shoulder-in, when you arrive at the middle of the short side, turn onto the center line in the position of this shoulder-in; in this position advance a little and without changing the position of the inside aids, put your outside leg back a little, slightly, and push with small touches. When the horse goes sideways two or three steps in the position of half-pass, release the reins and praise. Ask for just a few steps at a time, praise and pat the horse a lot.

A very important detail about the turn onto the center line: when you proceed in the position of shoulder-in, at the moment when you change to half-pass, the inside leg very softly pushes the haunches to the outside; the outside rein by an action toward the inside sends the shoulders in the direction of the half-pass. All of this must be done at the moment that you advance [to the half-pass]. The bend of the horse is already in the direction of the half-pass thus making the sideways movement of half-pass much easier. Little by little, ask for more steps [of half-pass].

João Oliveira, riding Caruso, Half-pass left on the diagonal. *Oliveira Archives.*

Pay attention that when the horse yields, the outside leg also yields and the inside leg becomes, at this moment, the main leg. Acting in the girth area, the inside leg has a spasmodic effect that causes in the horse the tendency to turn his head to that side. Therefore, this leg is indispensable in maintaining the bend, in the conservation of the angle of the half-pass and the forward movement. The inside rein must be slightly lighter than the outside rein and as the horse does more steps of the half-pass, he will later arrive at the side of the arena more supported by the outside rein and by the inside leg. This is how to avoid horses from doing half-pass with their heads tilted.

Every time the horse wants to overtake his shoulders with his hips, the action of the outside rein, in the direction of the movement, will fetch the shoulders back in that direction. Every time the haunches of the horse do not engage enough, it is the opening of the outside rein towards the opposite side of the movement that helps. The inside rein remains quiet and together with the leg on the same side in the girth area, this rein helps to maintain the bend.

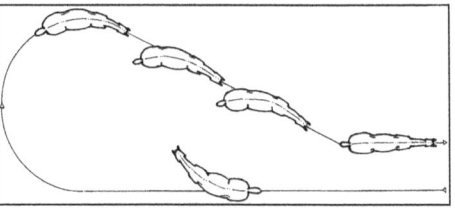

Begin in shoulder-in along the wall, pass through the corner in shoulder-in, in the middle of the short side turn down the center line in the position of that shoulder-in. In the same bend and flexion, without altering the position of the inside aids, apply the outside leg lightly and push the horse sideways in half-pass for two or three steps. *Courtesy of Colonel Fernando de Abreu.*

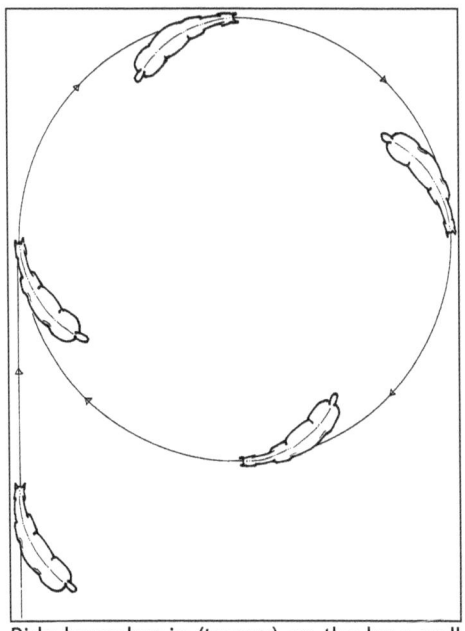

Ride haunches-in (travers) on the long wall and then continue the haunches-in on a large circle. *Courtesy of Colonel Fernando de Abreu.*

When the horse is capable of doing half-pass from the center line to the long sides easily, while conserving the same angle and bend, then start to do half-pass from the beginning of the long side to the center line and then continue on the center line, with the horse very straight. In the corner, you secure the bend and you advance two or three steps with the same bend, trying to observe the same precautions as on the center line, just as in the previous part.

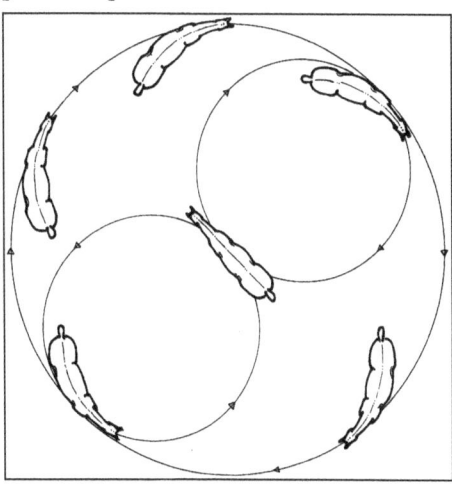

From haunches-in on the large circle, form a figure eight inside the large circle. Ride haunches-in on the small circle and at the center of the large circle, straighten the horse at the point of changing rein and proceed in haunches-in in the new direction on the second circle of the figure eight. *Courtesy of Colonel Fernando de Abreu.*

As was done for shoulder-in, after two or three correct steps of half-pass on the center line, with the horse very straight, sometimes release the reins and at other times begin to trot.

When the horse knows these two ways of doing the half-pass well, begin to bend him in the corner and, with his head towards the wall, ask for some steps of half-pass. One calls this movement travers. When the horse starts to do the travers with ease, now and then ask for a halt in the position of this exercise. The horse should stay calm on this angle (towards the wall) and, remaining at this angle, begin to walk again. Afterwards, do the same exercise on the other rein. Pay attention to always keep the shoulder near the wall.

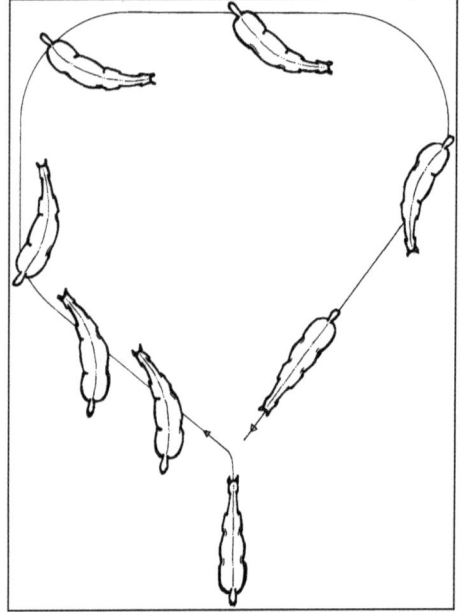

Ride half-pass up to the wall; shortly before reaching the wall, hold back the shoulders and let the haunches move out towards the wall, move on in the same bend and flexion in haunches-out, renvers on the long wall, through the corner, and after the second corner, allow the horse to stretch out on the diagonal. *Courtesy of Colonel Fernando de Abreu.*

When all these ways of doing half-pass are easy, start to ask travers from the long side to travers to the short side and afterwards ask for a big circle in haunches-in. Take care in this exercise that the haunches do not come too much to the inside, overtaking the shoulders. Little by little, make the radius of the circle smaller and after doing it on one side, do one or two steps going straight and ask for it on the other side.

Another exercise to do afterwards is, on the center line, half-pass towards the wall and when you arrive at the wall, hold back (support) the shoulders and make the croup go towards the wall. In old times, this would be called *affermir l'appuyer*. The horse starts, with the croup near the wall, to do half-pass on the long side. The bend stays the same and the exercise takes the classical name of renvers. When the horse does this easily on the long side, continue with the same exercise on the short side. When you pass the corner, keep the shoulders back and make the croup advance more so that the horse stays in the same angle. The first time one asks for this exercise, upon arrival at the other long side, ask for the horse to stretch across the diagonal; because the horse has accumulated impulsion, he can give a good stretch.

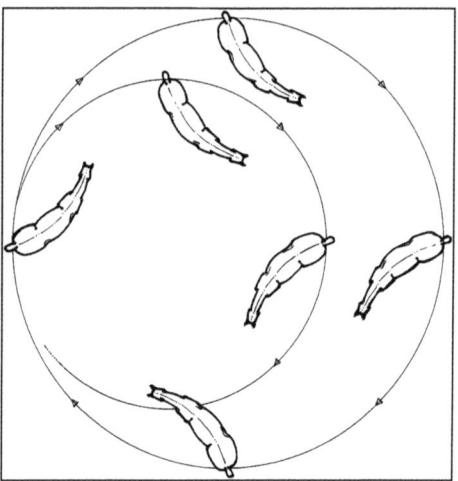

Ask for haunches-out on the circle and gradually decrease the size of the circle. *Courtesy of Colonel Fernando de Abreu.*

Later on ask a complete circle of half-pass around the shoulders; reduce the radius of the circle progressively.

Once the horse knows the different ways of half-pass, one asks for the "change of hand." Half-pass from the beginning of the long side to the center line; when you arrive on the center line, return to the long side in the opposite half-pass. At the moment when you will change to the opposite half-pass, it is the inside leg that will act first. For two reasons: acting while sliding towards the girth, it helps the new bend, but before arriving at the girth, it puts the haunches slightly in the opposite direction (or, to say in a better way, it prevents the haunches from going too much in the new direction) which causes the horse to take the angle of the next side, similar to the angle of the first side.

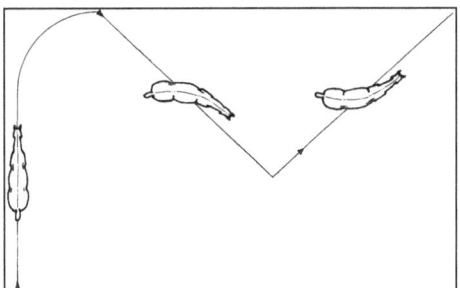

At the beginning of the long wall, begin half-pass on a diagonal to the center line; then change bend and ride half-pass in the other direction back to the same wall. *Courtesy of Colonel Fernando de Abreu.*

When the horse knows how to do this first counter-change of hand well, one will ask him, on the center line, some steps in the direction of the wall from where he came, double the number of steps in the other direction and finally go towards the center line with the same number of steps as the first half-pass, then continue really straight on the center line.

The rider must, in all these exercises of half-pass, pay attention that his body is neither on the inside nor on the outside. The weight of the rider must stay in the middle of the horse. To avoid the body from staying on the outside, slightly put more weight on the inside seat bone. The shoulders of the rider should, when turning across the school, in shoulder-in, half-pass and also first in the circle, remain parallel to the shoulders of the horse. The shoulders can, for a moment, move in the opposite direction to stop the horse from rushing or to give a half halt in the position of the exercise.

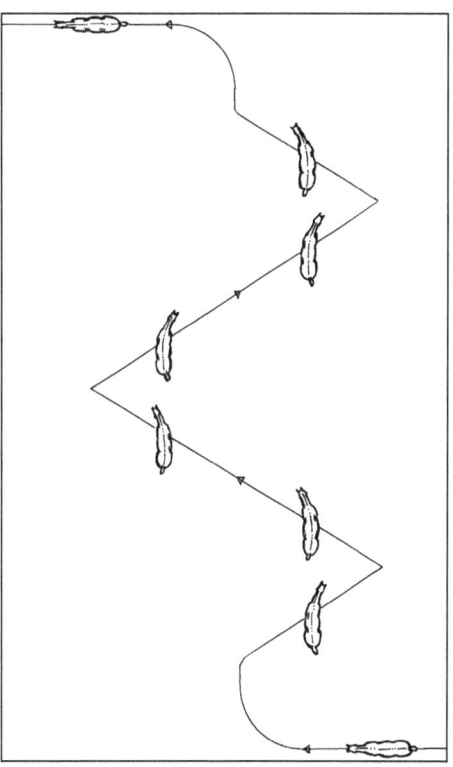

From the center line ride half-pass for a number of steps towards the wall, change direction and bend then ride half-pass in the opposite direction for twice as many steps, change direction and bend again and half-pass in the other direction for the same number of steps as the second half-pass, change direction and bend again and half-pass back to the center line; follow straight on the center line and track in the opposite direction from the original direction. *Courtesy of Colonel Fernando de Abreu.*

As for shoulder-in, after the horse knows how to do the exercises in the walk, you can ask for them in the trot. The rhythm of the trot must be established in the circle and the serpentines and when one asks for the trot half-passes, I think one should start them from a shoulder-in, always in the same rhythm. Later on, to make the spine more supple, the transitions of shoulder-in on the circle to haunches-in and vice versa are excellent exercises.

While performing all the lateral suppling movements, such as shoulder-in and half-pass, one should often, during a lesson, take the center line and go really straight. The horse, through the lateral suppling, always performed in a controlled rhythm, starts to balance himself and becomes rounder and lighter.

In the next chapter, I will speak about halt, rein back and about the half pirouette at the walk; after that, the horse has surpassed a phase and instead of the rhythm, I will speak of the cadence.

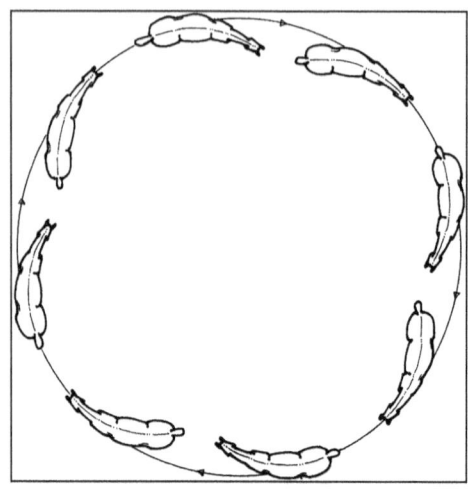

Changing from shoulder-in to haunches-in and back to shoulder-in on a circle in the center of the arena promotes suppleness of the spine.
Courtesy of Colonel Fernando de Abreu.

Chapter 4: About halt, rein back, half pirouette at walk

Until now, the halt has only been a halt, where one was only concerned about the calm immobility of the horse, more for the mental relaxation. It was not a square halt. As one asked for a halt several times from a position of shoulder-in and from a position of travers, the horse started to halt more round. Now, after he has acquired a certain roundness and has become lighter in the exercises of shoulder-in and in the half-pass he is ready to start to halt square and not before.

Invencível, bred by Dr. José Menezes, in Pirouette at the walk. *Photo by Francine Halkin.*

Now is exactly the time for some half-pass in the direction of the long side where, a few steps after arriving at the wall, the rider can ask for the square halt.

How does one ask for this?

The rider, sitting deep in the saddle, with the reins at the right length (not too short and not too long), with the elbows next to the body, will halt the horse by pushing with the buttocks and the back and by lowering the waist. Through this movement, the arms will follow the upper body and not make isolated movements. In this way, the body of the rider, positioned like a balancing point of a scale, puts the weight of the horse on the hindquarters and the horse halts square and not on the shoulders.

When the horse halts, do not forget to release the fingers, without losing the soft contact, so that the head of the horse does not go behind the vertical. Now send the horse forward with the same soft contact, really straight, the legs of the rider framing the horse's body. Later on, the horse will learn the *effet d'ensemble* with the spur at the halt, which will make the horse submissive through this powerful action.

When the horse can halt square, on his haunches, and recommence in the same light walk or trot, without changing the position of the head and neck, it is the moment in which to start asking for the rein back.

How does one proceed?

With the horse at a light and square halt, the legs of the rider move back a little and touch for a tiny fraction of a second, this touch immediately followed by the upper body, the waist and the reins and when the horse does the first suggestion of rein back, caress the horse, let the reins go and allow the horse to move forward freely for the first few times.

Later on, when the horse knows and executes some steps of rein back easily, he must advance (with the use of the buttocks, upper body and the legs) straight, with the same rhythm and gait that he had before the halt. If the horse moves back crookedly, straighten him by putting the shoulders in the same line as the hips using the opposite rein. If the horse moves away from the wall, make a small circle and come back to the same place as many times as necessary until he stays straight on the wall.

Later on, from the walk to the halt, rein back two or three steps, and recommence in the same gait. First, do this next to the wall, later on across the diagonals, on the center line, and later still, on a circle, keeping the line of the bend equal. Even later on, do the same at the trot.

Something very important in these exercises at the walk and the trot is that rein back should be easy, but slow, and the readiness for beginning the forward movement must be immediate.

When the horse easily does the preceding exercises, on one of the long sides of the arena ask a half pirouette after a light half halt.

If the rider's hand is not hard and does not block the forehand of the horse, the buttocks and the legs aid each step alternately, the horse can execute the half pirouette without blocking the hindquarters.

With this, another stage in the training of the horse has finished.

Slowly but surely the horse rounds himself, his weight is less on his shoulders and more on the hindquarters—of course, still very lightly—and, thanks to the succession of all these movements, and the concern of the rider to keep a light contact through the continuous opening and closing of the fingers, the horse will start to hold his expression and collect himself.

This is the start of cadence.

Chapter 5:
Cadence and Extensions

What is cadence? Cadence is rhythm with energy, gestures that are more sustained, with more vigor and muscular tone which are acquired by the preceding exercises. The horse stays more round, more receptive, ready to change from one movement to another, from one exercise to another, and starts to collect himself.

Studying deeply the rhythm of the natural gaits of each horse, when he is calm and free, also shows you the precise notion of the rhythm you should work in, in the previous preparations, so that you arrive at the appropriate cadence for every horse. Some are slightly slower than others and to have the horse in a really good collection, you need to work him in his own cadence. One must know what the cadence is of a collected walk, what the cadence is of the collected trot and of the longer trot (which is nowadays inappropriately called the working trot).

It is precisely by maintaining the appropriate cadence of every movement that you keep the lightness, with the weight on the haunches, and that one arrives at collection.

In the end, it is when the horse remains well-rounded, with a flexible back that rounds up and does not hollow, that we can really start the medium trot and the extended trot.

Before, needless to say, we have allowed with freer reins the horse that is naturally well-balanced, and only

Ousado in extended trot. *Oliveira Archives.*

this one, the one that does not rush when we do rising trot, to make this lengthening in a conditioned freedom, almost as a relaxation.

The horse that naturally puts his weight on his shoulders, and rushes in the lengthening, is a horse that should not be worked in extended trot.

We have created, through the preceding exercises, a balance where we can foresee the lengthened trot as well as the piaffe. In the first case, with impulsion, the horse pushes with the hindquarters that are pliable and he covers ground in balance. In the second case, also later on with impulsion, with active hindquarters and balance, the horse expends his energy trotting on the spot. In both cases, the impulsion is a result of the succession of the suppling exercises that puts the weight on the hindquarters and makes them active and flexible in the joints, especially in the fetlock that lowers.

Zabrod, increasing cadence in collection, beginning the piaffe. *Courtesy of Lucy Jackson.*

Now, true extension of the trot is only the lengthening that results from collection, where the horse stays lightly on the hindquarters.

Lengthening of the trot with flashy gestures of the shoulders, where the back stays hollow and the hindquarters stay at the back and often spread apart, has nothing to do with Equestrian Art.

A very important point in the lengthening, when the horse needs it, is to know how to increase the impulsion in the collected trot, with the use of both the hand and leg aids, in order to then make use of this increased impulsion at the moment the extension starts.

At the moment one takes the diagonal it is necessary to pay attention that the weight does not fall on the inside shoulder, the reason for that being that we must remember that going through the corners is each time a little bit of shoulder-in.

In the lengthening obtained after having acquired basic skills of collection and cadence, the horses have their backs supple and the riders can sit without bouncing in the saddle as one sees many times in the lengthenings asked for prematurely. Above all, one should not want to go beyond what each horse is capable of giving, within his own maximum extension. One must always, during an extension, think of returning to collected trot, with the haunches lowered and in lightness, not on the shoulders with rigid steps.

If the horse rushes a little on the diagonal, one can correct it through either coming back to the exercises of suppleness in the collected trot, for example, shoulder-in on the circle, or halting and reining back quite a few steps on the same diagonal and afterwards returning to the lengthened trot. With horses that do not have very expressive lengthenings, one can obtain results by increasing the impulsion.

This is how to proceed: from the center line ask half-pass, in the collected trot, and when you arrive at the other side, stay in the half-pass, continue along the rest of the wall and the small side in renvers, then take the diagonal, really straight, and let the horse lengthen.

Before we continue to the next chapter on the canter, I want to advise the riders that in the beginning, they should not work systematically for a long time in walk and then afterwards a long time at the trot. It is obvious that in the beginning, the longer one works in walk, the more the horse calmly learns the exercises, the more the horse will, in a manner of speaking, have thought about it. Later on, the combination of trot with moments where you return to walk is very good for flexibility.

Book 1 Classical Principles of the Art of Training Horses

Farsista in **extended trot**. *Photo by Pedro Villalva.*

Chapter 6:
Canter, departure to canter

It is obvious that until now, the horse has not only done walk and trot; he cantered from the trot, more freely, like a relaxing canter, with the reins as loose as possible, without any hint of collection. Using almost opening reins, he has done large circles and returned to the trot by abandoning the reins and with the use of the voice. Now the horse is ready to start collecting himself in the canter, to start to shorten his stride, to sit on his haunches, and to learn the departure to canter from a walk.

How should we proceed? Most of the riders start immediately with teaching the departure to canter from a walk. Much easier for the horse is to start through transitions from a trot, very collected, into canter, allowing the horse to gradually make more strides in a canter that is somewhat collected already, and return to a walk by abandoning the reins. When the horse is increasingly able to stay in the more collected canter, and he can canter for a longer length of time, one will also start to return delicately from the canter into the collected trot.

One can now start in the trot to establish the aids that one will use later on for the departure to canter from the walk: the outside leg slightly to the back (very slightly), put weight on the outside buttock and move the outside shoulder back a bit. When one feels the horse will do this very easily on both reins from the collected trot, stays calm during the canter, and returns easily to the collected trot, this is the moment to start the departure from the walk.

In the walk, the horse has more tendency to be crooked.

First, one asks for a shoulder-in on the circle, and then, at the moment one nears the wall, straighten him and then ask for the canter. When the horse gets excited or goes crooked again, repeat the movement as many times as is necessary until the horse departs into the canter straight and stays calm.

First, as in the trot, return to the walk by abandoning the reins.

When the horse can comfortably maintain the collected canter from the

Teach the horse the aids for striking off to the canter: Place weight on the outside buttock... *Courtesy of Colonel Fernando de Abreu.*

walk (some horses lose the impulsion more easily and others get excited due to the effort made in the hindquarters), one can start to ask the transitions from canter to walk. Here one should stay very attentive to the release of the rider's back. One must return to the walk through the waist and upper body of the rider and not through an isolated contraction of the reins. The horse must learn to return to a collected walk by remaining light. It is in the perfection of the transitions from canter to walk that lies one of the big secrets of achieving correct flying changes and later on consecutive ones.

When the horse can do the departures well into the correct canter, straight on both reins on the long side, start to ask for that on the short side and when he does them well everywhere in the school on both reins, with good transitions back into the walk, one can start to ask for counter-canter.

What is the best way to ask for that?

Take the center line, do half-pass to the wall, and when the horse arrives at the wall, ask for the counter-canter departure. Repeat frequently and return to walk before the corner. Start to ask the departures at the start of the short side and return to walk before the next corner. When the horse can do them easily, start to pass the first corner in a position that resembles shoulder-in without asking for an outside bend and stop before the next corner. Ask for these departures later on in the same way at the start of the small side and pass through the next corner and at the beginning of the long side, take the diagonal, return to walk and praise the horse. Once it becomes easier for the horse in the counter-canter, ask the departures anywhere in the school.

Always pay attention that the transitions into the walk are easy and correct.

When the horse finds the departures into counter-canter difficult in the beginning, it is also helpful to ask them from a half-pass in a collected trot before asking them from the walk.

Now that the horse has learned to do the departures anywhere in the school from walk to canter on both reins, it is the moment to start asking the same departures on the diagonals, on the center line, and later, on large circles at both ends of the school, paying attention to keep always a line with the same curvature.

It is beneficial to often reward the horse by walking on long reins, and also, between the departures to canter, to do some lateral suppling exercises in the walk as well as rein back and then moving forward again.

... place outside leg slightly back and outside shoulder slightly back.
Courtesy of Colonel Fernando de Abreu.

The horse now starts to maintain the collection in the canter. This is the moment to start to ask half-passes in the canter, starting on the center line, going towards the long side, to start to give, in the counter-canter, a very slight bend on the rein that the horse is cantering in, a bend that one always tends to exaggerate, and to start with large circles in the counter-canter.

In the canter half-pass, it is necessary to remember that the horse must jump sideways and not slide.

In this also lies one of the great secrets of the preparation for the canter pirouette.

First one must feel, in the half-passes in the canter, that it is the hindquarters that push the body forwards and sideways, and no weight falls on the shoulder in the direction of the movement. It is very good to be able to halt in the middle of a half-pass, come back to a walk in shoulder-in on the opposite side, and depart again into canter and ask for the half-pass once again.

When the horse starts to do the half-pass easily from the center line to the long side, ask it from the beginning of the long side, needless to say like before in the walk and trot, going through the corners in shoulder-in position, in the direction of the center line, and pay attention to do the rest of the line really straight.

Now it is the moment to ask the horse to halt in the canter. Here it is necessary, more than in the other movements, to pay attention to the relaxation of the waist, to be able to halt without blocking with the hand. When the horse can do this easily, one can ask two or three steps of rein back, and after two or three steps forwards in walk, once again depart into canter.

Later on, when the horse can remain easily and calmly in this exercise, depart immediately into the canter from the rein back. Here the aids must be very delicate and very precise for the horse to do it calm and straight, and above all the hand must stay extremely light.

The horse can now start to do two different exercises after all this preparation: shoulder-in and travers at the canter and big circles with half-pass around the haunches.

Shoulder-in, correctly trained shoulder-in in the walk and the trot, makes it easy for the horse to do it in the canter. Ask very progressively for more strides.

One must not forget that, as for shoulder-in at walk and trot, the inside leg acts on the girth and the outside leg acts a touch more to the back.

It is very helpful to have a light hand that sometimes moves (both hands) to the outside and comes back to the inside very subtly and delicately.

When the horse can maintain the shoulder-in well in the canter along the long side of the arena, continue through the corner in shoulder-in to the short side and from the center line change rein in shoulder-in, and change from this shoulder-in into half-pass to the other side in canter.

Start also the travers in canter at the beginning of the long side after passing through the corner in a semblance of shoulder-in. Later on, halt the horse in the position of travers in canter, rein back two or three steps in the same angle, depart to the canter and, when the nose is close to the long side, continue in travers. Straighten the horse, walk straight and on the other long side return to the shoulder-in.

Later, when the horse can maintain this travers in canter easily, go through the corner, continue in travers along the

Farsista, left canter with haunches-in. *Photo by Pedro Villalva.*

small side and do a big circle in half-pass around the haunches, a circle that first is the size of the small side. One has to make this circle gradually smaller, at a rate that the horse does not have to be forced.

Et voilà, through wise and very progressive building up of the exercises we have put the horse in a state where he can start the flying change and the canter pirouette without jerking one or forcing the other from him.

You have established through all of these exercises the collection of the canter. The shortening of the canter, the collection of the stride, was all done very progressively and the horse, while keeping his weight on his hindquarters can, without losing his balance, lengthen, shorten the canter, turn, do half-pass, and halt easily.

The learning of the flying change and the canter pirouette is another stage.

Chapter 7: Flying Changes

There are different ways to ask for the first flying changes.

Most of all, what is necessary in the moment of asking for a flying change is that the horse is sufficiently prepared to do it with light aids and not with aids that are too strong, so that the horse stays calm after the flying change.

In so many cases, I have seen a horse ready to do his first flying change easily, and his rider, instead of asking it with caution, gave the aids too strong. What happens then is that the horse remembers this for months and gets overexcited every time he thinks that the flying change will be asked, or with some horses they stay agitated for a long time every time they go past the spot where the change was made, or before arriving at this spot, always thinking they are going to be asked again with these strong aids to do the flying change.

This is how I usually proceed:

After having collected the canter well using the appropriate exercises, for example, the half-pass, halts and rein backs, I make a big circle in one end of the riding school.

When the canter is cadenced and light, I take the long side very attentive on the fact that the horse is well-cadenced and straight, really straight.

At the end of the school, I return to walk, I do a big circle at the walk, always staying attentive to maintain the cadence, lightness and impulsion.

I then proceed on the long side and do rather frequent transitions between walk, counter-canter, walk.

At the end of the long side, I go through the corner in counter-canter and do a big circle.

I return once again to walk in the circle and at the beginning of the other long side, four or five meters after the corner, I ask the counter-canter. I let the horse do four or five strides in this canter, return to walk and return to the same spot various times to ask the counter-canter.

When I feel the horse is receptive and round, I do a circle in the true canter at the end of the school before the spot where I asked the counter-canter, I ride through the corner (very important), I put my inside shoulder slightly back and on the spot where I asked the counter-canter, keeping the shoulders well back, (and above all, the inside one a little more back) I momentarily close my fingers without pulling the reins and a fraction of a second later I touch the horse very lightly but very quickly (an electric touch) with my leg on the same side where my shoulder is more back.

When the preparation has been made with the sequence of what I have just told you, the horse will have done his first flying change.

When the horse has done a few strides, very few, immediately return to walk and release the reins, caress the horse. After some time of relaxation on long reins at the walk, return to the same end of the school, do a correct canter again, and calmly canter past the spot where you just asked for the change. The same care and preparation should be taken for the other rein, then after caressing the horse, dismount and return him to his box.

On the next day, at the end of the lesson, when you feel that your horse stays calm, attentive and receptive, repeat the two flying changes, but not on the same spot, rather do them on the other side of the school. Just for a few days, be satisfied that the horse does only these changes from canter to counter-canter, varying the spot where you actually ask for the change in every lesson.

As the horse does the changes more easily, ask for them further and further from the corner. Always pay attention to pass the same spot with the horse really calm in the true canter. With time, instead of just asking for two flying changes per lesson, ask for four, and then six. For example, in the beginning ask for two changes, without preparation before, in the middle of the long side. Praise the horse, and do some suppling work at the walk, then ask for the next two changes with preparation between them.

When the horse can stay calm before, during and after asking for the flying changes from the canter to the counter-canter, it is time to ask the horse to change from the counter-canter to the canter. The preparation must also be as carefully done and in the same manner but in the opposite way.

I ask for the first flying changes from counter-canter to canter at the end of the long side at the moment just before the nose of the horse reaches the corner. Praise the horse and then ride past this corner two or three times in the counter-canter.

When the horse can do the flying changes easily and calmly after this careful preparation, I also start to ask them progressively a little further from the corner each time.

The horse has learned to do two flying changes on the long side, which will, later on, be asked for alternatively; the first from the canter to the counter-canter, and the second one from the counter-canter into the canter, or the first from the counter-canter to the canter and then the canter to the counter-canter.

Now we can start to ask the changes away from the wall, across the diagonal. If you are not impatient, all the preparations with departures on a perfect diagonal will help to make correct and straight flying changes. It is necessary, when you take the diagonal, to look in the direction where the horse should arrive at the end and not allow the weight to stay more on one shoulder or the other.

Now the horse will calmly do single flying changes, well-spaced, both on the long side and on the diagonals.

When one is really a purist, it is now the moment, before bringing them closer together, to ask for the single changes on the small sides and in big circles on both sides of the school.

Now the horse is ready to do timed flying changes.

The progression must be slow and there are two really important points I want to remind you of:

- When you start to ask, for example, flying changes every four strides, it is necessary that during the strides between the two changes, the canter aids (of the canter the horse is in) are subtly reinforced at every stride, and inverted at the precise moment of the new flying change.
- The other point is that for changing every four strides you need a certain amount of

Bunker, collected canter.

collection, for every three strides, just slightly more and for every two strides a touch more.

A mistake that I see most of the riders make is not keeping the outside rein quiet. Do not forget that the outside rein maintains the collection of the canter, and the best way to keep its action is to put your outside shoulder slightly more back.

Now the horse is ready to start flying changes every stride.

Here the horse must have a higher degree of collection and vibrancy.

This is how to proceed:

In one of the long sides, start the canter, either correct or counter-canter (it is necessary to think about it beforehand, which is the easier change, if it is from the right to the left or from the left to the right—for all horses have one slightly easier side). If, for example, it is easier for your horse to change from right to left, you put him on the right rein, but in counter-canter. Be aware to keep the impulsion and collection and the position exactly straight; you give the aid for the flying change from counter-canter into canter and when this change is not yet completed, you give the aids for the change from canter into counter-canter. Your legs must be perfectly free and relaxed so that they act quickly without being harsh.

Now the horse has done two flying changes every stride, praise him with long reins at the walk and when you feel it is necessary, work him a little bit at the collected walk before asking the same on the other side. When he has done that, dismount and return the horse to the stable.

You continue to ask for only two changes every stride on both reins for a few days.

Alternate sometimes from the canter to the counter-canter and back to the canter, and other times from the counter-canter to canter and back into counter-canter. The same slow progression is used until you obtain three changes every stride easily on both reins. Spend more time schooling only these three flying changes every stride. When the horse does this easily and calmly, ask for four changes and when he does these four easily, he is then virtually ready to increase the number of strides. Here it is also necessary to proceed slowly and do not finish the lesson with flying changes every stride, but, after praising and walking with long reins, finish the lesson with flying changes every two strides.

Do not forget that the degree of collection in the flying changes every two strides is less pronounced than that of the flying changes for every stride.

When the horse knows the flying changes well and does them calmly without changing his canter, he has also moved on to a new level.

Chapter 8: The Pirouette

The pirouette is no doubt one of the most difficult exercises to execute correctly.

Few are the horses who can execute pirouettes without being crooked in their necks and remain round and light.

For the pirouette to be done correctly it is also necessary that the preparation is made progressively and carefully.

Because the horse already knows the circles around the haunches, one would think that when one reduces the size of these circles little by little, one gets a pirouette. That is not true.

To obtain a very correct pirouette, you also need other preparatory exercises.

First, reduce the canter more than for any other exercises and do voltes on the haunches that are progressively of a smaller radius, in a canter where the horse lowers his haunches more. Halt the horse in this position, ask for a very small circle in shoulder-in at the walk, change from this small circle in a turn on the haunches in as small a circle as possible, almost a pirouette at the walk; from this position, ask for a transition into the canter and then do a quarter or almost half a pirouette in the canter, then send the horse forward really straight in the same canter.

Repeat frequently on both reins, making sure that the horse always returns to the same place for the shoulder-in at walk in the small circle. Shrink the circle slowly until the horse does a half pirouette easily. From the half pirouette advance into a three-quarter pirouette and proceed like this until the horse does the pirouette by lowering his haunches and dividing it like the sections of an orange.

The action of the inside leg is very important since it must support each section, stop the shoulders from falling in and keep the impulsion. The upper body of the rider must lightly lean more to the back than in the other exercises, must turn a little bit to the inside, the head turned to the rider's inside shoulder, looking slightly to the side and back. The outside leg must act without force for the horse to enter into the pirouette perfectly relaxed, collected but not crouching.

A serious fault is the exaggeration of the bend to the inside; if this is exaggerated, the horse will have more difficulty to lift his forehand in each section. Bend him of course, but not more than necessary.

The *descente de main* is indispensable if one wants to execute it without even a touch of up and down movement of the neck in this exercise.

The regulations of the F.E.I. state that one must be in a certain canter, execute the pirouette in this same canter and leave the pirouette and continue in the same canter. I agree completely, but most of the time the riders arrive in the pirouette in a canter that is not sufficiently cadenced and collected, with aids that are too strong, then they ask for a pirouette that is very crouched and made with a different mechanism of the canter and leave the pirouette in another canter. It is for this reason that I give you the advice to shorten the canter more than for any other exercise, enter the pirouette with the help of soft and delicate aids, and during the pirouette practice the *descente de main* so as to prevent the up and down movements of the neck, which is a sign that the horse is crouched, and not with haunches that are relaxed allowing the hind legs to flex in all of the joints.

During the execution of the pirouette, the buttocks of the rider must be flat and open, sitting in the center of the horse, and it is only with a slight turn of the waist that one puts the shoulders in the position that I have advised before.

When the pirouettes are asked for in a lesson, it is necessary to be very discreet in the beginning and continue very slowly, for it is an exercise in which the horse makes a considerable effort. In this exercise, more than in any other, the horse immediately demonstrates how this exercise was being asked. If the aids of the rider are harsh, the pirouette will be incorrect, but if the rider asks with delicate and precise aids, the horse will remain round and supple in his pirouette.

A well-informed spectator or a perceptive judge can, in the execution of this exercise, recognize how the rider uses his aids.

Euclides in canter pirouette from Michel Henriquet's book: *30 Years with Master Nuno Oliveira,* [Xenophon Press 2011] page 74. *Oliveira Archives.*

Chapter 9: Piaffe

The piaffe is one of the most brilliant airs that a horse can perform when it is high and slow. Not all horses are capable of arriving at such a piaffe. However, the small, faster piaffe is within reach for almost all horses.

If the horse has been properly worked in hand after you've broken him in, you could ask him in hand to start the piaffe, mobilizing him on the spot.

With some elongated and badly balanced horses, this is a good system, for this beginning of piaffe will make them round, and some of this work in hand, asking the start of piaffe every day before riding, is excellent, with the condition that this command does not damage the walk. It is necessary to observe the horse well, in order to decide if this is the right thing to use. If the horse already knows a little of this in hand, he will easily do the piaffe when ridden. It is a question of associating the action of the whip with the action of your upper body, your hands and your legs, and progressively withhold the use of the whip, once the horse has understood the association of the whip with the appropriate aids for piaffe.

If the horse does not know the piaffe in hand, one must also meditate to see in what way one can ask for it, so the horse can remain relaxed in his head and not tense up, as this will cause the piaffe to always be strained and the horse will want to avoid the exercise; the piaffe will never be a brilliant result of collection but a clumsy trick that was taught to the horse.

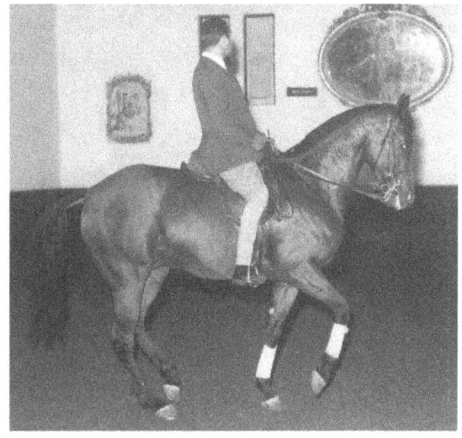

Tout-en-court, French-born Thoroughbred, executing a well-collected piaffe. *Oliveira Archives.*

I am not talking here about the horse that can "do" piaffe naturally, the one that is so well-balanced that a tactful rider, with perfect coordination of the aids, can achieve this piaffe at any moment and phase of the training. It is more important for this horse to first learn to do passage and when this passage is well-established, sustained and cadenced, one will arrive to a good piaffe if this passage is progressively shortened, whereas if one asks first for the piaffe, one risks to get a less suspended passage.

In the case of a phlegmatic horse, it is better to teach the piaffe first and when he does these steps of the trot on the spot relatively easily (that are not yet a real piaffe) one must start to teach the horse passage immediately, and continue to ask for the piaffe, without necessarily combining them at first. One will combine them when the passage is really short and light, the horse remaining seated, and when the piaffe is slower and slightly more suspended.

With a horse that is neither too phlegmatic nor too sensitive but with the normal nervous input, the piaffe can be developed to the maximum slowness, elevation and suspension that the horse is capable of offering without becoming tense, and from this piaffe advance into passage.

One does not always have the assistance of someone who can handle a lungeing whip or a long whip behind the horse to help. This assistance must only be used by a master, who knows how to use the lungeing whip or the long whip, but mainly who knows the horse through observing him.

In this case, the use of one or two dressage whips by the rider must be made tactfully and with extreme delicacy. Sometimes it is not a touch but a small sound or movement of the whip at the side of the hindquarters or on top of the croup, without touching the horse, that can give results. The big difficulty most riders encounter in obtaining the piaffe is always that their hands are not light enough.

Also, one of the great secrets of getting the horse to easily do the first steps of piaffe is not to forget the formula "prepare and let it happen," that is to say, the energy and the roundness of the horse are such that the moment the horse arrives on the spot, through the fact that you leave him alone, he continues the motion.

This formula is very difficult to understand for the riders who are not permanently preoccupied with lightness. It is for this reason that the piaffe remains an enigma for them.

The main point in the first requests for piaffe is to have the wisdom to stop before the horse wants to stop. The horse must learn to do the piaffe, needless to say, with energy, but in his head he must be as calm and confident as if he is doing work at the walk. In time, asking more steps, with more development of elevation, must be done very progressively.

To rein back when the horse is not sufficiently seated could be very useful.

In the piaffe, the upper body of the rider as aid is most important. The waist must be able to function as an accordion.

It is a grave mistake, at first, to step from piaffe into medium and extended trot, with a childish pretension to make the horse go forward. It is through stopping and letting go of the reins, and by leaving the piaffe in a walk or a collected trot that one establishes a desire in the horse to remain in the piaffe.

Needless to say, having achieved the piaffe, when the horse remains slow, high and cadenced, and above all, relaxed in his mind, then one can depart from this piaffe into whatever movement, which will be brilliant due to the accumulation of the balance and collection of the piaffe.

This piaffe deserves the name of piaffe.

The piaffe in which the horse is contracted and departs with tension is not part of equestrian art, it is a mockery.

I do not wish to elaborate more on the piaffe.

Naturally, I have seen horses where it was almost impossible to do piaffe. In most cases, they had been asked clumsily, putting them on the defensive and sometimes provoking terrible defenses each time they suspected the piaffe was being asked of them. Unfortunately, in all these cases, I have noticed that the riders wanted to arrive at the piaffe without any preoccupation of collection in lightness. The progression of collection in lightness leads the horse into a state of grace, which makes the piaffe easy.

In the development of the movement, it is necessary to know up to what point the horse can go. When you go beyond this point, you will ruin everything. It is obvious, as I mentioned before, that there are aids such as the qualified person behind to help, long reins, the cavesson, the pillars, etc. All of this, when used well, can help the horse which we want to teach the piaffe if this horse has not been worked in lightness and a rational progression. However, the tactfulness and the combination of the aids of the rider are normally sufficient.

Impostor, Piaffe, 1970, Quinta do Chafariz. *Photo by Pedro Villalva.*

Chapter 10: Passage

The passage is the most artistic form of the collected trot. When the horse already knows this collected trot well and is capable of maintaining it in lightness, one must, with the discerning alternating actions of the legs, first create the cadence of the passage in this trot, which carries within itself a light touch of suspension. Reward immediately at the smallest indication.

Ask often, be happy with little at a time and reward immediately.

Little by little, the horse gives more steps and little by little, he also shows more suspension. In the beginning, you must not ask too many steps. The first steps will be good, but the last will be less collected with less moment of suspension, and this is also one of the great secrets for later going easily from the passage into piaffe.

It is necessary, in the development of the passage, to feel that this passage stays short and seated, to feel the energy moving from the bottom upwards and not forwards.

It is obvious that, once the horse is capable of moving from passage to piaffe and vice versa, without losing the collection in the transitions, one would be able to teach the horse all the nuances of passage.

Unfortunately, a rider that is unacquainted with this art believes that large movements that look more spectacular at the beginning of the teaching of the passage are the results of his divine intelligence.

In circles and changes of direction in the passage, it is not the hands that determine that circle or change, but framing the horse with the legs of the rider. A horse that has been classically trained must know that the legs give direction as well.

The ultra-fine horse, who can naturally do the piaffe, will arrive at the piaffe through the progressive shortening of the passage in lightness. First, he will do passage on the spot, more or less two or three strides, later he will increase the number of strides and later still, on his own, he will lower his haunches and do the piaffe high, slow and brilliantly.

I have tried in these two chapters, the piaffe and the passage, to bring you to think that although one has a preconceived idea in one's head to decide which one of these movements to tackle first, that one must know for which type of horse it will be, to later join these two movements together.

In the transition from passage into piaffe it is not the hands that make it happen, but the increasing collection of the passage, arriving at the piaffe through an ultra-subtle action of the back of the rider with the reins very light. The last strides of the passage embrace the piaffe.

The lowering of the fetlock through the flexion of its articulation must be observed, for this is the proof that the horse is seated in true collection in the passage. Obviously, the passage must be high, but when the requested height

Nuno Oliveira on Rigoletto in passage. *Oliveira Archives.*

compromises the time of suspension, this height is wrong. One must always know the potential of one's horse and never want to go beyond his capabilities. It is necessary to give each horse all the brilliance he is capable of, but not more.

Euclides, Passage.
Oliveira Archives.

Chapter 11:
A rider's main endeavor, to always keep his horse correct

Voilà! Now we have a horse that already knows the Grand Prix movements, so his rider needs to be sparing and not demand the repetition of all the movements that the horse knows in every lesson. Naturally, it is necessary to combine the movements according to the rules of the test, and from time to time to repeat the test, but what is necessary above all, as the primary concern, is to maintain the collection.

Always practice the basics and devote more time to them than to the advanced exercises. *Edmond Reynaud Archives.*

But what does this mean?

- Basic concentration, calmness, relaxation, correct frame, cadence, energy and immediate response to the aids.
- To always return to basic exercises, spend more time doing them than the more advanced exercises, and ask them for a short time when one feels the horse is ready.
- To conserve, in order to use little, but well!
- To know that the spur is not only the strongest expression of the leg but can be a way of relaxing or a way of calming the horse.
- To feel that the back of your horse might some days be stiff, maybe due to a bad way he was sleeping in his stable.
- To feel if one leg is more tired, to know where this tiredness comes from and to know how to engage the leg without forcing it.

The horse is not a machine, it is a living being. Of course, one teaches him and he never forgets any movements he has learned, but what is necessary is to demand them correctly, without harming the body of the horse.

In each lesson, when one starts to work the horse, it is necessary to sense how he feels on the day, and to know how to adapt the aids according to the sensations one receives, and to know how to proceed with suitable work for the day. It is always necessary to finish the lesson thinking that the horse will be at his best form on the next day.

To close this chapter I want to tell you about an experience that I had a few months ago: I was standing in a corner of a famous school, watching a rider

Nuno Oliveira on Ulisses in passage, checking correctness riding with one hand, on the curb only. *Photo by Pedro Villalva.*

working. He stopped, came to me and in the beautiful French language, a most elegant French, gave me a knowledgeable and detailed explanation on the difficulties of the mechanics of the movements of his horse.

He invited me to sit on the horse, I did a few movements and at the end, judging that I obtained results, he expected that I would make a complicated, erudite speech, but I simply said the following: "try to relax your hands more and have a lighter contact."

I have been giving riding lessons for more than 40 years and this is what I persistently repeat to the students who show me their difficulties from all over the world.

Think about this, and everything will be easier, and more importantly, the horse will thank you.

Chapter 12: Work in hand

Working in hand is a valuable aid in the training of the horse, for he learns with this work, when it is done correctly, to sit and round himself, go forward in balance, move laterally, to bend, to rein back, and mobilize himself.

It is very delicate work, and if done badly, instead of producing results, can make a horse fearful of the whip, overexcite him and make him feel cornered. Some horses are almost impossible to work in hand, like some Thoroughbred stallions. Only a master with the help of someone who is also experienced, who can help in holding the cavesson, will be successful.

Start the work in hand with the horse in halt, and stroke him with the whip and show it to him on different places of his body. Observing the eye of the horse is very important, and one must make very discreet movements so as not to scare the horse. When the horse remains calm and relaxed when the whip nears his body, put him along the wall and try to make him walk forward by touching with the whip alternatively on the spot where the rider would have his leg or sometimes on the thigh. Repeat this on both hands until the horse very calmly advances in a slow walk.

Take the inside rein, a few centimeters from the snaffle; the outside rein should be over the base of the neck, and not in the middle, holding the whip in this hand as well, like it is a fencing foil. It is necessary to find the balance in the action of the two reins, in order to keep the horse straight.

Let the horse go forward a few steps, slowly, halt through a subtle action that has a tiny vibration of the snaffle. Continue these tiny vibrations on the snaffle until the horse flexes his poll a little, then release and in the halt, repeat until the flexions of the poll are sufficiently easy and the horse keeps his head in place and immobile.

I have spoken of the vibration. To do the vibration it is necessary to let the rein go very little to commence the vibration without weight. These small vibrations in place are no more than a quivering of the wrist. Once the horse, with his head in place, relaxes his jaw by swallowing, one asks him again to move forward a few steps and then halt once more. Repeat this on both reins as many times as necessary until the horse can easily go into halt, yielding his poll and easily relaxing his jaw.

How to hold the reins and the whip and how to position your body for work in hand. *Courtesy of Colonel Fernando de Abreu.*

Now it is time to be concerned about going into the walk while maintaining the two flexions, of the poll and of the jaw. The trainer works slightly behind the head of the horse and must, little by little, move backwards and stay at the level of the horse's shoulder.

Each time the horse resists, the trainer makes tiny vibrations and holds the horse by lowering his middle and spreading his legs apart, one foot more forward and the other to the back. Because the trainer goes back, the horse goes forwards.

The horse has learned to move forward at a slow walk, in hand, and lightly, and to return to the halt lightly and go to the walk again lightly.

We start to do circles (the trainer keeps going back and the horse goes forwards). In these circles, once they are well-established, halt the horse and once he stands, slightly tap him on the flanks or the thigh and attempt to move his haunches and his body one step to the side. Praise and drop the reins at the least sign of understanding.

Move on very slowly until the horse starts to do two or three steps easily. When he does these well, on both sides, put him really straight next to the wall, let him move forward with his neck imperceptibly bent to the inside and start with the greatest delicacy to try two or three steps of shoulder-in. If the horse wants to come to the middle, vibrate the inside rein from the bottom to the top until he remains with his croup near the wall. Once again, the whip touches the horse or is shown to him, depending on the circumstances and the sensitivity of the horse, and little by little a shoulder-in will be obtained along the wall where one halts the horse often in the position of the exercise.

Later on, when the horse does this rather easily on both reins without rushing or leaning on the hand, stop him in the position of the exercise, praise him, go to the other side, put him in the angle of the other shoulder-in, and ask him to do it on this side, always taking care to have the croup near the wall.

Repeat often on both sides with a halt in between.

Afterwards one will start to ask the horse to move through the corners in shoulder-in, taking care when going through the corner that the hips advance more and the shoulder less, to keep the angle the same on the side that follows.

When the horse is capable of going around the school in a calm shoulder-in on both reins, in smooth steps, ask him

Advance the waist and give small vibrations on the reins when the horse resists.
Courtesy of Colonel Fernando de Abreu.

Let the horse step sideways on the circle.
Courtesy of Colonel Fernando de Abreu.

If the horse performs shoulder-in without difficulty, ask him to stand still in the posture of the same exercise.
Courtesy of Colonel Fernando de Abreu.

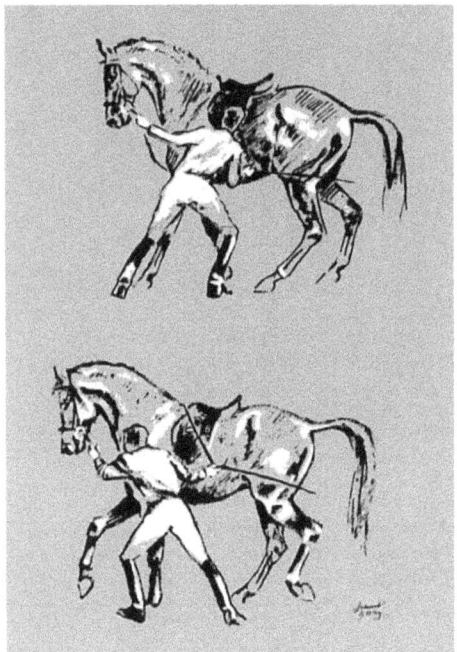

Let him go backwards for a few steps, then forward and back again.
Courtesy of Colonel Fernando de Abreu.

at the beginning of a long side to leave the wall in shoulder-in and move halfway across the diagonal, always maintaining the same bend; when arriving at X, the trainer takes longer steps (not faster) and turns the horse towards the wall, maintaining the previous bend. The horse turns lightly around the haunches, and because the trainer takes longer steps, he sends the horse's shoulders faster in the opposite direction of the bend. When arriving at the wall, continue in counter shoulder-in, go through the corners of the short side in this counter shoulder-in and at the beginning of the long side, with great tact and delicacy, try to change the bend and gently start a half-pass across the diagonal. When arriving at the wall, do two or three steps, and then halt.

In the beginning, when you change the bend, the rein (on the new inside) that holds the whip can open and the wrist rotating correctly will make the whip rotate with precision.

When the horse knows the half-pass across the diagonal, one will exchange the counter shoulder-in and the half-turn in this shoulder-in for a half-pass along the wall and a big half-turn [in half-pass], lightly moving around the haunches.

Progressively make the figures smaller, make them bigger again and alternatively make them smaller again.

Now is the moment to ask for rein back at the wall.

How to proceed:

Halt the horse, flexed in his poll, with his jaw relaxed. The trainer stands at the height of the horse's shoulder, legs wide apart, and with a vibration and a small tweak on the reins towards the back at the same time as the trainer leans his upper body towards the horse's croup, putting more weight on the leg on that side; the horse moves back one step, release the reins and caress the horse. Take the reins again at the spot where he halted, ask flexions of the poll and jaw and ask him to step back one or two steps again, halt, release the reins and praise. Take up the reins again and this time ask the flexions and walk forward, attentive and slow. Repeat progressively until the horse is capable of doing the rein back a few steps without rushing.

In case the horse rushes, the trainer pushes him forward with the whip on the thigh (at the same time the outside hand releases the rein), and the inside hand moves to the front of the nose and pulls the horse a little forward.

To progressively move from the halt (where you are next to the horse's shoulder with your legs well-spread and firmly on the ground) to the rein back, use delicate pressure on the reins for the rein back and then touch delicately with the whip on the thigh to move forwards; the trainer's upper body leans to one side then the other and allows the horse to do two steps forwards and two steps back alternately.

When this exercise can be done easily, with the vital condition that the horse remains flexed both in the poll and the jaw, we are ready to approach the trot on the spot (let's leave this term be and call it piaffe). Small, fast, subtle and electric touches with the whip, on the thighs or the hips, the top of the tail or on top of the croup (and the rider has to find what position suits the horse best), and a hand that for a few moments allows a limited freedom (that takes and gives for a tiny fraction of a second), will make the horse present the first hints of piaffe.

Proceed progressively, ask little every time, and don't forget that the true trainer must always have in his pocket sugar or some other tidbit that the horse likes.

This is all I want to say about the work in hand, which can be an extraordinary aid in the training of the horse but on the condition that it is done with irreproachable correctness and precision.

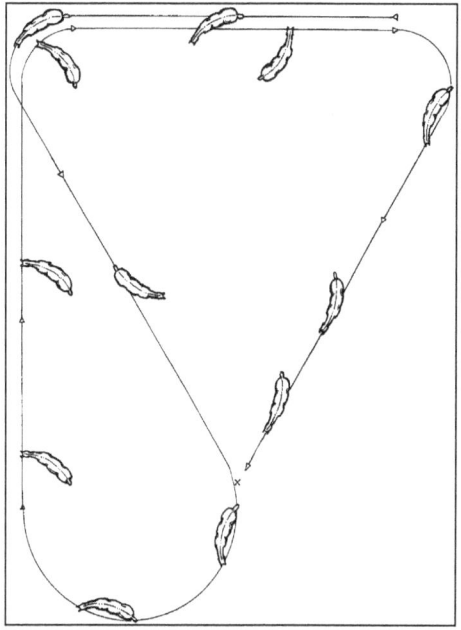

At the beginning of the short wall, start with shoulder-in, proceed on the diagonal in shoulder-in and upon reaching the center at X the instructor walks a little faster, the horse turns slightly around the hindquarters on a large half circle. Continue along the long and the next short wall in counter shoulder-in [shoulder-out] and upon reaching the long wall after the second corner, change the bend and half-pass on the diagonal.
Courtesy of Colonel Fernando de Abreu.

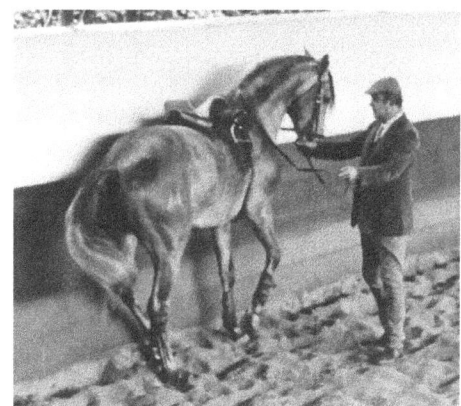

Piaffe in hand with a young Lusitano-Arabian cross, from *The Legacy of Master Nuno Oliveira*, Xenophon Press 2014 by Stephanie Grant Millham.
Courtesy of Kathy Cleaver.

Tenor, Alter Real [breed], executing piaffe in hand with João Oliveira.
Oliveira Archives.

Chapter 13:
About the lightness in the action of the rider's legs

"I would like to remind you once again about the rider's legs: they propel, they soothe, they frame, they relax..."

- Nuno Oliveira

One always speaks about the lightnaess of the rider's hands but one forgets to speak of the lightness in the action of the legs. If the legs act with pressure and they stay stuck, what happens?

Because of this pressure, the rider in the first place contracts the muscles of his thighs, contracts his back and finally also the rest of his body a little. In the second place, it is important not to forget that the horse breathes, and with

Lightness resulting from daylight between the horse's sides and the rider's legs: Soante in the piaffe. *Courtesy of Yvon Bourgois.*

the legs stuck, the breathing is compressed in his flanks.

It is also necessary to remember that most of the time when a horse is not correct in the hand, it is because the hand receives the faults of the legs.

Although the legs of the rider should remain next to the horse's flanks, they should be free, loose, and capable of giving tiny touches from the calf down to the spurs through the relaxation of the ankle.

When a rider has short legs and rides horses with a deep girth, the rider must know when his spurs are in contact or not. I would advise these riders to put the spurs lower on their boots.

One must have the ability through the relaxation of the legs to give touches quickly, whether they are lighter or stronger, like electric touches. Let the leg go in order to touch, touch and let go, all that with enormous speed and without shifting the legs. In certain cases, one must also know how to leave the legs in contact for a few seconds, completely loose and relaxed, feeling the flanks of the horse well. One must know how to round the legs in order to use the spur without the leg. All of these are nuances that, when used by a rider that knows how to use them, the rider has much more ease to teach his horses than the rider who uses his legs badly.

The latter gets the horses confused and is incapable of turning lethargic horses into fine horses. The first rider can get along with both of them.

One must know how to touch at the moment when the horse puts down a diagonal or leg, to influence it from the start of the lift of the other diagonal or leg, and thus to provoke the extension or suspension of its action.

One must finally know (this is so difficult to do that only the riders who have a perfect and very relaxed seat, that have perfect mastery of the coordination of their hands and legs, can approach it) how to do the *leçon des attaques*[3] to refine the horses, make them rounder, more brilliant and appear to be floating.

---

[3] *Leçon des attaques*, an expression from François Baucher; see Chapter 7 of the book *From an Old Écuyer to Young Riders*, by Nuno Oliveira: (…touch the horse quickly with the spurs…)

Chapter 14:
Descente de Main et de Jambes

The rider must always have the idea in his head that to ride a dressage horse is to push, take and give and so on.

Push through minute actions of the rider's back and buttocks the collected horse, close your fingers with a motionless hand (that is the result of the arms correctly placed and the elbows next to the body, which is in unity with the flexion of the waist and the position of the torso), relaxing all as soon as the horse yields. The fingers open and the contact is softer, the horse remains in the vibration of the movement or the exercise, his poise has not changed; let him continue for some moments with slackened reins and no action of the legs, sustained only by the axis of the balance, namely the torso, where the waist is relaxed.

You have to know how to take the reins again without being brusque.

The longer *descente de main et de jambes* lasts, the horse staying in his own balance, the greater is the proof of impulsion.

"Descente de main" or lowering [yielding] the hand: Tenor, Alter Real, piaffe in self-carriage ridden by Joao Oliveira. *Oliveira Archives.*

Impulsion can be given various definitions, but I think that which suits a trained horse is when he can stay for as long a time as possible in the same posture, cadence, and always using the same amount of energy, without the rider asking him with his aids.

The *descente de jambes et de main* is the proof of true collection and collection is a beautiful poem of impulsion.

Chapter 15: The *Écuyer* as Teacher

To know how to teach and give all that you have learned through practice, to know how to explain that, transmit it to a student, one needs some psychological knowledge to understand the character of the student and to see in which manner it is needed to explain for him to understand.

It is also necessary to be aware of what state the horse is in when ridden by this or that rider. To get the student to obtain a certain result with his horse, it is first necessary to deeply observe the capacity of the student to transmit in the best way for the horse to understand what is demanded from him.

To know when to talk at the right moment and above all with the tone of voice that is suitable. The voice of the teacher must know how to calm, give energy, confidence and never put the student or the horse (through the association of the influence of the voice on the state of mind of the rider and consequently of his aids) in distress or despair.

One has to know when one has a result even when it is not yet what we are expecting. To see if this or that student needs to be encouraged or another needs to be told it is not yet that. One has to know how to use images that can help the student to understand what one wants. Without being on the horse, one has to have deep knowledge of what one is teaching, and almost feel the horse that the student is riding.

One has to know how to talk a lot to a student that needs continuous explanations because silence will intimidate him and know how to speak very little but to the point with another student with a spirit of introspection. One has to know how to go around a question in certain cases when one sees that the difficulty is insurmountable for the rider. Go around the question without giving the rider or the horse the idea that one gives up and the other wins.

The teacher that can manage this is the one that has deep knowledge of his art and this person, only this person, deserves to be called *Écuyer*.

Finally, as the last resort, one can ride the horse to resolve a difficulty, although in a way that will not give the student the idea that he is incapable, and not be as foolish as to have a superiority complex and the vanity of being a genius; on the contrary, in great simplicity know how to explain to the student, from horseback, to get [the student] to observe and try to quickly get the horse in a condition where he can be ridden by his rider again and that the latter is capable of immediately solving the problem.

One must know when to stop in the exact moment when the student obtains a good result when one is not sure that the student will be able to get this same outcome without great difficulty.

The true *Écuyer* is not subordinate to any system or regulations. He must know that different roads lead to Rome.

Nuno Oliveira at the Cadre Noir in Saumur. *Oliveira Archives*.

The *Écuyer* is the one who has trained many horses, the one who has spent hours and years on the backs of horses meditating, reflecting and enriching his knowledge, this knowledge that he tries to transmit in the best way he can.

The *Écuyer* is the one who, as he gets older and loses his physical capabilities, knows how to appreciate that of his colleagues or students that are younger, and is the one who will be happy when one day, one of his students, due to his teaching, will have superior equestrian qualities to his.

The *Écuyer* is the one who knows how to remain humble and through his professional honesty will make a friend out of his student.

In my opinion the true embodiment of the *Écuyer* my master Joaquim Gonçalves de Miranda, a pupil of a disciple of Baucher and *Écuyer* of the Portuguese Royal House. His idea of the *Écuyer's* role and the immense talent he performed it with gave me forever the cult of this profession. *Oliveira Archives*.

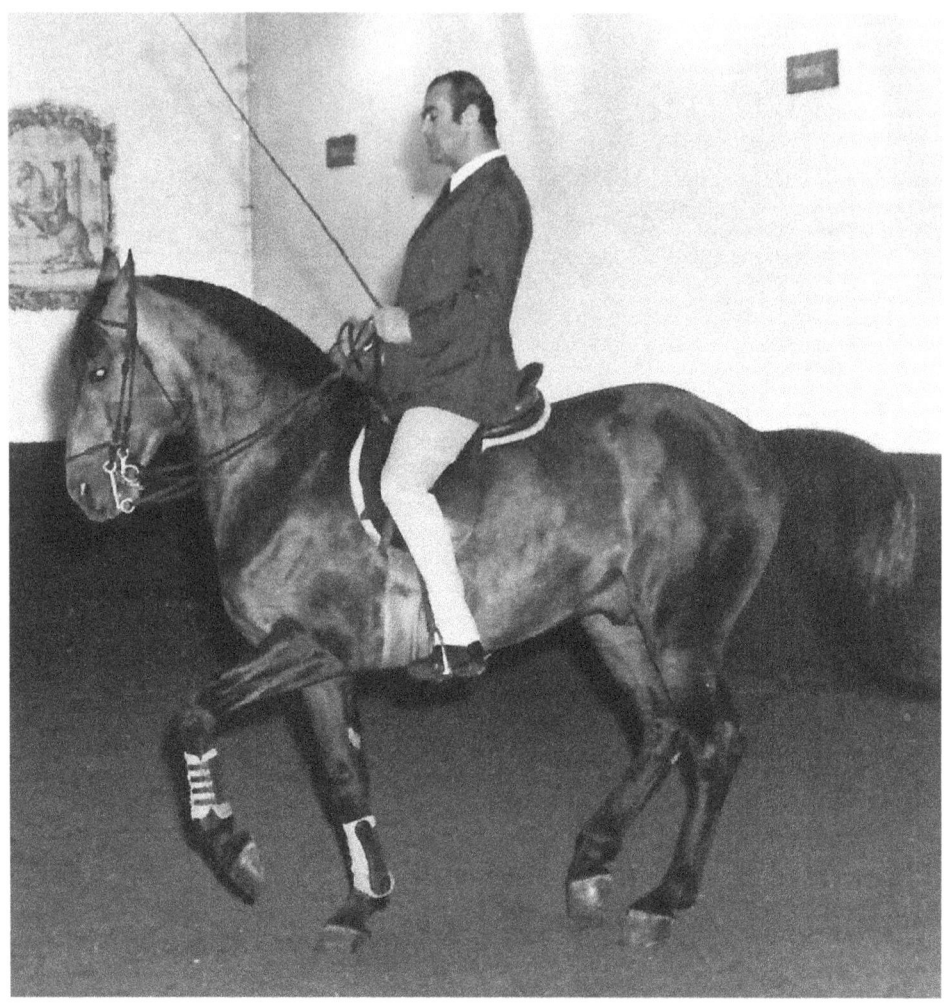

Nuno Oliveira on Impostor in piaffe, 1970. *Photo by Pedro Villalva.*

When you listen to my music, I do not ask you to "think" but rather to "feel." If you do not feel it, then either I am incompetent or you are a Philistine.

- Ludwig van Beethoven

In Closing

In the previous lines, I have not wanted to impose a method or to convince you that it is only in this way that you can train a horse correctly.

Many years of practice, meditation and studying made me have the certainty that you can only have horses that have pleasure in their work while remaining obedient when you are not using continuous force.

I have wanted to transmit the idea of looking for lightness to riders who are interested in dressage, which has always been the major preoccupation of all great *Écuyers* that have enriched the art of equitation with their experiences and their teachings. Each of them, in the written works they have left us, have put the concern of lightness and delicate use of the aids in the first place.

Unfortunately, at present, this notion is a little lost. If some riders who read me will meditate on this subject, and try to have their horses light, I would feel extremely rewarded, and I would have been able to turn the valiant horses that they ride into happier animals.

I have wanted to give those who start to ride their horses a view of a progression; there are, obviously, special cases where, to surpass them, it is necessary to have profound knowledge. Observation, reflection and reading (not only what people write nowadays but also the works and treatises of *Écuyers* of the past), with practice, will give you this knowledge.

Photo by Francine Halkin.

In this small work, I have wanted to pass on the fruit of forty-some years of practice, observation, reflection and reading, to be able to help the riders, and that amongst all the daily concerns of life, every rider could, thinking of the beautiful moments he has passed with his horse or horses, be sure that *Equitation is an Art*.

12-2-1983
Ocean Grove, Victoria, Australia

Nuno Oliveira and Beau Geste executing a classic levade. *Photo by Pedro Villalva.*

Book 2
Horses and Their Riders

*"When you write, do not worry about what others do
and do not try to imitate them.
Write what you feel sincerely and without bias.
In Art, what matters is sincerity and not ill will."*

- Advice from Giuseppe Verdi to Umberto Giordano

Contents

Foreword by General Durand..59

As a Beginning...60

Chapter 1 Choosing a Horse..61

Chapter 2 Breaking-In a Young Horse...63

Chapter 3 The Next Phase in Training...69

Chapter 4 The Circle and Serpentines..71

Chapter 5 Accustoming the Young Horse to Spurs..................................73

Chapter 6 The Young Horse and the Cavalletti.......................................74

Chapter 7 Teaching the Beginner Rider...75

Chapter 8 Notions That the Instructor Must Instill
 in His Pupil's Mind from the Beginning................................78

In Conclusion...79

Foreword

I always consider myself lucky when our friend Nuno Oliveira entrusts us with a little more of his experience and talent, which he uses in training horses. Filled to the core by French tradition, his riding skills are their direct legacy. His fundamental knowledge of the great masters of the eighteenth century, his deep understanding of the genius of [François] Baucher, his loyalty to the great principles expressed by General [Alexis] L'Hotte, and his constant endeavor to breathe life into them make him one of the great *écuyers* of the present, who perpetuate a riding art whose legacy fills us with pride.

These lines about riding are particularly characteristic of the spirit in which Nuno Oliveira begins the training of the horse: Gaining momentum in calm and searching for balance, a condition *sine qua non* [without which, it could not be possible].

"The rider only brings into play and uses those forces that are useful for the horse in the intended movement...."

Colonel (now General) Pierre Durand, Director of the École Nationale d'Équitation, Saumur

As a Beginning

Photo by Francine Halkin.

Once again, I have taken my pen to write about horses and riders.

Fifty-eight years on horses' backs and forty-odd years of teaching riders makes it impossible for me not to pass on to others what experience, observation and a great love of horses have taught me. I even feel that I have the moral duty to transmit to younger people what so many years of experience and research have taught me.

It is once again on the other side of the world in Australia, where I find myself teaching riders, who are full of enthusiasm and who want to learn, that I take my pen again. This time I am going to talk about, amongst other things, the breaking-in of the young horse, how to start teaching a new rider, and a little about how to give these lessons.

General L'Hotte, in his wonderful book, *Questions Équestres*, [*Equestrian Questions*, L'Hotte/Nelson, Xenophon Press 2021] says, "Horses always recall their first habits." Like him, I dare say about riders, "Riders always recall their first habits."

Breaking-in the horse correctly simplifies later training if it has been done with the idea of creating in the horse's mind the will to collaborate with his rider.

A rider who has had his first training with advice from an enlightened teacher, whose character has been observed, who has been taught according to this observation, and who has not followed a rigid method, will later find that he can approach more advanced work in a simple and relaxed manner.

Equestrian Art belongs to our cultural heritage as much as to Art itself, but no Art deserves this name if one is content with mediocrity.

May these following lines help riders who, by working their horses, arrive progressively to give the spectator the impression that there is no rider, and by the gentleness and correctness of their seat and their delicate aids, present their horses in balance and all their beauty as if they were free or riderless.

Chapter 1: Choosing a Horse

Of course, the choice of a horse must first be a love affair.

When I choose a horse, I look first to see if I like his general appearance, his beauty and the expression of his eyes. I look at him through half-closed eyes, as he is led in hand towards me, to see if his general appearance is well-rounded. Finally, I look more closely at all of his gaits and then his legs.

I always prefer to buy a horse that is not too well-nourished because, being thin, I can see his defects better, as well as seeing how he will develop later on.

I am more interested in the form of the canter rather than seeing a trot with too great an extension. The trot can be improved more easily than a naturally bad canter.

I watch how the back functions in all the gaits. The back is the bridge between the fore and hind legs and the part that carries the rider's weight.

It is important to observe the state of mind of the horse while he moves without being excited or pushed, and observe how the neck and withers are attached. In every breed of horse, one finds both good and bad horses. Some breeds have a greater number of horses which are more appropriate for one thing or another. However, in all breeds, one finds good qualities of gaits, balance and strength among many individuals.

Of course, due to its conformation, being high at the withers and to great lateral suppleness, the Iberian horse is more apt to stay on the haunches and to turn on a shorter base than most breeds; however, the extensions of the gaits are less pronounced in the Iberian horse than in some other breeds. In saying that, some Iberian horses do have good extensions.

In the Thoroughbred, there are different types. One also finds, in a certain type of Thoroughbred, some horses well-adapted to lower their haunches and which by their natural energy can become wonderful horses of *Haute École*.

The tragedy is that in most of the cases in Europe, one sees Thoroughbreds cast off the racetrack, that have been trained too young and do not have a healthy back, and even sometimes have compressed vertebrae.

In the United States where they breed Thoroughbreds to be saddle horses, one sees some wonderful Thoroughbreds. In New Zealand where they start racing Thoroughbreds only when they are three years old, I have seen some excellent horses too.

In Latin countries where jumping is more popular than dressage, one is ready to pay more money for a jumping horse. However, many of these subjects would be very good dressage horses.

Speaking of Thoroughbreds, one must observe that the racing horses we can buy for dressage are seldom the winners.

I remember a few years ago while attending the races at the race track of

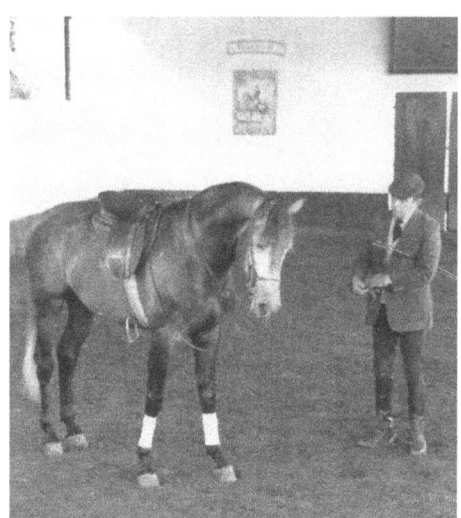

"Of course the choice of a horse must first be a love affair." Nuno Oliveira with the young Luso-Arab stallion, Ingemisco. *Photo courtesy of Stephanie Millham.*

Lima, Peru, watching Thoroughbreds prancing before the start of the race, I watched those who had the most ability to round their backs. By coincidence, they always were the winners.

One should not confuse an excess of sensitivity in the horse with the real finesse that a horse of *Haute École* must have.

When horses are too highly strung, it is always due to a lack of strength. I have trained some horses like this that have fascinated me. However, the result of training, although brilliant, is less valid than with a stronger horse.

The degree of finesse of a horse must also be related to the degree of finesse of the rider's aids.

Of course, I have seen small people ride big horses as well as big people riding small horses, and both riding well. Anyway, there is a law of proportions for the pair to be harmonious.

The back of a small rider has less influence on a big horse than the back of a big rider on a big horse. Unless he is a genius, the rider with a big back riding a small horse has, most of the time, too big an influence on the horse's mass.

The correct dressage, of course, must refine the horse.

Nevertheless, to practice subtle equitation one must have a sensitive horse. Unfortunately, it is not the prerogative of the present day's so-called dressage competition. The "tride"[4] develops also with good training of the horse, but if the horse has natural "tride" from the beginning, the result will be better.

I am sure that a great pianist can make bad pianos sound good. However, on an appropriate one, his interpretation will have another class and another beauty.

---

[4] *tride*: a French equitation word that Baron d'Eisenberg, in *The Art of Riding a Horse, or Description of Modern Manège in all its Perfection* [Xenophon Press 2017] explains: "Refers to a walk, a canter, a movement of a horse whose amplitude is short and whose cadence is rapid." - Translator's note [Strong and swift. - Editor's note.]

Chapter 2: Breaking-In a Young Horse

There are, in small stud farms, breeders who have one or two mares who are used to living near human beings and being petted, and so do not fear man.

On the other hand, there are countries where breeding is still practiced with large herds of mares. These horses, when three years old, have never been held with a halter, and some have never had a person near them to pat them.

In the first case, breaking-in the young horse is quicker because the horse is less frightened by people. In the second case, the first part of breaking-in the horse is for him to be calm in the stable and to get used to people around him. Primarily, except for the halter, the horse must accept being patted over all his body and pick up his feet as if for the blacksmith.

He must allow himself to be patted on his ribs, at the girth and all of his head, including the ears. He must allow you to push his head down by a gentle pressure on his poll. I know that there are horses who take a long time to let you caress their ears. These horses, although taking longer, will by the gentleness of the rider, and with the help of tidbits and patience, arrive at a good result.

Becoming irritated is not the same as being firm (firmness at the precise moment and for a fleeting moment) and often ruins everything. It is only when the horse is calm in his stable and

Joscelyn Gunter bridling Zabrod. *Photo courtesy of Lucy Jackson.*

allows himself to be groomed and patted all over without fear that he is ready to be taken to the riding school.

He must be taken there with a padded cavesson and a fairly long lunge-line which are not too heavy. The person holding the horse on the left side must try to keep a cadenced walk, with his hand holding the lunge-line about twenty inches from the cavesson, with a loose rein to allow you to vibrate it if the horse is difficult. He should have tidbits to give the horse after a few steps and a halt.

Try again until the horse follows the person, walking calmly. The horse must be followed by a helper holding a whip, showing it to the horse without frightening him if the horse will not advance. Accustom the horse to the riding school by walking him around on both reins, with halts until he is completely calm.

Begin straight away with the horse in hand going into the corners correctly, taking the center line and the two diagonals, and always staying on the inside of the horse so that he is against the wall. The helper should walk behind the horse but on an inside track.

When the horse knows this lesson, you must stop him in the center of the school and the helper with the whip should very delicately and tactfully caress all the horse's body with the whip.

The person holding the lunge-line should pat the horse and feed him tidbits or vibrate the lunge-line, according to the horse's reaction. He should talk to the horse in a comforting, or if necessary, a stern voice, but never shout.

The horse can now go back to the stable where he should be accustomed to being bridled with a snaffle. This should be done several times and be rewarded with pats and tidbits. The horse should then be left bridled alone for a short time in his box. When you remove the bridle, caress a lot.

For the next lesson, you bring the horse to the school with his snaffle and the cavesson. Repeat the same lesson as before and once back in the stable, take off and put on the snaffle again several times.

For the following lesson, you will need a third person. This person should have a lunge whip and should stand on the center line, fairly near the short wall if it is a small riding school and further down in a large school.

At the other end of the school, the person with the lunge-line should walk the horse on a circle the width of the school. The second helper with the lunge whip follows the horse. Progressively, the person with the lunge-line little by little lengthens it, and the helper with little movements of the whip pushes the horse into a trot.

The third person, on the center line, should watch the horse attentively and with small movements of the whip accompany the horse from one side of the school to the other.

If this operation is done tactfully the horse should quickly be trotting on the lunge-line in a perfect circle. You then repeat the exercise on the other rein.

The helper at the end of the school must be particularly attentive when the horse turns on the rein that is more difficult for him. When the horse has turned correctly on both reins, stop him, make him come towards the person holding the lunge-line, pat him and give him a tidbit [treat]. Take him back to the stable and repeat the exercise with the bridle, taking it on and off several times.

In the next lesson, after the horse has executed several circles correctly, the

Starting the young horse on the lunge with aides on the circle.

Illustration Jean-Louis Sauvat.

person lungeing should walk straight down the center line to the other end of the school so that the horse goes large, and then repeat the circles at that end.

The helper at the end of the school walks down the opposite long side to the horse and takes his position on the center line, on the short side.

All this should be done with long, calm strides so that the horse stays calm.

It may be necessary to walk a little faster if the horse loses his cadence. Slow down as soon as he obeys you. Repeat the same exercise on the other rein.

If the horse is calm at the end of the lesson, he should be stopped in the middle of the school, away from the walls.

The person holding the lunge-line pats and gives tidbits, whilst the helper shows a roller to the horse and lets him smell it. If the horse stays calm, put the roller on his back and rub him gently with it behind the withers. Pat and give tidbits. Take the horse back to the stable, where you repeat the exercise with the bridle, and if he stays calm, rubbing him with the roller.

The next lesson, repeat the previous one, trotting on the circle, which may now become three circles: one each end of the school, and one in the middle.

When this has been done calmly on both reins you choose the easier side for the horse, and at the end of a long side just before the corner, the helper who is pushing the horse should with the whip push the horse into a canter. If he takes the correct lead let him canter and follow with the whip, which pushes him forward but never frightens or rushes him.

If he takes the wrong lead or is disunited, the person holding the lunge-line should vibrate it and say "trot ... trot ..." to the horse until he trots, and then push him into the canter again in the corner. This should be repeated until the horse is relaxed and cantering calmly on the circle. Repeat this exercise on the other rein. The helper at the other end of the school should be very vigilant as the horse passes in front of him. Stop the horse in the center of the school and rub his back with the roller. Then take him back to the stable, where you should recommence the exercise with the bridle and the roller.

In the next lesson, you repeat everything to get the horse used to passing from the trot to the canter and vice versa.

The person holding the whip should adapt the amount he uses it to the orders given by the person holding the lunge-line. The whip pushing or the lunge-line vibrating must harmonize with the vocal command, "Canter" or "Trot," and be used simultaneously, taking care that the tone of the voice corresponds to the order.

If the horse disunites his canter and he is not too excitable, push him with the whip until he is cantering correctly. If, on the other hand, he is highly strung and has a tendency to become excited, it is better to return to the trot and push him back into the canter when he is calm.

At the end of the lesson, show the horse the roller again and rub him with it. Then with a long whip delicately start him on side steps on a circle. Ask for these first few side steps with a whip that touches the flank or the thigh whilst the person holding the lunge-line walks in a circle facing the horse, vibrating the lunge-line and giving a tidbit at the least submission. Repeat this exercise on both reins, asking very little each time and rewarding often. As before take the horse back to the stable, repeat the exercise with the bridle and the roller, and reward.

The next day, take the horse to the riding school with the snaffle and the cavesson. At the halt, repeat the lesson with the roller, showing it to him and rubbing his back with it. According to his reaction, either caress him or vibrate the lunge-line.

When he accepts being rubbed with the roller calmly, lunge him at the trot and the canter longer than usual. Bring him back to the center of the school and again show him the roller, etc.... More pats and tidbits. Lunge him some more at the trot and the canter. Stop him again in the center of the school and give a tidbit. Put the roller on his back. The helper (from the short side) approaches the off-side of the horse and takes the end of the roller. The other end is held on the near-side by the helper (who pushes the horse on the lunge-line). Whilst patting the horse, the off-side helper drops the end of the roller and near-side helper takes it under the horse without touching him. Gently and progressively, he touches the horse with it, at the girth, and if the horse stays still, he attaches it and tightens it. It should not be too tight, only enough so that it does not slip backwards.

The near-side helper takes his whip, the off-side helper goes back to his place on the short side, and the person with the lunge-line lets it lengthen gradually, whilst the helper gently pushes the horse forward. Some horses go forward jumping in the air, and some horses stay on the spot. By the way that you use the lunge-line and the lunge whip, you must control the horse so that he goes forward readily, even if it is a little rushed.

When the horse calms down and is used to the roller, bring him to the middle of the school, pat him and give him tidbits. Tighten the roller. Lunge him again, taking the same precautions until he goes forward calmly at the trot and the canter on both reins.

Stop him again, take off the roller, pat him, put back the roller, and tighten it. Lunge him a little more. Once again, stop him, take off the roller and pat him. Now ask for a very few side steps on the circle with the whip. Back in the stable, take on and off the snaffle and caress. This lesson should be repeated three or four times until the horse is completely relaxed on the lunge-line with the roller. Now the horse is ready for the saddle.

To put the saddle on the horse the first time, you should use exactly the same procedure as with the roller. The first few times, the stirrups should be run up and it is only when the horse is completely relaxed with the saddle that you should bring him to the center of the school and let them hang loose.

When he is calm at the trot and the canter, stop him in the center of the school and caress him.

The two helpers approach the horse on either side and gently move the saddle, bang on it and rub the stirrups over the flanks of the horse. The person holding the lunge-line vibrates it or pats and gives the horse tidbits, according to his reactions. Talk reassuringly to him, paying attention to the tone of your voice. Take the saddle off and repeat the side steps on the circle, then put the horse back in the stable. Repeat this lesson three or four times.

When the horse is relaxed with the saddle, bring the side reins and attach them to the snaffle. To begin with, they should be very long and loose. Progressively shorten them a little so that the horse can take a contact with his head forward, far from a vertical position. At the end of the lesson, repeat the exercises with the stirrups, rubbing them on the horse's flanks, moving the saddle and then ask for a few side steps with the saddle and side reins.

Start the next lesson by lungeing the horse. You then take off the lunge-line and the horse should go large followed by the three people with lunge whips. There should be a person at each end of the school and one in the middle. Thus, if the team works correctly, you can make the horse execute circles, go large and change reins by altering the position of the helpers. Be careful not to frighten the horse by a person being in the wrong place. When the horse does this exercise, changing the reins etc. going forward calmly, put the lunge-line back on the cavesson. A helper can now start, gently, to take the reins of the snaffle for a few side steps. Obviously, the person holding the lunge-line must still control the horse, vibrating the lunge-line and patting as necessary.

Bring the horse to the center of the school and again give the lesson of moving and banging the saddle, and rubbing him with the stirrups.

The person holding the lunge-line should now be very attentive, as the near-side helper who is going to mount the horse should put his left foot in the stirrup. Repeat the movement several times, putting that foot in and out of the stirrup. Pat the horse, give him a tidbit then lunge him again, for a while at trot, and canter. Once again, you stop the horse in the middle of the school and attach a stirrup leather around his neck.

The near-side helper again puts his foot in the stirrup and puts his weight on it; he then lifts himself a little way off the ground, being careful not to stick his toes in the horse's side. Pat the

With the guidance of the aides, let the horse trot, then canter and change direction across the arena without the lunge-line.
Illustration Jean-Louis Sauvat.

horse. If he is quiet, the helper continues his movement until he seats himself lightly in the saddle. The person holding the lunge-line pats the horse. The off-side helper passes behind the person holding the lunge-line and picks up the lunge whip. This should have been left on the ground on the near-side and behind the horse.

The rider should take hold of the stirrup leather with one hand, and with the other, pat the horse on his neck. If the horse is calm, the person holding the lunge-line should let it lengthen and the helper behind the horse with the lunge whip should gently push him forward into the trot. The rider must pat the horse's neck and then behind the saddle on both sides.

Continue to push the horse at the trot until you feel that he is relaxed and going forward easily. You then ask him to canter. The rider continues to pat the horse and the person lungeing talks to him. Stop the horse, bring him to the center of the school and repeat the same exercise on the other rein.

Finish the lesson by the rider dismounting and mounting the horse three or four times on each side. Take the horse to the stable with the saddle and unsaddle him there. Reward him with tidbits.

By now, the horse should be calm on the lunge with the saddle so that for the next lesson he can be tacked up in the stable.

He should first be lunged without the side reins and then with them, then be let off the lunge-line and worked loose with the three people with whips. The lunge-line should now be put back on and the horse worked in hand, executing his side steps on the circle. Lunge him a little more and then the rider should mount. Work the horse on both reins at the trot and the canter and finish the lesson by mounting and dismounting on both sides several times. In the next lesson, the horse will begin to relax under the weight of the rider. The person holding the lunge-line should, at this time, give a whip (neither too short nor too long) to the rider. At the halt, the rider should pass the whip, in an upright position, from one side to the other, over the withers of the horse. The person holding the lunge-line should be attentive, either vibrating the lunge-line or patting, according to the horse's reaction.

He should then push the horse forward into a trot (with the side reins attached but loose) with the lunge whip. The rider, holding the stirrup leather (which is around the horse's neck) with one hand, following the movement of the lunge whip, should start to push with his whip and heels, together and separately. Thus, the horse starts to understand the aids that will drive him forward. You repeat the same exercise on the other rein, with the whip always on the inside.

In the next lesson, the rider should hold the reins and the stirrup leather so that his hands stay still.

When the horse accelerates, the rider should rise to the trot, and as he slows down, the rider should be seated.

Bring the horse to the center and the rider should change reins, using the rein on the side that he is turning to, with short actions and relaxing it immediately.

According to how the horse accepts this lesson, you either now or a little later take off the lunge-line. The horse should then go large at the walk, change reins and make large circles aided by the two lunge whips (as in the preceding lessons without the rider). Repeat this at the trot. You finish the lesson by repeating the side steps with the rider still on the horse. Use the whip of the person on the ground in time with the leg and the whip of the rider. Before taking the horse to the stable, mount, dismount several times and reward.

For many long years, I have been breaking-in horses in this manner.

The observation of each horse that you break in will determine when you can proceed to the next stage in his training.

One must always react at a precise moment and not later. When the horse is quiet in the riding school, this last lesson should be repeated in an outdoor school.

With each lesson, the horse should have a better understanding of the rider aids: the legs, the hands and the body.

You should only go outside when the horse understands that the hands of the rider slow him down and stop him, and the legs send him forward and sideways.

A horse trained like this will always be easier to work than one where no care has been taken with the relaxation and calmness in the breaking-in. A horse goes forward when he is relaxed. A horse who rushes is not relaxed and therefore does not go forward. The horse who does not submit to the rider is being ridden under protest.

Chapter 3:
The Next Phase in Training

At this stage of the training, the young horse now accepts the rider on his back, and he starts moving in a relaxed manner and turns easily.

Before starting to collect the horse, he must be able to go calmly and easily from one gait to another in both upwards and downwards transitions. Calmness must be obtained before anything else.

Before you can have the weight of the horse transferred back onto its haunches, you must accustom the young horse to working calmly at the three gaits in a more horizontal balance without letting him lean on the reins.

One must accustom the horse to trot calmly on a large circle and ask transitions to the canter at different places on the circle, with few aids of the legs and with still reins. One must be certain that the transition from the canter to the trot is obtained more by the body than by the reins.

Do not stay too long, either at the canter or at the trot.

It is necessary that, without getting nervous and with few aids, the horse always keeps on the same circle and goes very easily from the trot to the canter and vice versa.

This is a basic exercise that riders forget to ask. They start collecting the horse too early which provokes nervousness of varying degrees, depending on the sensitivity of each animal.

In this phase of training, you establish by calmness the impulsion, which will increase gradually as collection increases.

Jane Turley riding Airoso, Lusitano, beginning collection in the trot.
Photo courtesy of Lucy Jackson.

The horse which is constantly solicited by the rider's aids and which gives visible but rigid gesticulations is not a horse with impulsion. Impulsion stems from the physical and mental relaxation of the horse.

One must also be attentive to ask for calm halts.

Once the horse halts, relax your hands. Then see if, by a very light action of the reins, the horse slightly rounds his neck. If he does, push him forward with your seat that slides under you, whilst relaxing your hands again.

With the two preceding exercises, one will accustom the horse to accept the influence of the rider's back, either pushing the horse forward or slowing him down.

Of course, during this phase of training, the rider can continue the work in hand.

Joscelyn Gunter riding Zabrod, canter on the circle. *Photo courtesy of Lucy Jackson.*

He will be able, in that manner, to ask more collection of the horse without the weight of its rider.

In the training of a young horse, from the breaking-in to the *Haute École*, one must not neglect any step.

It would be the same as starting to construct a building on the third floor before building a sound foundation. The horse's body and mind must both be prepared for the next phase of training.

Horses that reach advanced exercises and that, before reaching certain levels of the lesson, put their weight on the reins, are rigid, or take too much time to relax, are not really trained horses. They have been obliged to act a part, no more than that.

Go and observe, in the big international dressage competitions, the warming up of the horses before they enter the arena. Then think, for instance, about Baucher with Capitaine, Buridan, and Neptune who were mounted behind the curtains and who entered the arena obedient, well-balanced and light.

Another exercise that is important at this phase of training is the exercise of a broken line along the long side of the riding school, obtained with the same rein. The horse becomes accustomed progressively to understand the action of the outside rein.

Later, practice this lesson either walking or trotting, sometimes with the reins in the left hand, sometimes with the reins in the right hand. The horse must be accustomed from the start to do without the gesticulation of the arms of the rider. The rider does not need to make gestures with his hands; that is for the conductor of an orchestra.

In this phase of training, you must do a rising trot and sit when the horse is well-relaxed and cadenced. When you feel rigidity again, go back to the rising trot. Resume the sitting trot when you feel that the harmony is re-established.

From the start, the horse and rider should be as one. By the relaxation of the rider's waist, his body should not move more or less than the horse's back.

The length of the lesson must not be conditioned by your watch, but rather by the sensation you receive and by the perception of the state of mind of your horse. Always finish the lesson, thinking about the next one, so that the horse will be pleased to start his work again the next day.

Chapter 4: The Circle and Serpentines

The circle is a figure of the utmost importance when working young horses. The circle must be a perfect geometrical figure. The rider must make his horse follow the circle, adapting the arc of its spinal column to the arc of the circle.

One must enter into a circle with the outside shoulder of the rider going forwards, parallel to the outside shoulder of the horse and not with an action of the inside rein. The contact on the two reins must remain even.

By the contact of the legs, one must accustom the horse to following the line of the circle without going either inside or outside it.

Often riders are not careful enough not to let the horse put the weight of either the forehand or the quarters inside or outside the circle. The horse must follow the arc of the circle equally well on both reins. He should be able to make circles, in spirals, making them bigger or smaller by the rider's legs, which guide and control the horse's body on each circle.

One must also be able to increase or slow down the pace of the gait, always following the arc of a geometrically perfect circle. One must also be able to stop the horse on the arc of the circle and start him again on the same circle. Again, one must also be able to correctly execute the large circle that is a circle the size of the arena's width and also a small circle that is a circle the size of half the arena's width.

Rubin with João Oliveira: Beginning self-carriage in the lateral movements.
Photo courtesy of Lucy Jackson.

If the circle is equal on both sides, if the horse goes equally easily on both sides, keeping the rhythm and the impulsion, he will be straighter on the straight lines. If the circle is correct while cantering you will feel that your body and your seat are not pushed either inside or out.

Prepare the straight lines with correct circles on both reins.

The serpentine is also a valuable exercise. In the serpentine, the rider should try to feel or savor both sides of the horse. One must execute them without altering the rhythm, even in the bends.

Preparing the turn to the right with rigorous attention to bend on the young horse. *Courtesy of Stephanie Millham.*

You must prepare each of the bends by moving forward your outside shoulder and having the horse turn around your inside leg at the girth.

Of course, we are now working the horse in the second phase of his training. However, when I say one must turn without the action of the inside rein the rider must be attentive and ready to act with it at the precise moment if the horse refuses to turn.

However, if the preceding preparation has been well-executed and the rider has been concerned with the rhythm, everything will go well.

The horse is now able to do a circle and to turn. Later on, you will ask the shoulder-in and the travers always taking the same care to keep your inside leg close to the girth in such a way as to avoid the horse leaning or escaping with his inside shoulder.

Chapter 5: Accustoming the Young Horse to Spurs

In his book, General Baron Faverot de Kerbrech [*Methodical Dressage of the Riding Horse*, Xenophon Press 2010] explained the way of having the young horse accustomed to spurs very well.

At the halt, using spurs without rowels, gently put the spurs in contact with the horse in such a way that the horse stays calm. Then you start him forward with a gentle pressure of the spurs. As soon as he starts forward, you remove the pressure of the spurs. Normally that is the way I accustom a young horse to the spurs; however, some horses are more ticklish and more difficult.

With these horses, I use the cavesson, the lunge-line and the whip to work in hand, the horse being ridden by his usual rider. I start by asking for shoulder-in, on the circle, and when the horse is calm during this exercise, I ask the rider to press gently with the inside spur, while I stay attentive with the lunge-rein, which must vibrate if necessary, and while with the whip I ask the shoulder-in. When he submits, caress and halt. Then do the same work in the other direction. When he submits, caress and halt. Afterwards, walk the horse on the lunge-line and ask the rider to press both spurs and the

Balet, the young horse begins to carry himself. *Photo courtesy of Lucy Jackson.*

person holding the lunge-line either vibrates it or caresses the horse according to his reaction.

I have also used this method for many decades with horses that are very fine, very sensitive or very apprehensive. At this stage in the training of a horse, the spurs must be very light and the use of spurs must be moderate. At this stage of training, the spur is the strongest expression of the leg. If the legs are sufficient, use only the legs; if the legs are insufficient, then use the spurs with moderation.

Chapter 6:
The Young Horse and the Cavalletti

Set up a cavalletti in the middle of the long side of the riding school. Bring the horse to the school on the lunge-line without a bridle or a saddle.

Lunge the horse on both reins, at both ends of the riding school, and when he is calm and relaxed, lead him near the cavalletti. Let him lengthen his neck and look at the cavalletti. Do this on both reins.

Lead the horse at a walk to the cavalletti on the rein that you know is easier for him. By using your voice or by using the lunge whip delicately behind him, make the horse jump. Then stop him, caress him and give him tidbits. Repeat this after having lunged the horse at the end of the riding school in a very cadenced gait.

When he goes easily over the cavalletti on both reins, at the walk, repeat the same exercise in a very measured trot. When the horse passes the cavalletti well on both reins, move the cavalletti towards the end of the long side of the riding school and put another cavalletti parallel to it on the opposite side of the riding school.

Still on the lunge-line, push the horse on a circle, first at the walk, then at the trot, over the cavalletti, making sure that the horse stays on the arc of the circle. Do this on both reins. Then halt, caress him and give him tidbits. Later, after two or three lessons like this, put another cavalletti on the short side of the riding school with a fourth cavalletti parallel on the other side of the circle. Lunge the horse on this circle, at the walk and then at the trot, until he passes the four cavalletti calmly.

The following lesson should be given in loose schooling after having ridden the horse so that he will be calm. Place the cavalletti in the middle of the long side of the riding school.

If the horse jumps the cavalletti on both reins, then put a cavalletti on the other side and have the horse jump it calmly. When the horse performs this calmly on the lunge-line, at loose, repeat these lessons in the same manner, mounted, at the walk and at a measured trot, the reins half relaxed.

Chapter 7: Teaching the Beginner Rider

The teacher in charge of a beginner must, first of all, know the horses very well, be calm, with completely steady nerves and must be intelligent enough to understand his pupil's character. Unfortunately, one sees in many countries of the world instructors who have not been prepared to observe their pupils, nor choose the horse suitable to them, and do not know anything else but the repetition of generalities of only one method.

To teach a beginner does not necessarily mean to fill the complete hour's lesson. The lesson can be shorter or longer according to the individual. First, one must create self-confidence in the pupil. Twenty-five years ago, I trained many new riders. I believe that, at that time, my pupils were very relaxed and secure on a horse.

First, I put them on a calm horse on the lunge-line and with a vaulting surcingle. They are started by doing many gymnastic exercises to make their bodies suppler.

They learned to take their hands off the surcingle and stay in the correct position. Afterwards, when I put them in a collective lesson, I was very careful to choose a horse that was best suited to each rider and I was also always taking care to place in the lead a horse who had a good cadence and gave the correct pace for the other horses.

I tried to instill into the beginner the notion of the forward movement without using force. It is a rule without exception.

Bettina Drummond with Harpalo Prince, Half-pass at the walk. *Oliveira Archives.*

Of course, one must also create fast reflexes to be able to react rapidly, at the right moment, with firmness, but without brutality.

Some riders must be slowed down in their impetuosity, others have to be awakened. It is up to the teacher to observe the character of his pupil. The work without stirrups is also important under the condition that the leg falls naturally without forcing the heel down, as I often see it done by some teachers. Observe later those who have been instructed in that manner and see how they use their legs in the most difficult airs of the *"Haute École."*

To sit well and to be correctly seated on a horse is not the same as looking nice on a horse. One is looking nice on a horse when the horse looks nice because the rider does not interfere with him either with his hands or with his legs or with his body that stays too straight and rigid.

If a young beginner is enthusiastic for one or another discipline, either jumping or combined training or dressage, he must first be supple on a horse. He must feel the movement of the horse, to be able to jump obstacles, to be able to gallop on the outdoor run, to jump a ditch or a gate and to know what one used to call the aids for the "*Basse École.*" If one trained beginners this way, one would not see barbarians in the jumping discipline and stiff rheumatic people in dressage.

Equitation is the same for all the disciplines of horsemanship. For instance, one rider will jump two meters whilst another one will do flying changes every stride in a serpentine.

Schools that I often see in different countries and that one pompously calls Dressage Academies are completely ridiculous because all one can learn there is to instill in the rider's head that the horse must do such and such a merry-go-round and no more than that.

I remember a famous International Jumping Competition in Lisbon in about 1961 where Brigadier General Henrique Calado entered the arena to compete in the Grand Prix with the horse Xomac doing the flying changes every stride. The horse did them perfectly with invisible aids from his rider.

Only a few days ago, I saw a film of so-called 'great' dressage riders of our time whose legs in their flying changes every stride wandered everywhere, and with horses leaning on their reins.

In conclusion, the instructor who teaches beginners must, by his understanding of his pupil, create an all-round rider, who will choose later, the discipline he likes best.

I remember a few years ago giving a lesson to a group of riders among whom were two young professional instructors. I asked each one, in turn, to stay in the middle of the group or to lead the lesson. I noticed the tone of voice they were using and I showed them the type of voice to use for the various movements, on various occasions and for the various horses. The voice of the instructor must be reassuring, soothing, encouraging, rapid if necessary but without nervousness.

What I have just written is very important.

So many times I have seen instructors shout at random without realizing the state of mind of the riders. Forty years of giving lessons have taught me a lot!

In addition, an important point is to know if it is more suitable for the pupil to work by himself or in a group. Some riders feel less confident when alone and are more motivated and interested when in a group, while others, on the contrary, prefer to be alone. The teacher must understand the temperament of his pupil and make him progress while keeping him relaxed in his mind and his body.

One must be able to say, "Very good," to encourage the pupil. Very good for his level even if it is not perfect yet. One must be able also to tell the pupil it is bad without discouraging his enthusiasm. The profession of riding instructor requires great preparation. Unfortunately, one often sees this noble craft either practiced by ill-prepared

A riding school must be run by someone who deserves the name of *Écuyer*. Nuno Oliveira on Ousado in passage. *Oliveira Archives.*

people, without equestrian knowledge, or psychologically ill prepared to be good pedagogues.

The student rider must first learn on supple and well-balanced horses to have the correct notion of what riding is. Only when he is at ease on such horses, and has correct knowledge of what a well-balanced horse is, will he be able to ride a green horse.

For a riding school to be worthy of the name, it must have horses capable of teaching the pupils. For this, the one who directs the school must either be competent or have competent people to train horses and to keep them trained. This is the way my school has always functioned. It requires more work and the profit-earning capacity is less, but only under these circumstances can one call it a riding school.

A riding school must be run by someone who deserves the name of *Écuyer*. I remind you that Monsieur [Antoine] de Pluvinel,[5] the first person to be given this title, was among other things: professor of etiquette of the King of France and Ambassador of France.

---

[5] [*The Maneige Royal*, Xenophon Press 2010]

Chapter 8:
Notions That the Instructor Must Instill in His Pupil's Mind from the Beginning

What is asked from the horse must be conditioned by the state of mind of the horse and the sensations received from his body. In all living creatures, one must ask for a certain mixture of stimulation and relaxation of his nerves so he is not disinterested nor too excited, in such a way that will maintain the rhythm, for instance, the horse always develops the same dose of energy.

One must always be quick so as not to intervene too late.

Always reward the horse and do not forget that it is a reward for the horse for the rider's action to be stopped. One must always be careful about the amount of action of the legs to the amount of action of the hands and vice versa.

Always remember the harmony of the aids!

The hand of the rider must hold the horse without him pulling on the hand, but also without pulling in the horse's mouth towards the rider!

One must, when starting an exercise, ask it with a certain intensity of aids. However, one must, during the exercise, feel how much the horse submits and reduce the aids according to his submission.

One must obtain from the horse a constant attitude, cadence and vibration for as long as possible, without the help of the aids!

One must instill in the rider's mind the notion to choose the best moment to change from one exercise to another or from one gait to another.

The quality of the next pace depends on the quality of the pace you are in.

Patience is one of the human virtues that develop with the practice of Equitation.

The rider must know the physical abilities of his horse so as not to go beyond them. When one goes beyond them, one risks a fight of which one is not always sure to be the winner.

Finally, training the horse is not to make a robot or a machine of him, but to render him obedient and collaborating with you, whilst keeping his freshness.

In Conclusion

Euclides displaying good cadence in the Spanish walk. *Oliveira Archives*.

I hope that what I have written here will be useful to the riders beginning to break in young horses. It is the foundation for the rest of the horse's training.

All the horses that I have broken-in at my riding school were always easier to train further than horses who arrived already broken-in. The training of a horse must be done with the same philosophy from the very beginning.

A person who has never broken a young horse does not merit the title of *Écuyer*. He cannot completely know the horse that he is training unless he has worked with him from the very beginning.

I still remember a young horse, Torras, which I rode some fifty years ago, under the direction of my riding master Miranda, after he had the horse worked on the lunge-line.

The horse is a marvelous animal, which merits a rider that understands his character and his possibilities.

Equitation is a school of abnegation and humility. Practicing it, if it is done properly, betters the human being.

"As to small defensive actions in their attitude made by young horses, which are not preceded by physical defensive actions, they are in fact, just surprises. It will be easy for a clever and patient rider to anticipate or repress them, whilst gradually getting the horse used to hearing and seeing everything and accepting everything within his limits."
- Henri Baucher from *Aperçus Équestres*, page 26

Book 3a
Notes on the Teaching of Nuno Oliveira

Compiled by Jeanne Boisseau

Piaffe in the classical manner. Photo from the book, *Wisdom of Master Nuno Oliveira* by Antoine de Coux, Xenophon Press. *Oliveira Archives.*

- Editor's note

Some of the photos used in this section are from the Crépin Leblond edition and others are from the later French editions published after Master Nuno Oliveira's passing. Translation of part of the preface of the Crépin Leblond edition is as follows:

"The riders who illustrate this work are friends and students of Nuno Oliveira, of whom he himself had requested the photographic material (and come from the private collection and Francine Halkin).

The photos of the Master come from his personal collection and those of Maxime Le Forestier."

Contents

Foreword by Jeanne Boisseau..84

Foreword by Lieutenant-Colonel [now General] Pierre Durand.......................85

Chapter 1 Equitation - Dressage - Tact...86

Chapter 2 Position..88

Chapter 3 The Aids and their Uses...90

Chapter 4 Impulsion, Cadence, Collection, Lightness.................................94

Chapter 5 Gaits, Exercises, Straightness...96

Chapter 6 Transitions - Extensions...98

Chapter 7 Shoulder-In...100

Chapter 8 Half-Pass..102

Chapter 9 Canter Work...105

Chapter 10 Flying Changes...108

Chapter 11 Piaffe, Passage..109

Chapter 12 The Young Horse..112

Foreword

Black eyes and hair, impressive figure, a resting force: Nuno Oliveira, professional rider.

A life dedicated to the horse and to work in the riding school. Getting up at 5 a.m., from 6 a.m. on horseback, lessons, often into the evenings with a glass extended to the delight of his friends and students, trips abroad, wherever he is called, exchange of ideas from morning until late evening. His daily routine, fully occupied by the horse. No holidays. Never. Inexorable with his students, demanding and tender with his horses, rough to snobs and the vain. The man is a typical southern European, polite and generous, serious and spiritual, sometimes bitter: "in my life I have been criticized too much, and praised too much." The rider is extraordinary: the shine, the lightness, the concentration of his horses is astonishing.

But the aim of this little work is to give some insight into his teaching. The Master is patient, at times enthusiastic, often quiet, yet he knows how to communicate. Images and parables sometimes merge, the clues fall with accuracy, intuition and a remarkable knowledge of horses. So here, in some chapters, the basics, the definitions and aphorisms are repeated, always written down after his oral lessons. This reproduction is certainly not exhaustive, since the Master teaches continuously and each day discovers livelier, more precise, and also more poetic approach to his students. There are several of us who carefully kept our notebooks, but this work would undoubtedly not have been created without the extraordinary, long-lasting diligent work of Antoine De Coux [*The Wisdom of Master Nuno Oliveira*, Xenophon Press 2012], faithful witness of Nuno Oliveira, who at every meeting never ceased to hear the statements of the Master, noted and written down. We thank him for entrusting us with the fruit of this harvest. I hope that his generous contribution will allow all of Nuno Oliveira's students to rediscover what they may have forgotten over time, and enable those who do not yet know him to sense the richness of an exceptional teaching, mirror of an Art that has seldom been mastered.

Jeanne Boisseau

Foreword by Lieutenant-Colonel [now General] Pierre Durand

It was in 1962, while taking part in the Concours Hippique International in Lucerne, that I made the acquaintance of Nuno Oliveira. Dressed *à la française*, he introduced horses to *Haute école*.

On this occasion, we forged friendly bonds and, from then on, we kept them warmly entertained through regular correspondence and reunions at longer intervals, especially in Lisbon during two sporting stays, when Nuno Oliveira received the French team with his characteristic generosity and dignity.

As a competition rider, convinced of the unity of the art of riding, I was impressed by the style of this rider, which was exclusively dedicated to artistic perfection. In no way is it about the search for a grateful photographic motif, but about respect for the *mental and physical unity of the horse*, the *primary concern for impulsion* and the *cult of lightness*; these three factors whose harmonious interplay beyond all boundaries and disciplines when in perfect balance make up the art of good riding. In view of the responsibility of running the *manège* at Saumur, which has to combine its traditional principles with the requirements of modern competitive riding, I wanted the École Nationale d'Equitation to welcome the most talented riders. Our Portuguese friend was one of the first. Because of his lessons, whose notes I have, faithfully collected by Jeanne Boisseau, I consider myself lucky to present to the readers, and shed light on an idea that is dear to me.

"In the art of riding, everything is in the manner."

Lieutenant-Colonel [now General] Pierre Durand,
  Écuyer en Chef, Saumur

Chapter 1: Equitation - Dressage - Tact

The tragedy in riding is that despite all the rider's knowledge, the horse has faster reflexes than man.

On the horse, do not cease to observe.

Riding is not an exact science. We must "feel" and not have a "system" in one's mind.

There are no tricks in riding. There are simply riders who have more or less equestrian tact and...*the others.*

There are two things in riding: the technique and the soul.

Riding is made up of many small details that must all be respected.

Equitation is not the search for public success, nor should it be self-satisfaction once having obtained some applause from an audience, nor trying to please at all costs to a jury. Equitation is a one-on-one dialogue that you have with your horse, the search for harmony and perfection.

No real method can exist in Equitation, because each horse is a unique case.

Dressage is not about executing difficult movements but about making the horse easier, more flexible and for the rider to allow for the horse to have better balance.

Dressage is the search for roundness. Dressage is the development towards perfection of the three natural gaits of the horse. The equestrian art is the poetry of all of this put together.

A trained horse is a horse that is supple, pleasant to ride, happy, and not a horse merely performing gesticulations.

Technique may take you to a certain level; beyond that, however, there must be a psychological acceptance by the horse.

Equestrian art is made of an infinite number of small details and of the rider's feeling.

Equestrian art begins with the perfection of simple things.

Equestrian art is, for the rider, to stay quiet and keep his horse straight.

You must abandon the technique a little and ride with your heart.

As a rider, you need to be able to feel and go towards emotion.

Equestrian tact is not only the lightness of the aids but also the sense of how to choose which aids to use, and also, the softness of the whole action.

When asking for an exercise you must make sure that the horse goes willingly into the exercise and not under coercion.

Look for the purity of the three gaits. The rest will come easily.

Do not allow the horse to lead but make sure that there is no fight, so prepare your horse accordingly to avoid the fight.

Make a habit to pat the horse when the horse gives of himself.

When a horse gets nervous as a new exercise is requested, we must calm him in the exercise, otherwise, he will get

Horsemanship begins with the perfection of the simple things. João Oliveira with Radames. *Oliveira Archives.*

nervous each time we ask him something else or something new.

If your horse becomes nervous, do not become upset. Pat him, and soothe him with your voice.

When a horse tends to get excited, we must introduce the exercises with such diplomacy that he does not notice that we are about to make him execute them.

When riding, don't be insistent on constantly being the boss. The difficulty is to feel which degree of intervention to use.

Do not require or be insistent that the horse gives his maximum to you at all times. Learn to wait for him to be capable.

If a young horse is doing a simple job well, it is important to be able to appreciate his willingness; if an old horse overcomes his stiffness to satisfy you, you must appreciate it too.

If you are only looking for scores from a judge, if this is your only criterion of satisfaction or disappointment, then my equitation does not interest you.

I often meet well-dressed gentlemen, with a beautiful tie and good manners. However, when you put them on a horse they begin to hit and to poke their horses and I do not understand this metamorphosis. Could it be that, on the ground, they only appear to be civilized men?

Chapter 2: Position

The academic position is the only one that allows the aids to be independent and performed with finesse:

- Shoulders down
- Navel in the direction of the horse's ears
- Tip of the buttocks not protruding backwards beyond the vertical line of the shoulders
- Coccyx towards the pommel of the saddle
- Thighs down, with relaxed muscles
- Relaxed joints
- Flat calves in contact (with the horse's sides)
- Heels in line with the rider's neck and shoulders

It is not enough to have an elegant position; your position has to be useful. For this, your position must follow the horse with suppleness.

The academic position must be free of stiffness; we must place our own body so that it follows the horse's movement.

The forehand and hindquarters of the horse are the two plates of a balance and the rider's upper body is its beam.

We must envelop the horse with the medial side of the knee, as if we were sitting on a barrel, and have the same spacing between the feet as we do in ordinary walking.

Do not hang on the reins, do not lean on the stirrups, just sit in the saddle, with soft calves in a caressing contact with the horse.

Clamping legs, even slightly [unyielding], contract the body of the rider as well as the body of the horse.

The most important position is not that of the upper back, but the position of the part going from the center of the back through the back of the knee.

I want to see torsos and bodies that are relaxed on the horse and legs without tension in the muscles.

The same way the leg begins at the hip, the arm starts at the shoulder.

When we say, "have a relaxed hand," this is also true for the wrist, the arm and the shoulder. When riding, remember to also relax your face and to grow your upper body.

To have long legs does not mean "lean your leg towards the back," it is so the thigh is as straight and as vertical as possible, with the knee well down.

Being linked to the horse is not only to be seated but sitting so as not to fall off in case the horse makes a happy jump.

Being linked to the horse is to follow the horse's back with our back.

Your shoulders should not swing and the waist stay fixed, it should be the other way around: the shoulders must be immobile and the waist flexible.

Round the wrists as if you were holding a candle in each hand.

Make your elbows part of your upper body, with relaxed wrists.

Only the academic seat grants refinement of the aids. Nuno Oliveira on Impostor, passage. *Photo by Pedro Villalva.*

Generally speaking, keep your shoulders parallel with the horse's shoulders.

Have heavy buttocks and light back, not the opposite way around.

When trotting, it is the waist that should trot, not the hand.

The optimum positioning of the hands is a small space in which the rider is the most comfortable and in which the horse accepts them most easily.

It is important to make yourself light on the horse's back. A small and thin rider can be heavy on the horse, and a heavy rider can be light.

Chapter 3:
The Aids and their Uses

Bettina Drummond on Soante in the transition from passage to piaffe.
Oliveira Archives.

The secret in riding is to do little but at the right moment.

The more we do, the less it works.

The less we do, the better it goes.

You must *feel* your horse, not ride him as you would on a bicycle, with an insensitive seat.

I don't want to see riders that move. Do the work with your mind.

It is useful sometimes to ride with your eyes closed.

To adjust the reins is to establish a soft contact.

You must have a steady hand with mobile fingers.

Your hands should be like cement when the horse resists and like butter as soon as he yields.

With a trained horse, the fingers must rarely be tightened.

The little finger and the ring finger can release, never the thumb.

The *descente de main* is not to perform a move but simply to stop acting with the hand.

With the *descente de main*, the rider opens his fingers and the horse must keep the same gait, the same attitude, the same cadence.

In Equestrian Art, any excuse is good to release with your fingers. Between *support* and *pull*, there is a whole world.

You must not have ruling hands but hands that are natural, relaxed, with flexible wrists.

Act with the reins at the base of the neck, not at the middle, so that you don't break it.

Any action of the hand must be preceded by an action of the upper body, otherwise you are only acting on the horse's head.

Do not vibrate with your fingers on a tight rein, rather give in a bit before you vibrate with them.

Do not let your horse fall asleep on the hand, do not have a dead hand.

Look for the position of your hands, within a small circular space, that the horse accepts better.

The hand must be a filter, not a plug or an open faucet.

To have a fixed hand is not to pull, but rather to adjust and stay quiet. When riders act excessively, it is often because they act too late rather than at the right time. Many riders act during the exercise that they approached without enough previous impulsion, when it is the opposite that should be done.

It is better to run the risk of losing some contact rather than not releasing it.

Leg action does not necessarily mean action of the calf since the rider's leg begins at the hip. Often it is enough for the hip to act, meaning that the rider has a stronger seat.

Unstable ankles, particularly in sitting trot, is the surest way to wreck the gait.

The legs should be comfortably "close enough" to act quickly and gently, not by tightening but by light touching.

If your legs are hard, you risk receiving a hard horse in the hand.

Do not inflict pressure with the leg in an isolated way; use separate actions.

If you are always acting with your legs, you do not allow the horse to go by himself, thereby you are required to hold more, which results in a lack of finesse and being ineffective with your aids.

Spurs have a lot fewer virtues than we think.

Pressing the spur continuously does not send the horse forward but instead, makes him acquire the habit of holding back.

Even the most violent attack with the spur must be made with a flexible leg. If we touch the horse with stiff legs, he stiffens.

It is important to remember that the legs (just like the hands) can take and give.

Any mistake that you make with your legs you will pay for in the horse's mouth.

[Demonstrating] the exercise of the halt, 1967. *Laurenty Archives.*

Keep in mind that it is the back of the waist and the legs that push the horse forward and the hands' purpose is solely to transmit this power through the aid of discreet reins.

Follow the horse's mouth through your back.

It is with the back of the waist that the rider dominates the horse. The upper body is the centerpiece of the rider, the arms and legs are merely the accessories.

When riding you must move your waist towards the hands and not the hands towards the waist.

Use your hands and legs frugally and compensate with your seat.

Push forward with your back, slow down with your back. One must feel the back and follow the mouth but should care more for the back than the mouth.

A horse needs to be balanced in order to be relaxed and for this to happen he must not be contracted in any way.

Doing without the aids is not to abandon the horse and let him go by

Euclides, Lusitano in passage, Gala de la Piste, Paris 1966. From the book *30 Years with Master Nuno Oliveira*, Xenophon Press 2011.

himself, but rather keeping the contact with the horse while acting as little as possible.

Do not use force with your legs, your hands or your back. There is no need to act constantly.

The *Effet d'Ensemble* (Combined Effect) is a reminder to order, it must always be followed by a giving of the hands and legs.

On the horse, we must rest, not struggle.

During all moments and the horse's life:

- your hands must take and give;
- your legs should intervene every time there is a risk of losing the impulsion.

Learn to do without the use of aids.

The inside rein curves, bends; the outside rein envelops, sits.

If you want to follow your young horse's walk, do it with your waist, not with your hands.

If your horse resists under a left rein action, replace this rein action by using the left leg.

We should not begin riding by learning the effects of reins but by learning to feel.

Warning, danger! When we talk about impulsion to riders, they tend to rush; when talking about lightness, they tend to abandon.

The rider who, in the name of lightness, abandons his horse does not work, he wanders.

Those who jab and pull are barbarians.

It is easier to obtain than to maintain.

At the beginning of a lesson, adjust the intensity of your aid to your horse's mood.

You must arouse the interest of your horse by the discretion of your aids.

When riders act excessively, it is often because they act too late rather than at the right time.

We should not begin riding by learning the effects of reins but by learning to feel. From the book *30 Years with Master Nuno Oliveira*, Xenophon Press 2011.
Oliveira Archives.

Chapter 4: Impulsion, Cadence, Collection, Lightness

Impulsion is a moral and physical disposition of the horse to obey as quickly as possible the rider's orders, to move forward and maintain his propulsive force without the help of aids.

The horse that has true impulsion is the one who keeps the same attitude, the same cadence and the same amount of energy in a given gait, without being carried by the rider.

Between over-excitement and impulsion, there is a world.

Impulsion is a small vibration in the horse, it is not running. Some horses that are unwilling to move forward, though, require you to have to push and sometimes even accelerate a little.

Impulsion is the maintenance of energy within cadence. The more we reduce the extension and speed of the gait, the more we increase impulsion.

If a horse is truly forward, he does not have the time to create difficulties.

The difficulty is to maintain impulsion without using force.

When you ask an exercise of a horse that has impulsion you only need to give him an indication of what is required and after that you only need slight adjusting.

Many riders act during the exercise that they approached without enough previous impulsion, when it is the opposite that should be done.

Since exercises are supposed to relax the horse, how can we supple him if we act all the time?

There are two kinds of impulsion: one where the rider hits, pricks, and obtains furious gestures, or the true one where the horse is in harmony with his rider.

Do not let your horses, in the name of flexibility, begin exercises with laziness. They must be active without being contracted.

Steadiness is part of impulsion: it is its result.

There is no impulsion without cadence and no cadence without impulsion.

A horse in cadence is not a sleeping horse; it is a horse that is reposing [7] to the rider but still vigorous.

To obtain cadence, first create good energy, then act as little as possible; the horse will then cadence himself.

It is very important to obtain a regular cadence; without it, the horse cannot be calm because there is a continuous rupture in his breathing rhythm.

Without cadence, there is no genuine equitation.

Whenever the rider forgets to control the cadence, it is the horse that commands.

The horse becomes supple when he is cadenced and becomes stiff when he precipitates [rushes].

---

[7] maintained in a particular position. - Editor's note.

The cadence of walk that is suitable to each horse is when, without effort from the rider, he walks relaxed and in a correct position.

A good trot cadence is that in which the horse is the most flexible, the most relaxed, lighter.

I'm not saying "put your horse on the bit," but let your horse "drop" on the bit.

At the beginning of a lesson, setting the horse on the bit should be made gradually.

The *ramener* must be proportional to the degree of engagement of the hindquarters and inversely proportional to the velocity.

It is a mistake to keep a horse too long on the bit. One must regularly relax him by doing the transition to walk, long reins, and then gently retake the reins.

It is the horse who, by the impulsion and the engagement of his hindquarters, must come to search for the contact.

Equitation must be a set of exercises that bring the horse on the hand without any weight resistance.

To make the horse come on the hand is a feeling that:
- The neck flexes,
- The back rises,
- The hindquarters engage.

You must look for softness, relaxation. It is better to have a lower neck than a contracted horse.

The relaxation of the mouth alone is not enough, it can be misleading because it does not necessarily result in lightness.

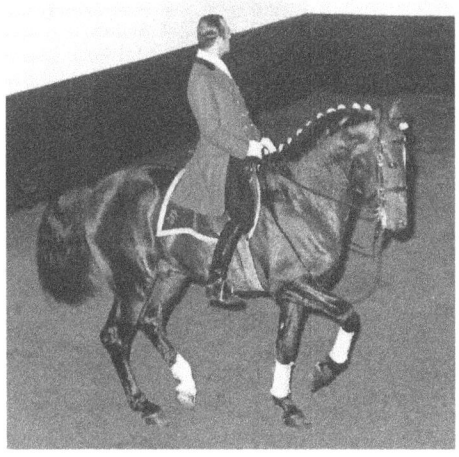

Farsista, piaffe. *Photo by Pedro Villalva.*

It must be accompanied by the relaxation of the whole of the horse. If he gives his back, it will unfailingly have a repercussion on his mouth.

To collect the horse, do not fumble. Strengthen the academic position, with legs that send the horse on a smooth hand.

The feeling of collection is when the rider feels that the horse's tail passes between his legs rather than the horse's head going towards the back.

Positioning the horse's head is not enough. We must feel the movement of the horse's back as if we were riding a feline.

A light horse is not an abandoned horse.

Lightness is the result of impulsion and collection.

People talk a lot about collection, lightness, but I tell you: "Your horse has a head that vibrates. Try, thanks to the gentleness of your hand, to keep the vibration of this head."

Chapter 5: Gaits, Exercises, Straightness

One of the basics of dressage is the regularity of the gaits. You must think about it all the time.

The quality of the preceding gait will determine the quality of the gait that follows.

The walk is a gait that allows the horse to mentally accept many things.

It is in the calmness of the walk that the rider and the horse take the time to meditate and prepare the quality of the trot and the canter that follow.

The walk is good when you can count four equal beats and you can feel his back working with his legs.

When we start trotting, we must have the feeling that it is the hindquarters that push the horse.

Try to get a trot detached from the ground, not along the ground.

When starting an exercise, make few preparations, be concise and fast.

Before starting an exercise, first put the horse in the required position.

When the horse begins an exercise well, stop acting, but without losing the contact.

When you are performing a figure, it is not the horse you have to look at, rather, look at where you are going and where the horse must arrive.

When we ride a circle, it is not for the fun of going in circles but to improve something. Use this opportunity to

Ansioso, beginning the transition from passage to piaffe. *Photo by Pedro Villalva (Póvoa de Santo Adrião).*

improve the balance, the impulsion and the roundness of your horse.

On the circle, use the inside rein as little as possible. On the circle, make sure that the horse does not put weight on the inside shoulder. Your buttocks must have the same contact on both sides. On the circle, stay on the [central] axis of the horse, with the outside shoulder forward.

Going correctly through the corner encompasses many things: impulsion on the straight line, the beginning of a proper circle or a shoulder-in… On the circle, the spine of the horse must fit the curvature of the circle.

In voltes and serpentines, make sure that the horse keeps the same contact on both reins; that is the proof that he does not break his neck.

The horse performs the Spanish walk more easily and correctly, if the walk and the school walk are perfected beforehand. *Photo courtesy of Lucy Jackson.*

Serpentines are a valuable exercise for the study of sensations: we must feel that there is no more resistance in one loop than in the other.

Regularly take the center line in the three gaits to check the straightness of the horse.

When turning down the center line do not allow a change in the speed.

When, on a straight line, the horse is not completely straight, slightly swing the hands right and left to oppose the shoulders to the hips, and stop when you feel him straight.

A straight horse is not only straight in his shoulders and hips but also straight in his ears.

The horse is straight when:
- He keeps the cadence,
- He is not heavier in the hand on one side than the other,
- On the center line, he can on the spot initiate a 6 meter volte, either to the right or to the left.

Before asking for a halt, we must put the horse into a ball.

When halting, do not bring the hands towards the back but send your waist towards the hands.

Rein back is a useful exercise provided it is calm and straight.

To teach the horse to rein back one must make him understand this movement using simple means, on the ground for instance.

The arena is similar to a drawing paper where the horse draws figures like a compass: look for the geometry of these figures.

Chapter 6:
Transitions - Extensions

Jean Magnan de Bornier, Faraó.
Oliveira Archives.

In transitions, ensure the steadiness of the front end. If the steadiness is lacking, it is because there is not enough impulsion. A horse that increases or decreases his speed while raising the neck is the antithesis of equitation [and lacks impulsion].

Concerning the transition from walk to trot, all the books say that the horse must keep the neck at the same height, but I prefer that the horse completes this transition by keeping the same mindset.

If your horse transitions from walk to trot without changing the position of his head and neck, it means the walk had a correct impulsion. To switch from trot to walk, keep the impulsion and give immediately but keep the contact.

In transitions between different trots, watch the following:

- Having a stable position of the neck,
- Maintaining the cadence,
- Requesting the transitions by using the upper body and not the hands.

An extension is a shifting of contact frontward and downward, it is not letting go of the reins.

We can, by pricking and pulling, obtain extensions. However, to be a useful exercise, the extension should not be forced, otherwise we lose the benefits of the preceding work.

A horse cannot give an extension with his head in the air, he will only precipitate [rush] with a hollow back.

Make sure that the horse does not raise his neck when starting the extension. The neck must remain flexed.

In the extension, it is important not to lose the sensation of the cadence.

In an extension, we must be content with what the horse can give.

In the extension, the horse should extend a bit the neck but remain rounded.

In the extension, have the waist forward but without putting the shoulders too far back.

When in extended trot, if the horse gives spectacular movement, it is great, but what matters for me is that he stays relaxed.

You must not 'push' during the extension, or you will lose the cadence; it is before that you have to push.

When leaving the long side to initiate a diagonal in extended trot,

Extended trot at the presentation of the Alter Real horses in Palácio das Necessidades, Lisbon - 1967. *Oliveira Archives.*

make sure that the horse does not move away on his inside shoulder.

For an extension on the long side or on the diagonal, everything is actually prepared on the small side where we must request extra collection and control the passage of the second corner.

Here is one way to prepare for a trot extension:

- Start with some variations between collected and medium trot,
- Ask for a very active renvers with more contact on the snaffle rein, especially on the outside rein,
- Straighten the horse after the second corner of the small side, with a straight neckline,
- If necessary, push, but only in the first two or three steps of the extension.

Chapter 7: Shoulder-In

The shoulder-in is the aspirin of riding: it heals everything.

The corner of the arena, the volte and the shoulder-in are a love triangle.

The shoulder-in is not only a suppling exercise but also a means of domination.

The shoulder-in is a corner passage that extends until the end of the long side of the arena.

It is not so much about the horse walking sideways but that he walks with a bend.

Contrary to the rule where the hindquarters need to be engaged before starting an exercise, shoulder-in is not a precondition, it is a consequence: it is the exercise that makes the engagement of the hindquarters.

The goal is not to force the horse to do the exercise but to do it with a relaxed horse. A shoulder-in that is not properly executed is absolutely useless: it is twisting the horse in contraction.

Requesting a shoulder-in is rather about controlling the outer side than pushing the inner side.

In shoulder-in it is the croup that pushes, it does not drag behind a broken neck.

The shoulder-in is easy to execute if you start it gently. If you do too many things, the horse resists.

By fear of lack of impulsion, do not ask for a shoulder-in in a fast and precipitate walk. It must be asked in a slow, cadenced walk, so the horse can engage and flex his joints.

In the shoulder-in the outside aids control and support.

In the shoulder-in, feel:

- that the horse supports himself
- that the outside rein receives all the actions from the inside rein
- that you help your horse by alternately passing the weight of the inner buttock on the outside buttock
- that the horse puts his weight on his inside hind leg and not on the outside shoulder.

In shoulder-in, the inside leg acts close to the girth (so that the haunches do not slip), not by compression but using soft pressures. The outside leg may play a momentary role behind the girth to curve the horse.

If, in the shoulder-in, the horse gets behind the hand, it is because his neck is broken.

Once you started the shoulder-in, open the fingers of the inside hand (*descente de main*).

In the execution of the shoulder-in, the outer hind leg should not move sideways [outward] too much: it should not go past the leg of the rider.

Do not bend the neck of the horse too much; his head should not go past the imaginary line separating the front legs.

Don't pull the horse's head too much to the inside. Sue Oliveira, shoulder-in. *Oliveira Archives.*

João Oliveira on a young horse, introducing the shoulder-in. *Photo courtesy of Lucy Jackson.*

The hand begins at the shoulder; in the exercise of shoulder-in, do not raise the [rider's] inside shoulder, relax it.

In shoulder-in, send your body towards your outside elbow.

If, in the shoulder-in, your horse yields to your inside leg, cease to act; otherwise, you will rush the pace.

If the horse puts too much weight on the outside shoulder, bring both your hands slightly to the inside.

If, for example, in a right shoulder-in, the horse pulls away from the wall, send him back [to the wall] first by bringing the left hand to the left, and only then [secondarily] also bring the right hand to the left.

If the shoulder-in is well-executed, the horse should reach the end of the long side more flexible, more relaxed. If it was forced, he will arrive at the end even more rigid.

Chapter 8: Half-Pass

Lateral work is only valid if the horse is in a state of impulsion, cadence, lightness.

Half-pass is not about rushing sideways, which would be one way of the horse protecting himself, but walking with flexibility.

Do not begin a half-pass if the horse is not energetic in his gait.

One of the utilities of the half-pass is to mobilize the hindquarters which must push the mass.

To correct a half-pass is difficult: its success depends mainly on the conditions that are in place at the start.

In the walk half-pass, the horse should not leap, he should walk.

Start the half-pass with an impulsion that allows you to maintain the same cadence, without slowing down or speeding up.

If the half-pass is well-prepared, you will only have to be concerned about the lateral progression.

In the half-pass, the horse must move towards the hand on the side where he is going.

During the half-pass, feel that it is the outside hindquarter that pushes the mass.

In the half-pass send your hip and your body towards your inner elbow, which replaces a lot of the use of the inside leg.

If, in the half-pass, the haunches advance too much, replace the action of the outside leg by that of the outside rein.

In the half-pass, look at where you want to go; this will help you to put your shoulders parallel to those of the horse.

Send the horse towards the inside rein. If the forehand is not working enough, push it with the outside hand.

Do not over-bend, otherwise, you will block the shoulder on the side [inside] where the horse goes.

To improve a half-pass or to overcome resistance, change from half-pass to shoulder-in until the horse yields his inner side, and then return to the half-pass.

In a real half-pass, the horse should not put even one extra gram on his inside shoulder. So, make sure that the horse remains in the axis up to reaching the wall without rushing the last steps.

Before starting a half-pass, thoroughly check the impulsion so you do not have to push all the time during the half-pass.

In the half-pass, the inside leg is the most important. It is the one that receives the horse, holds the bend and, if needed, maintains the impulsion.

Although in the half-pass each rein has a different position, make sure that they both have the same tension, otherwise, you are going against the movement.

Use your outside rein to settle your half-pass issues.

Ingemisco, half-pass at the walk on the diagonal. *Oliveira Archives.*

Lucy Jackson riding Baritone, beginning to work in half-pass.
Photo courtesy of Jane Turley.

Place the horse in the half-pass position and, once started, try to follow him just with your seat.

For the half-pass, also apply the rule of ceasing to act once the movement is started. It is a matter of psychology, rewarding obedience. Cease to act, certainly, but keep the legs near the horse to intervene quickly.

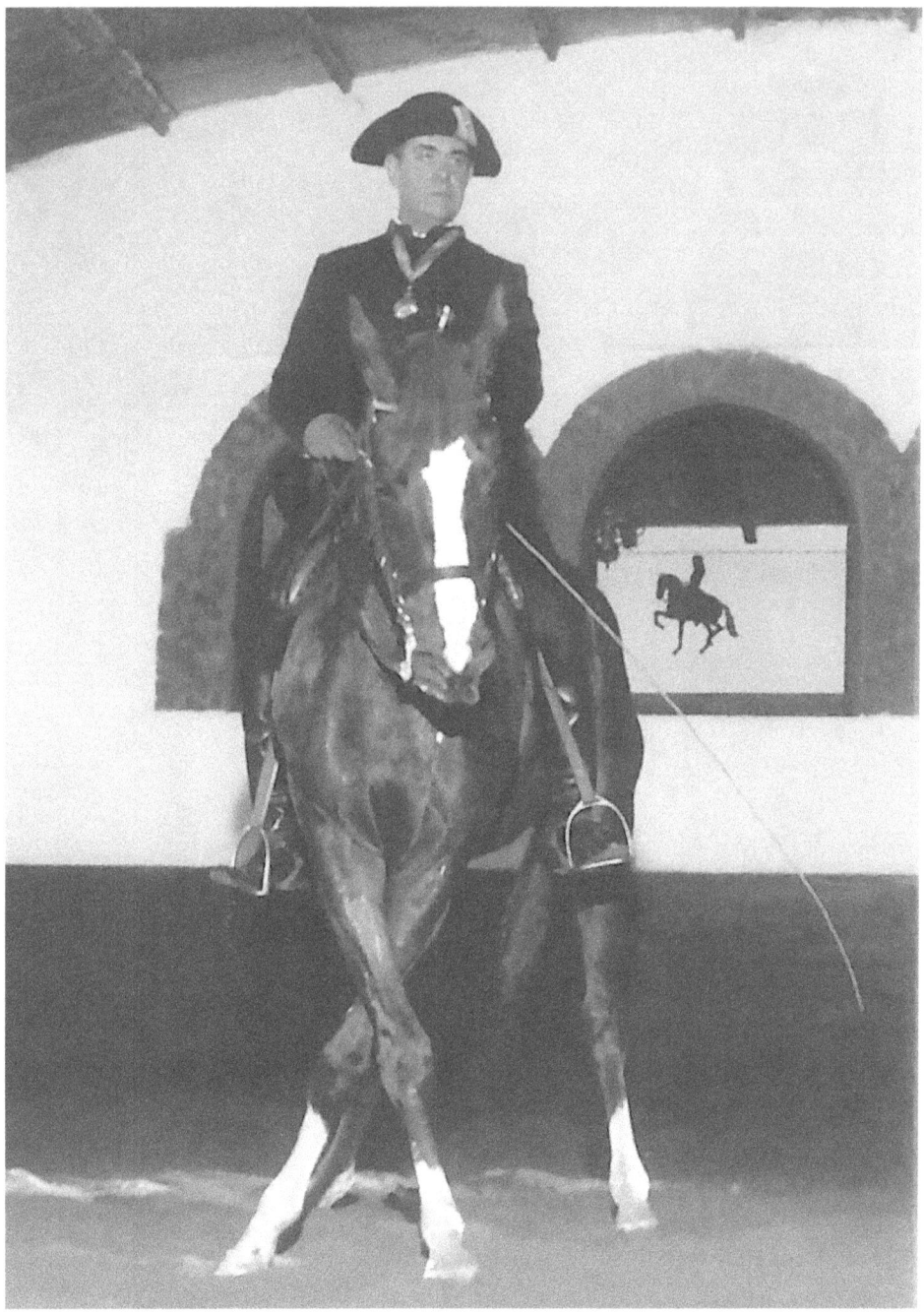

Svitok, in half-pass. When changing hands on two tracks the horse crosses his legs. Nuno Oliveira at Quinta do Brejo wearing the insignia of Offical of the Order of Infante D. Henrique. *Photo by Polana Studios.*

Chapter 9: Canter Work

Canter is a succession of three leaps, each leap containing the next one.

Rather than striving to obtain at any cost a flying change or to do a lot of things in canter, look for the purity of the gait. The rest is little things.

In canter, breathe deeply and calmly; dilate your chest.

The qualities of a good canter are round, impulsive, straight, cadenced, and light.

When starting the canter feel that the horse is raising his forehand and is not throwing himself forward.

The horse must not lift his neck either at the start or during the canter.

In canter, it is not the upper body that should move a lot, it is the waist that must soften.

Do not be content with any old canter transition. Improving the departure will result in the improvement of the quality of the canter.

In canter, be seated, and that is all.

Do not try to cadence a canter of a horse that is not collected, you may extinguish the impulsion.

The more a horse slows down his canter, the more he needs impulsion.

For a horse to be able to have a good swinging motion in his canter he must be straight. So, avoid over-bending him.

People often tend to exaggerate the bend when cantering: the horse struggles and contracts himself.

Canter work carried out to perfection is on the highest level of training.
Oliveira Archives.

To keep the cadence of the canter, the horse must have his shoulders at the right place.

For a good canter transition, do not advance the inside leg; leave it at its place.

If you need to touch with the legs while cantering, avoid letting the rider's knee come up.

In canter, the outside rein seats the horse, the inside rein extends the neck down.

In the counter-canter tracking left (i.e., on the right lead) send the horse's body on the right hand.

In canter, if the rider moves little, the horse cadences himself better.

In canter, the horse should carry himself with the same amount of energy as in the other gaits and not be carried by the hands and legs of the rider.

Vizir, son of Euclides. The young horse shows total attention to his trainer as he demonstrates left flexion while passing through the corner of the hillside arena at Quinta do Brejo. *Oliveira Archives.*

Canter in such a way that, in case you give the reins, the horse does not increase his speed. This requires a swinging and relaxed canter.

If your horse tends to rush in canter, play more with your upper body than with your hands.

We must not try to place the horse in canter before he is well-established in the trot.

It is the outside rein that straightens the horse, by placing the shoulders in front of the haunches.

In canter, we should not do exceptional actions of the reins: the outside rein must act parallel to the body of the horse.

When cantering around the arena, it is helpful to consider each of the four corners as a small bit of shoulder-in; this is one of the secrets of developing a successful flying change on the diagonal.

If the horse puts more weight on the inside shoulder during a circle in canter it is good to support the inner side with the inside leg.

In the counter-canter on the circle, prevent the horse from throwing his haunches outward, hence the importance of giving only a light bend.

To canter on the circle, it is beneficial to replace, in some cases, the use of the inside rein with the use of the inside calf.

On the circle in canter, the rider's weight must remain in line with the axis of the horse. If the horse puts too much weight on the outside, use the outside lateral aids [outside leg and outside rein]: if he puts weight inside, use the inside lateral aids [inside leg and inside rein].

If your horse tends to rush his canter, play: do not block a single rein; take the left, give the right, take the right, give the left, take both, give both. Vary the [rein] support you provide.

With some horses we must ask for a canter extension to calm them; with others, you have to ask for this to have them be forward.

When we extend the canter and the horse is with the nose down, we should not keep our back stiff and leaning backwards, but follow the horse by tilting the upper body a little forward so as not to oppose the movement.

To go from canter to walk, do not use strength; straighten and grow your chest, close and open your fingers once, but without blocking them.

If you return to the walk after a canter, set up your walk to collect your horse and get a new, even better canter; this is the utility of transitions.

In the counter-canter on the short side, make sure the horse does not increase his speed.

The basic canter is a three-beat leaping gait. *Oliveira Archives.*

When, after a counter-canter, you take the diagonal to return to the true canter, do it by using the legs and your upper body, not by using your hands.

When, after a free canter, we take the horse back onto the circle, he should come back immediately into the position (*mise-en-main*).

The canter to walk transition is more important than the walk to canter transition. Coming back to the walk must be made calmly, without the horse sighing with tension, without him opening or precipitating.

In canter, use your hands as little as possible so that the horse remains straight.

The more the walk is collected the easier the transition to canter will be.

In canter, relax your back and do not move more or less than the horse.

It is sometimes useful to raise your hands a little to slow the canter and seat the horse.

Chapter 10: Flying Changes

When a horse can make canter to walk transitions calmly and can start canter on either lead anywhere in the arena, he is ready for the flying changes.

A flying change is a canter departure departing from the canter.

To obtain a good flying change we must, above all, improve the initial canter depart.

Ask for a flying change in the calm spirit of a relaxed canter; one should not hear a "huh" of effort.

To have good flying changes, the canter should be leaping, one must feel the horse's bascule.

It is preferable to do two good flying changes rather than thirty mediocre ones.

One of the secrets of the flying changes is to have the horse's shoulders in the same line as the hips, but many riders approach them with the haunches in.

It is not the intensity of the demand that matters for the flying changes, it is the form of the initial canter depart.

In the execution of a flying change, from right to left, for example, it is useful to slide the right buttock sideways towards the left, which corresponds to put the right shoulder back.

When you request a flying change on the long side, do not let the horse stick his shoulders to the wall.

It is a mistake to believe that it is necessary to bend the horse on the side to which he is changing. Take care not to twist him; maintain a straight neckline.

In the flying change, we tend to place the [new] outside leg too far back, causing a shortened movement.

If your horse is laterally very flexible, do not ask the flying changes with the leg too far back: it would make the hips swing and would also be an obstacle in the promptness to the request.

Do not let the horse "run" after a flying change.

When asking the flying changes along the long side, be sure to have more contact on the side of the wall. Otherwise, you throw the shoulders against the wall.

The more we bring the flying changes closer [together in count], the more we should control the cadence.

When we bring the flying changes closer, it is essential to keep the same tension on both reins, otherwise, the flying changes will never be straight.

Chapter 11: Piaffe, Passage

The rider should know exactly on what occasion to start the learning of piaffe. With some horses, it helps to start the piaffe early in in-hand work. With some others, asking for mounted piaffe too early can be a serious error for the entire life of the horse.

The piaffe should be a means at the disposal of the rider to round and dominate the horse.

The piaffe should always be a conquest of balance.

From the beginning of teaching piaffe, the horse must be absolutely straight.

The great pitfall of piaffe is that most riders want from the start to obtain too much action. They forget that, before he obtains elevation, the horse must remain as calm and relaxed as in walk.

When asking for piaffe, the rider must stop the horse a few steps before he will stop by himself.

With some horses that are not powerful in the hindquarters, it is better to ask at the beginning of piaffe that he starts with the head a little down.

In the training of piaffe, we must often stop and then let the horse calm down and lengthen his neck.

It is necessary to know the power that one horse has in his hocks in order to feel how much we can seat him in his piaffe.

One of the most important things in the tact of a trainer is to know exactly what dose of relaxation and

Bunker: In order for the horse to display all the vibrancy that he possesses when doing passage and piaffe, the lightness must be consistent. Quinta do Brejo.
Photo courtesy of Lucy Jackson.

nervous impulse is necessary to ask for the performance of a given exercise. For the piaffe we tend to ask for too much nervous impulse; as a consequence, whenever asked to piaffe, the horse is always a little excited.

Baucher was right: in the piaffe, a small swing of the hand from left to right and from right to left helps to straighten and cadence the horse.

In the execution of the piaffe, never forget the principle: put the horse in position and let him execute, *"placer et laisser faire."* When you feel that the horse piaffes with all his heart: *Descente de main and descente de jambes* [lower (yield) the rein and relax (yield) the leg aid - Editor's note].

The sign of a good piaffe and a good passage is the time of suspension of

Bunker performing a correctly learned passage. Quinta do Brejo.
Photo courtesy of Lucy Jackson.

each diagonal rather than too much elevation with little suspension.

For the piaffe, the ground work and the work on the wall must be very tactful and delicate. Before undertaking it, the horse must know the shoulder-in and the half-pass asked for on the ground with the help of the whip.

In the piaffe work on the ground, the help of the whip is very important. The horse must accept the contact of the whip on all his body, he should not be afraid each time the rider makes a gesture with the arm that holds the whip, and his eye should remain confident.

In the work of piaffe on the ground, it is necessary, for each horse, to know in which place to touch the hindquarter, see what attitude he takes when he is touched at this or that place.

In the long reins, the work of the piaffe can be very profitable for impulsion and straightness.

The premature teaching of the passage is a serious error. The neophyte who rides a horse tending to hover his trot and who takes advantage of it to put his horse in the passage—which is not at that time a collected passage but a gazelle passage—commits an error which will definitely spoil the trot of his horse.

At the beginning of the passage, some horses raise one diagonal more than the other.

Determine first if it is the posterior which has difficulty engaging or the shoulder that has difficulty lifting up. In the first case, the opposite leg to this diagonal must act at the right moment with more intensity. In the second case, it is recommended to bend the horse a little toward the more active shoulder's side, so that the shoulder of the lazy diagonal is more open, which facilitates its elevation.

The perfection of the passage cannot be achieved without having previously worked the horse well in the school trot.

Do not ask for passage/piaffe transitions before the horse is well confirmed in his passage on the circles, serpentines, figures of eight and all exercises.

It is a mistake to think that to execute a transition from piaffe to passage it is always necessary to require more energy. It depends on the horse. With some horses, it is necessary to gently put the hindquarters in position to make the transition and relieve them then.

With a sensitive and well-schooled horse, it is with the waist that we ask for the transition passage/piaffe and piaffe/passage. The rider's waist should be very relaxed and his back must feel the horse's back very well.

For the horse to give all the brilliance that his whole body is capable of ("…tout le brillant que comporte son ensemble"— Etienne Beudant [*Horse Training: Outdoors and High School*, Xenophon Press 2014]) in the execution of the passage and the piaffe, lightness must be constant and the legs of the rider have to be lowered. Then the horse points the ears forward, grows his front by the engagement of the hindquarters and looks proud, taking pleasure in his air.

Va Pensiero, Alter Real: Doing piaffe is always a balancing exercise. Quinta do Brejo. *Oliveira Archives.*

Chapter 12: The Young Horse

The breaking of a young horse must, above all, be addressed in his mind: it is about "preparing" him to be schooled.

Pay attention to the coordination of the aids in the work on the lunge; the lunge replaces the reins and the long whip the legs.

The goal of the work in side reins is to get the fixity of the base of the neck in the transitions.

When a young horse is "routined" in the lunge work, it is useful to make him jump small obstacles.

Work on the ground can give a great advance in the work and great domination, but it must be approached only by experienced riders possessing great tact.

One of the first principles to respect: never oppose the forward movement.

Never "corner" a young horse; he must be morally relaxed.

An example of a first mounted lesson:
- walk and rising trot.
- keep the horse along the wall by holding the outside rein open while keeping the whip against the inside shoulder.
- to turn: open inside rein.
- execute some steps of a faster trot.
- the next day, push him gently on in the rising trot so he can come into a large canter, on the circle.

Once the young horse performs some geometric figures well, we can ask, in the walk, using the inside lateral aids, for some portions of the circle with haunches-out. Progressively we will get to the long side with slight shoulders-in, then lateral work.

The golden rule for young horses:
- forward.
- nose on the ground.

The lesson of the nose on the ground:
- This work, especially recommended for horses with the neck too high and a hollow back, is good for all young horses.
- We can use the draw reins for this work, not to place the head but to lengthen the neck.
- With the horse on the circle (trotting at first), "play" with the inside rein until he lowers his head and raises his back. Reward immediately by ceasing the action of the rein.

Next, do the same work in the other gaits
- Then execute transitions walk/trot, nose on the ground.

If the young horse lacks energy, perform some transitions from trot to canter in the following way:

With the horse cantering to the right on a circle, for example, put his hips on the outside by opening the right rein to the right and down. The horse must throw himself on the right shoulder and fall instantly into a great energetic trot. Go back to canter and so on.

To perfect the trot of the young horse, execute many changes of direction which will mobilize him.

On the warm-up rising trot, pat the neck on the right and left, without

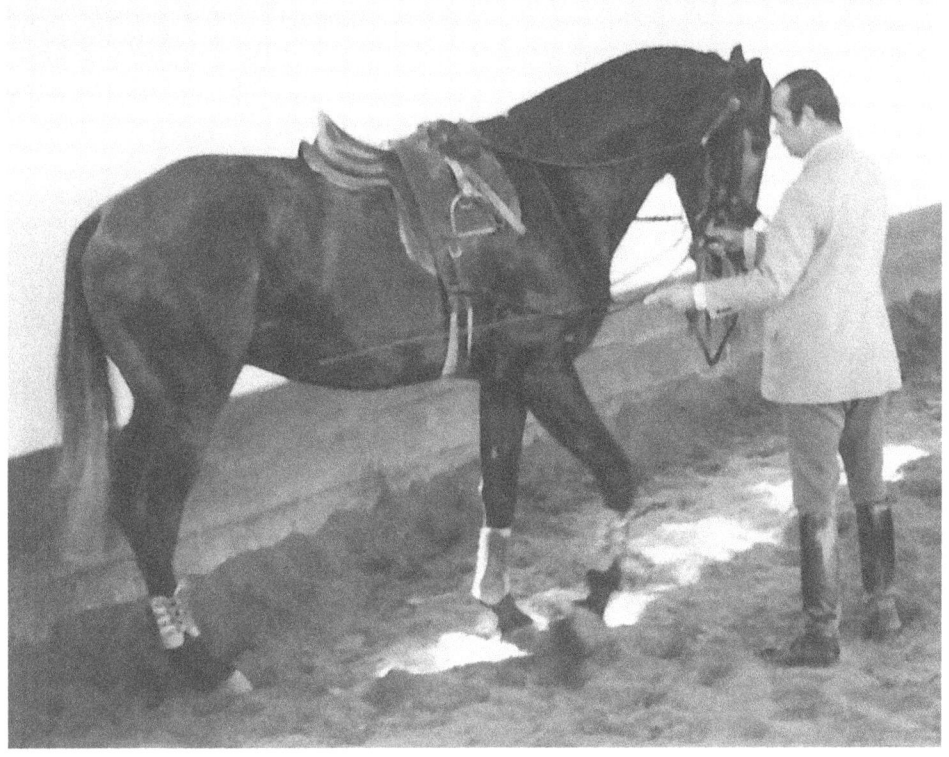

Vizir: work in hand after lungeing. *Oliveira Archives*.

letting go of the reins: it is a way to obtain an elongation of the neck.

With a young horse, work 85% at the rising trot and 15% at the sitting trot.

It is useful to frequently ask the young horse for some halts; the halt calms and relaxes. Halt by an action of the upper body and not by a traction of the reins, as straight as possible, without him falling on one shoulder or the other. Resume the movement with long reins.

Do not try to ask a young horse for the *ramener* before obtaining a relaxed and flexible back.

We cannot expect a young horse to be immediately placed (in *mise-en-main*), but we must try to obtain a constant attitude of the front with an almost immobile head. Even with a young horse, when going through a corner we must demand that he have the tip of his nose to the inside.

If one asks too early for complicated things before the horse walks, trots and canters quietly and with impulsion, we begin a fight which never ends.

Get the young horse used to reducing his speed by transitioning from rising trot to sitting trot and not by pulling on the reins but only by the fact of sitting down.

Small variations in the gait are more likely to keep a young horse active and fully attentive than kicking with the spurs.

With the young horses, apply the principle "Hands without legs, legs without hands" (do not use the *combined effect*). Hands only to teach him to know his mouth and to obey the reins, legs only to carry him forward without slowing him down.

Not having to resort to "methods" is done by taking care of all the details of the transitions so that one prepares the *rassembler*.

With a young horse, do not set the stirrups too low, you risk searching to find their base.

With a young horse, use unilateral aids [left leg and left rein together OR right leg and right rein together].

An excellent exercise for the young horse is to ask for a counter shoulder-in [shoulder-out] along the wall and, after the second corner, to change the bend and do shoulder-in. At the end of it, let the horse gradually lower the neckline.

With a young horse, do not approach the counter-canter before getting a balanced canter and calm departures.

The last impressions of the horse before returning to the box are very important. Try to make sure that at the time of the last halt, he calmly puts the nose on the ground.

Book 3b
Notes on Elementary Equitation

Intended for the riding instructors of the Manila Polo Club, Philippines

Nuno Oliveira on Ulisses in passage, September 1962 from *30 Years with Master Nuno Oliveira*, Xenophon Press 2011.

- Editor's note

The following lines were edited by Nuno Oliveira in February 1972 in Manila at the request of the instructors of the Equestrian Circle of the Manila Polo Club.

Despite the resemblance of some passages in the text to certain preceding notes, it still seemed interesting to publish the text in its entirety.

Contents

Preliminary Remarks..118

Work in the Riding Lessons...119

Impulsion..119

The Position of the Rider..119

Position According to the Movement..120

Flexibility Exercises of the Rider...120

Brief Principles of the Use of the Reins..120

The Impulsive Action of the Rider's Legs...121

A Beginner's Riding Lesson..122

The Choice of the Horse for the Beginner..122

The Length of the Stirrups...122

Study of the Conformation of Each Horse, of the Way He Moves,
    and Where to Tighten the Girth...123

The Geometry of School Figures..123

Cadence of the Gaits..123

Preparation Work of the Horse for Competition......................................124

Using the Snaffle Bit..125

Preliminary Remarks

Foremost, what the teacher must first inculcate in the pupil's mind is the love of the horse. He must also gradually observe the character of the pupil and see how quickly he must make him move forward. There are pupils who, due to their character and physical abilities, can progress fairly quickly, while for others, the instructor will have to be content making them gain confidence and seat very gradually.

To love the horse is not only giving him caresses or carrots and sugar. It is also, when one rides him, to feel that he walks willingly and if he is resisting. If most instructors wanted to observe, they would notice how many times the same horse, that refuses to walk properly in a lesson with some beginners, works well without being pushed or forced with another beginner. By observing a variety of cases, the teacher must choose the right horse for each student. It is imperative that before putting a student in the saddle and with two reins in hand, it is necessary to put him on a horse which, when lunged, can transition from one average gait to another without jerking or making sudden movements either with his neck or with his limbs.

With a *voltige* harness and without a saddle, the beginner can start to feel his horse, to feel his movements and to be able to relax without having to worry about driving the horse forward, which he otherwise could not do properly because of the instability of his seat. Thus, by alternating the suppleness exercises of the arms, torso and legs, the student begins to acquire the ease that will allow him to keep the horse in a close-to-correct position.

I insist on how the horse should be kept in the correct position for this job. The transitions from walk to trot, trot to walk, trot to canter, canter to trot or walk, must be made without precipitation [rushing] and without the horse putting all his weight on the shoulders.

On the lunge, the pupil must hold himself correctly (particularly in the transitions), while taking the surcingle first with both hands, then with only one hand, while the free arm performs exercises of relaxation, and finally repeat without holding onto the surcingle.

The teacher should explain to the student the function of the lower back and waist, which must lower and advance without rigidity.

Students should not be told to put their shoulders back, as there is the risk that they will develop the tendency to hold the torso rigidly. Instead, tell them to let the waist come forward flexibly. It is only when the pupil can sit correctly on the lunge that one can put him in a riding lesson with the others.

The teacher that has previously studied the student's character will use these observations to choose the horse that the student will ride in the lessons.

Work in the Riding Lessons

When in a beginner riding lesson, if there is none among them who can properly lead his horse in a regular pace in front of the others, then place a more advanced rider who can do so. In fact, it is the one who is in the lead that has the responsibility to maintain a regular rhythm in all the evolutions that the teacher recommends. Therefore, it is necessary that the horse in the lead has very regular and rhythmic gaits.

Impulsion

From the beginning, you have to talk to the student about impulsion. However, first you have to know what impulsion is. One must not confuse the state of over-excitation of a horse who gives falsely brilliant gestures with impulsion. Impulsion has its starting point in the horse's head.

Good impulsion is that of the horse who, in a relaxed attitude, can maintain the pace desired by his rider without the help of the aids, deploying the same intensity of energy and in a constant position.

It is obvious that the horse's deployment of energy in each movement depends on the degree of advancement of his rider. The horse ridden by the beginner will have and must maintain a degree of impulsion that is not the same as if it were mounted by a trained rider. Nevertheless, the impulsion must always be there. And it is the morale of the horse that one must first address and, if force were to be used, we enter a field that does not belong to Equestrian Art or civilized people.

The Position of the Rider

The rider must have a correct position. A good physical proportion of the rider makes this position easier, but it can always be correct with any physique.

Each part of the body of the rider must rest on the part that is below it.

The buttocks must open and flatten on the saddle. The shoulders should go down very well and relax because the shoulders are the beginning of the hand.

The wrists should be relaxed and the elbows should rest against the torso.

The thighs should be as vertical as possible and the legs adhering. It is not the knee that has to tighten against the saddle flaps, but the popliteal fossa[8]. The fat of the calf should be in soft contact, without being pressed.

---

[8] popliteal fossa is a diamond-shaped space behind the knee joint. It is formed between the muscles in the posterior compartments of the thigh and leg. This anatomical landmark is the major route by which structures pass between the thigh and leg. - Editor's note.

Thelma Granpré Molière on Anne's Folly: sitting upright in a high levade.
Oliveira Archives.

The feet must have the same degree of obliquity as in walking. The widest part of the foot must rest on the tread of the stirrups; the widest part is behind the toes.

The inner part of the stirrup should be slightly pressed; the heels must be more down than the tip of the foot but not by much, and without force. Take the reins as if you had a candle in each hand.

Position According to the Movement

This correctness in the position must be maintained in the paces, but not with rigidity. On the contrary, the rider must go with his horse.

You must always put your weight in accordance with the movement of the horse. For example, if the horse turns right, put a little more weight on the right buttock. Try to slip the coccyx towards the saddle pommel. Put the shoulders parallel to the horse's shoulders. Operate the waist so that the torso of the rider does not resist the undulations of the horse's back. Go correctly with the horse, do not oppose the motion. Follow the horse's mouth employing a flexible back.

Flexibility Exercises of the Rider

All suppleness exercises either of the arms or the legs of the rider must be done in cadence with the pace of the horse.

In addition, the rider must sit deeply while he is performing these exercises so that everything happens without contraction, fatigue, or hurried movements of the rider, who transmits to the horse all he does, good or bad.

These flexibility exercises of the rider must be performed efficiently on a horse that remains very calm, relaxed and at average gaits.

Brief Principles of the Use of the Reins

Each action of the rider's hand must be preceded by an adjustment of the torso to the movement of the horse.

1. To turn to the right with an opening rein, the rider's elbow must rest on his upper body, and the right wrist should turn outward so that the nails are turned upwards. The outer rein has to advance a little like the handlebars on a bicycle.

However, the rider must always maintain the same intensity of contact as on the inner rein. This assumes that the rider's outside shoulder advances.

2. To stop, move the navel to the hands while keeping the distance existing between the hands and the body of the rider. At this point, the thumbs must tighten on the reins.

3. These actions of direct reins are the only ones that should be used for beginners. Later on, more advanced riders should be taught that the action of an opening direct rein brings the head of the horse to that side and throws the horse's body outwards.

4. The action of the outer rein toward the inside brings the shoulders inward. The action of this rein must be done with a compensation of the inner rein so that the head of the horse remains straight and is not bent outwards.

5. It is very important that the torso of the rider precede the action of the hand. It is the only way to make the actions of the reins less hard.

6. When one uses an equal action of the two reins to turn, this intermediate action acts approximately on all the horse's body.

The Impulsive Action of the Rider's Legs

When the rider needs to use his legs to give impulsion to his horse, he must do it with the muscles of

Francis Laurenty on Império: active leg in the passage. *Oliveira Archives.*

the legs well-relaxed so that the horse receives touches that may be more or less strong, but still flexible.

In order to be able to touch this way, it is also necessary that the leg not be pressed [onto the horse's side] at the initiation of the request. Whatever the rider does with his legs, he is paid in return; he receives it back in the hand.

The actions can be more or less strong depending on the case but never contracted. When we contract one part of the body, we tend to contract the rest. The continuous action of the legs to maintain the impulsion is nonsense. The horse becomes accustomed to this continual action and falls asleep.

Touch, profit from this touching, feel the moment when it will be necessary to touch again; touch at the moment, and stop.

Touch with the legs, making them function from the back towards the front and not the opposite: it is very important. When the [rider's] legs function [correctly] from the back towards the front, the buttocks push; when one does the opposite [working with the legs from front to back], the buttocks tend to come back, which is in opposition to the forward movement.

A Beginner's Riding Lesson

So that the more timid and less passionate beginners enjoy the practice of riding, the teacher must be able to interest his students by his qualities of calmness, intelligence, dynamism and avoidance of monotony.

The instructor should explain without making big speeches; he should not ask for more than the students can do. He should know how to mix exercises of relaxation with varied school figures, and later he should know how to organize games; these are useful so that the students practice the leading and the control of their horse, but avoiding over excitement.

It is very important not to make the lessons monotonous and it is necessary to correct without making big speeches and without getting angry, to give energy to the lesson, remaining calm, without getting upset. That is all you need to do to get the student to progress by staying in mental relaxation.

It is always necessary that in his requests the professor is moderate and does not go beyond the possibilities of the pupil as well as the horse.

Do not lose sight of the fact that before asking for any new movement, you have to prepare the horse, give him time to put himself in a physical and mental attitude to undertake this new movement, especially for the canter.

The Choice of the Horse for the Beginner

In a lesson for beginners, the teacher must know a little about the character and temperament of his students, the same way he must have in mind the peculiarities of his lesson horses. A pupil who tends to get angry, to excite himself, should ride a phlegmatic horse. On the other hand, to a more phlegmatic student, it is necessary to give a more active though easily controllable horse.

The place to be given to each horse in a lesson is also very important. We must see which horse must be in the lead, and see the places to be assigned to each horse so that everyone, whether in front or behind, can walk properly without being upset or stopped.

The Length of the Stirrups

In an equitation school, the rider must have his legs well down, resting his foot on the stirrup, but without feeling that the stirrup shortens his leg. Nor should he have difficulty maintaining contact with the stirrup in case the horse makes a large or sudden movement. Normally the stirrups are adjusted as follows: having the legs well down and free, adjust the stirrup leather so that the surface of the stirrup is at the height of the rider's ankle bone.

In outdoor riding, one must shorten the stirrups two holes approximately, and in jumping three to four holes, according to the reactions of the horse and according to the height of the jumps.

Adjusting the stirrup leathers with the arm is too approximate. The length of the arms is not always related to the length of the legs. There are riders with long arms and short legs and vice versa.

Teach the student to know the horse, teach him how to approach him, the care to give him, etc. The beginner must not only learn to sit on the back of his horse. He must know a little what this brave animal is, how to approach him, hold him in hand, saddle him, bridle him, lift his feet, and also about his grooming and food. The teacher must teach the beginners how to lead a horse in hand, how to lift his feet, caress him, bridle him, saddle him, etc. Then, in the saddlery, teach him how to disassemble, reassemble, and clean the tack. It is essential that the beginner acquires all these notions and that the teacher knows how to interest him in all of that.

Study of the Conformation of Each Horse, of the Way He Moves, and Where to Tighten the Girth

It is falsely believed that all horses should have the girth in the same place and with the same degree of tightening. It is necessary to determine precisely if the saddle on a particular horse is not too much on the shoulders, which could hinder the movements of his forelegs and put the rider too far on the forehand. For other horses, we must see that the saddle is not too much on his loins, the rider being too far back and putting too much weight where he should not.

It is important to check which saddle is best for each horse. See that the saddle does not rest too much on the withers nor squeezing them too much. See that the girth, due to excessive tightening, does not cause in the horse a discomfort that could make him work contracted. Generally, the horse who works in the school at a moderate pace does not need to have the girth too tight, only snug enough so that the saddle does not slide.

The Geometry of School Figures

Right from the beginning, the instructor must instill in the mind of the student discipline in the way of making the school figures, even the simplest, because with this discipline he begins to be obliged to properly lead the horse and the horse himself, not deviating on the shoulders, works with more impulsion and discipline.

Cadence of the Gaits

It is important not to mistake cadence with laziness, nor precipitation [rushing] with impulsion. The horse must cadence the gaits while keeping his impulsion. Cadence is only possible when the horse is relaxed, decontracted. It occurs when the back of the horse is supple and the movement of the hindquarters corresponds to the movement of the front legs.

When the horse is contracted and rigid, his back—which is the connection between the hind legs and the front legs—does not allow the attitude of the hind legs to correspond to that of the front legs, and vice versa, due to the contraction.

Yet the back of the horse cannot be relaxed without his neck being in a relaxed position and the horse not fighting with his mouth. And usually, the horse fights with his mouth because his rider, not knowing what a walk, a trot, a gallop is, and whose back does not feel what happens in the back of the horse, pulls on the reins.

The moment has come to talk about cadence: what is a horse in cadence? It is a horse that is not sleepy, but also, it is the horse that maintains the same tempo, relaxed and without altering this tempo when he has to change rein, go down the center line or make a volte.

It is by teaching students to stay with gently quiet hands, without pulling in the horse's mouth that he relaxes, that he "gives his back" and that he does well the coordination of the movements of the hind legs and the front legs while remaining in the cadence.

The horse alters the cadence when fighting against the rider's hand; he contracts and hollows his back. This is where the vicious circle begins because the horse has a contracted back, the rider is badly seated, he is unbalanced, and pulls even more. The rider's hands should be as nice as possible.

Preparation Work of the Horse for Competition

1. Preparation of the rider

Assuming that the rider has already gained a good position and balance and can drive his horse in all three gaits, he is ready to start learning to jump. This learning begins with the exercises on the cavalletti.

Afterwards, the rider must learn to jump small obstacles ensuring the position over the obstacle and the comportment of his horse, which must remain calm.

After this, it should be outside on natural obstacles that he must acquire the feeling of galloping, the impulsion and the confidence of the horse. He must take care, especially, that his horse remains calm and controlled.

2. Preparation of the horse

The show horse must, of course, be good for jumping, but he must among other things have received training that allows control, to increase and decrease his speed without effort, to turn wider or tighter without pulling, and keep him in a well-rounded attitude that allows him to make efficient use of his back.

It is first on the lunge that we must start the horse on the obstacle. Put the horse in a relaxed trot on the circle, and when he is going well, make him jump on the circle in each hand. Later do the same thing in a well-controlled canter.

Everything must be done gradually; therefore, do not make him jump every day. When riding him, mix lessons of attitude correction and gait cadence with the horse's habituation to jump.

Using the Snaffle Bit

All beginners must ride their horses only in the simple snaffle bit. Faulty seat positions that lead to hand faults are much harder for the horse if he has a Weymouth curb in his mouth or a curb chain than if he is only in a snaffle bit. In addition, the beginner often clings to the mouth of his horse for balance, which means that the horse has a harsh piece in the mouth, and tightens himself, due to that clinging action. The simple snaffle is the bit suitable for horses ridden by beginners.

It is for the teacher, who must know his horses, to see the correct adjustment of the noseband (if there is one), but without ever tightening it too much.

The instructor must not forget that the impulsion of the horse ridden by a beginner is always weak or in many cases non-existent. In addition, if the horse is constrained by a more powerful instrument in his mouth, he will have no desire to go forward.

Book 4
From an Old Écuyer
to Young Riders

Beau Geste, Lusitano stallion, levade in long reins. *Photo by Pedro Villalva.*

Contents

Foreword..130

Chapter 1 Contact and Relaxation of the Reins................................131

Chapter 2 The Legs of the Rider..133

Chapter 3 The Inside Leg...135

Chapter 4 The Rider Must Use the Weight of His Body................136

Chapter 5 The Shoulder-in...137

Chapter 6 Effet D'Ensemble (Combined effect)..............................138

Chapter 7 The Lesson of the "Attacks"..140

Chapter 8 Development of the Natural Movements......................142

Chapter 9 The Running Reins...144

Chapter 10 Work on the Lunge...145

Chapter 11 Work in the Pillars..147

Chapter 12 Work on Long Reins...150

Chapter 13 The Mouth of the Horse: The Jaw and the Tongue....151

Chapter 14 Some Exercises that the Old Masters Executed and which are Precious to Improve the Balance..153

Chapter 15 The Degree of "Ramener" Appropriate for Work........155

Chapter 16 How to Hold the Reins..156

Chapter 17 Lateral Flexions...157

Chapter 18 The Center Line..159

Book 4 From an Old *Écuyer* to Young Riders

Chapter 19 In what Canter to Ask the First Flying Changes.........................160

Chapter 20 Horses that Swish Their Tails..162

Chapter 21 Neck Extention...163

Chapter 22 Knowing How to Establish and Confirm Good Balance..........164

Postscript...165

Memorandum...166

Foreword

Initially, I had decided not to write about equitation any more.

For centuries, countless riders have noted down the results of their research and their thoughts on this wonderful art that is the Equestrian Art. Some of these authors limited themselves to repeat what others had written, convinced that everything must be based on a system. There are of course rules and principles of a general nature that must never be forgotten. We must be aware that each horse is an individual, with a personality of his own, that is unique every single time; that each rider has neither the same reflexes nor the same degree of perception as another.

The man who has long looked to improve the sensations given by the horse, transmitted by his increasingly relaxed body and by the constant will to achieve greater harmony between two living beings, knows that each horse is an individual different from another in his reactions and behavior.

Moreover, if he spent many years teaching horse riding, he also knows that every rider is different from another, in his body, his actions, and his reflexes. In the computer era, I realize that many riders only think about a "method" and many of those who write about horse riding have a tendency to build a system out of everything.

Just as men are equal in essence but differ depending on their countries and climates, horses differ too. Compare for example a pure English Thoroughbred born in a cold climate (Northern Europe or the United States) with another pure English Thoroughbred born in South America where it never gets cold. I have often had the opportunity to work horses in very different climates and I have realized that one system cannot be applied in all cases. Each horse must be worked according to the classical principles of a general nature, but we should allow for his receptivity when we ask for this or that thing. That is the *equestrian tact* that all authors have spoken about.

This *equestrian tact* is not only due to the physical faculty of receiving the sensations given by the horse, and adapt to them or change them, but it is also made by the continual observation of minute changes, this at each fraction of a second. The teacher must really know what he is teaching, be attentive to everything that is happening to the horse and to the rider and know how to give the right advice, not by repeating conventional words, but because his observation is dictating what he has to say at the exact moment.

In my last book, *Classical Principles of the Art of Training Horses*, I tried to be helpful to riders who worked their horses and tried to give them a progression which seems wise, by talking to them about gentleness, not by asking anything with force.

It was still in Australia that I decided to write, observing young people full of enthusiasm but still having a systematic theory in mind, regardless of the horse.

In these few chapters, I will try to help riders of an era where the trend is to turn everything into precision machinery.

Chapter 1: Contact and Relaxation of the Reins

Some say, *"Send the horse to the contact and do not let him lose the contact with the reins."*

Others say, *"Give the reins to the horse so he gets accustomed to working free, happy and light."*

There is, of course, some truth in both formulas. It is necessary to know when to connect and when to let go, which can be done at very different moments depending on the horse one is working with. This depends on the horse's degree of willingness to go forward, his impulses, where his stiffness comes from, or his asymmetries. Some horses need to be supported in order to be relaxed, others need first to be relaxed before being supported.

To understand this well, it is important to know the interpretation you give to *impulsion*. Impulsion is not what many believe and preach: *"Push the horse on the bit, make him round, forward, energetic, and that is all!"*

The horse with impulsion is the one that moves at the gait that we want, always deploying the same energy, in the attitude that we want, without the help of the aids, for as long as possible.

The current dressage rider would be wise to know how his horse would behave on the trails of a mountain, or jumping over ditches and natural barriers; or (in case he returned to the

Saturno, Anglo-Lusitano-Arab stallion in piaffe. From *30 Years with Master Nuno Oliveira* by Michel Henriquet, Xenophon Press. *Photo by Pedro Villalva.*

past), defending his life, the reins in one hand, the sword or saber in the other hand…

Lightness does not only consist of the horse not weighing on the reins. It consists of having a horse that, by his happiness, his energy, keeps the attitude and the movement requested as long as possible without being solicited by the aids. To obtain this lightness, we should not only stay attached to the principles but especially to interpreting quickly the sensations given by the horse.

The hallmark of good training is the display of maximum strength while remaining calm. Beau Geste, school levade. Gala de la Piste, Paris 1967. *Oliveira Archives.*

Chapter 2:
The Legs of the Rider

Much has been written about the hands of the rider but few riding treatises address the problems of the legs. Most of the bad sensations that we get in the hands come from bad actions and demands from the legs. We tend to abuse the pressure of the legs. Here is a very simple explanation that will prevent you from doing it: the horse breathes and if the pressure of the legs is continuous, he breathes with a weight that compresses his flanks. The legs should be stretched down, near to the horse but soft, not moving, and they must quickly touch, relax, if still necessary they touch again and relax again, in a fraction of a second.

I see most riders, legs glued to the horse, the heel always impeccably low, spurs always placed too high, and they do not realize if they're touching or not. It is obvious that with such legs, you cannot receive an accurate sensation, either directly through the flanks or through the reins. What is serious, also, is that the rider does not realize that by pressing his legs he contracts his back, preventing his waist to act properly, and it is a vicious cycle. The legs should touch quickly, be light; and more energetic if a stronger touch of the spurs is needed. The spur placed too high prevents some subtle touches for which one needs to put the toe down (in order to have a flexible heel), with a spur that reaches the horse like the fingers of a guitarist on his instrument.

In the lateral work and half-pass schooling, you must touch at the moment of the stride, relax during the next stride, and give the horse the time to cross without precipitation, which in most cases happens indiscriminately, and this is the cause of insufficient crossing, because the horse does not have enough time to make it in cadence. If you think the spur only strengthens the leg, do not expect the horse will arrive to a high degree of impulsion and lightness.

In some cases, the spur can also relax and even, with an extreme delicacy of employment, act on relaxing the jaw through correlation of muscular and spasmodic effects. However, that does not mean that the same advice can apply to all horses. On some horses (that are not too ticklish or too hot), by using the spur moderately as an aid for relaxation, the rider will try to obtain a lightness and a roundness that will enable the horse to perform whatever he wants. On other horses, too cold or too hot, the use of the spur to obtain suppleness is a talent only bestowed upon very few riders.

I also recommend to most riders to use spurs without rowels because it causes less tickling and less defensiveness. However, as an aid to suppleness, the rowelled spurs are finer and more subtle.

In all the arts, there have been immortal works, mediocre works and atrocious ones. Each time they were accomplished by different beings. So it is with the riders, the system is not the same for all.

The horse builds up in collection and becomes more majestic. Farsista in the piaffe, 1968. Quinta do Brejo. *Photo by Pedro Villalva.*

Chapter 3: The Inside Leg

Practice shows us that a horse cannot give his back before having curved his side around the inside leg.

In order to achieve this the tiny voltes around the inside leg, placed close to the girth and sliding gently from back to front, are essential to get the yielding of the inner side, from the tail up to the head, bending towards the inside, getting relaxed and without getting crooked.

Although the inside rein acts, the main role, in this exercise, is played by the leg of the same side, it being essential that the horse is around this leg without putting more weight on the inside shoulder or the outside shoulder. Of course, the inside rein positions the horse but it does not pull. The role of the inside leg is to get the horse to turn around this leg without putting more weight on the inside shoulder than on the outside shoulder.

When I work my horses, it is rare, before asking something else, that I do not start with these small voltes on each side.

When the horse is well-bent around the inside leg, use this leg within tiny fractions of time whenever you feel a contraction or a stiffness in the inner side.

The great mistake that riders typically make is by overusing the inside leg when cantering, with all subsequent

The inside leg serves as a wall in canter. *Oliveira Archives.*

difficulties arising from that; they have not previously bent the horse around that leg, and they use the inside and the outside legs with the same intensity. The horse does not understand and becomes confused. In canter, the inside leg serves as a wall, preventing the horse from getting crooked; it can of course also have an action near the girth quickly and gently when there is any contraction or stiffness, but not otherwise. It would be interesting for the riders to read a bit of what the Marquis de Saint-Phalle wrote on this subject: For to the eye of the spectator, both legs are equally placed, but the rider who has tact knows that he uses them in a different way.

Chapter 4: The Rider Must Use the Weight of His Body

The rider who has tact, who is seated well down in his saddle, must feel in his spinal column everything that happens at the level of the back and limbs of the horse.

While remaining straight, he must be able to sit a little more on one side than the other in order to lighten or overload a particular part of the body of the horse.

He can press more on a stirrup than on the other, lean more on a buttock than on the other, lower a shoulder more than the other by using the waist, or put a shoulder backwards or forward.

He can also bend slightly forward to lighten the hindquarters or backwards to alleviate the forehand. Each action is different and it is due to "feeling" and ultra-rapid reflexes that you give the right aid at the right time.

Training a horse is mainly about feeling and trying, according to what we feel, to help, not force him. Right now, among my young horses in work, I have one who begins the piaffe which is becoming very high and suspended.

Well, not long ago, I would lean very slightly forward, feeling that his hindquarters could not yet stand up to the weight. As he got used to giving a good movement of the hind legs, I have then gradually straightened up my back.

Do not think that during the horse's training you might not change your position a little in order to help him. At that point when the horse becomes symmetrical and easy, the rider remains motionless, with a relaxed waist. While remaining straight, we must also know how to sit in a stronger or lighter way. One sits stronger by flattening one's buttocks and sits lighter by squeezing them. It is the sensations that the horse gives you that make you choose how you should sit at any given time. The theorist only thinks about the system. The rider knows what he must do because, through practice, he is used to feeling and acting quickly. The horse is a living being, with naturally quicker reflexes than those of a man. The rider's aim is to act as quickly as the horse, according to his own sensations.

Chapter 5: The Shoulder-in

We see people performing indiscriminately an exercise called "shoulder-in." I would rather call that contortion "overburdened outside shoulder." It would be really preferable to keep using the practice of geometrically well-executed circles rather than initiate this false shoulder-in.

Most of the time, riders begin this exercise by starting to act on the inside rein.

Yet the first movement to perform is to bring the outside shoulder to the interior with the help of the outside rein. It is only when this outside shoulder comes towards the inside that we give the degree of inside bend which is suitable to each horse and his training level. Some require more bending of the neck towards the inside, others less.

The shoulder-in performed in a presentation is subjected to rules and established elements, but the shoulder-in in which we work at different phases of dressage is conditioned by the necessity of obtaining the intended suppleness in the horse. Some horses need a more prolonged work in the shoulder-in; others, naturally more relaxed laterally, require less. This is further evidence that we cannot confine their work to a system.

Certainly, for centuries, riders practiced the shoulder-in without giving it that name but it was, of course,

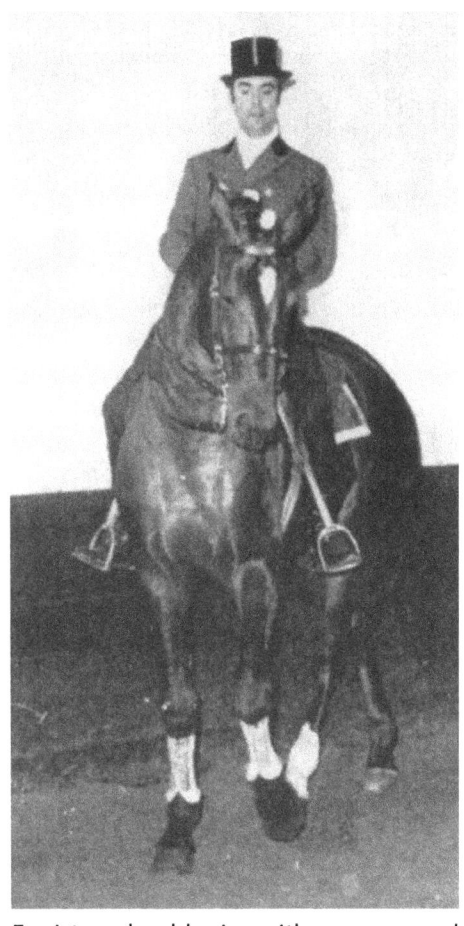

Farsista, shoulder-in with pronounced bend. *Photo by Pedro Villalva.*

Monsieur De La Guérinière that explained it. The theorists will tell you that Baucher has not practiced it. But what then are his lateral movements? Have they read his son, Henri Baucher's writings? Bending horses is a natural thing; it is still necessary to bend them well and usefully.

Chapter 6: *Effet D'Ensemble* (Combined effect)

The combined effect is a way to make the horse attentive, round, quiet and light. What is fundamental is that in the combined effect the action of the spurs be done in a different area than their usual place of action. I advise that the action of the combined effect is always held at the girth. If the combined effect is used correctly, piaffe ceases to be a mystery to many riders. Conversely, those who practice the combined effect with hard legs, not stretched down, and using strength in the hands, will surely fail.

A horse is not considered to be fully schooled until he has experienced the combined effect, but one must know at which point in his training that it should be taught to him. With some horses, do not ask it before you feel them relax in their bodies and their heads, and with the constant desire to move forward. With other very hot, distracted horses, who always want to move forward, it is advantageous to apply the combined effect really early. Again, no general rule. It is the rider's knowledge, gained through practice and reflection, that must decide when to use the combined effect. It is a very powerful way to resolve plenty of difficulties.

I remember that, around forty years ago, at a time when we could still ride horses in the Lisbon streets, I was asked to accustom a horse not to be afraid of cars, trucks and trams passing by.

There was a quiet little street overlooking the main street. Once the horse was used to the combined effect, I went every day to stop him at this place in front of the main street where there was all the traffic.

More attentive to the combined effect, he got used in two or three weeks to only pay attention to the approach of the spur. I would then go on the main street and whenever I felt he was restless or fearful, I would halt him using the combined effect. Gradually and without struggle, he was quickly able to go anywhere. He was then ridden in sidesaddle by a lady who went everywhere with him.

Colonel Lagarde told me some years ago that while he was holding a position in North Africa, Captain Beudant had to present his horse, Mabrouk, for an equestrian show previous to the Fantasia. The Arabian riders who were running late arrived in full gallop on the track where Beudant's horse was working in High School. Beudant halted him by the combined effect and he did not move an inch. After the Arabs moved past, he retook a majestic piaffe in perfect cadence.

This is the power of the combined effect.

Today, in the world of so-called dressage, champion horses behave like unbroken animals as soon as they come out of the dressage rectangle, facing the noise and the other horses.

Getting a nervous horse to stand still is a matter of feeling. *Oliveira Archives*.

Chapter 7: The Lesson of the "Attacks"

Bunker: cadenced passage in release of the hand aids (*descente de main*), ridden with the reins in one hand.
Photo courtesy of Lucy Jackson.

This chapter is only intended for the riders who have a perfect position, an experienced hand, and are well-practiced. It is by this lesson that we confirm the training of a horse, make him look brilliant and aerial, able to guess all the requests of the rider.

In case we give the lesson of the attacks before having the horse extremely *rassemblé*, light, straight, cadenced and familiar with the combined effect, we will only cause disorder, over-excitement, involuntary halts, jumps or running away. However, when you succeed, thanks to methodical and valid dressage, in being able to give the lesson of the "attacks," then you pinch the horse quickly with the spurs and the horse grows within his collection, he becomes more energetic and brilliant, looking as though he is not touching the ground.

Using the combined effect, you halt him in perfect calmness and you can start again. The horse who received the lesson of "attacks" acquired that way the energy that allows him, as Beudant used to say, *"to be given all the brilliance that lies within him,"* and looks like a real dancer in the execution of classical high school. The one who executes these same airs weighing on the reins and receiving continual aids looks like a poor unfortunate. Compare two horses in passage or piaffe, one in *"Descente de main" (descent of the hand)* with a relaxed jaw, the other with a rider hitting and pulling, as seen so often today, and you will see on one side Grace and the other Ugliness.

140

Euclides, Portugal, in collected trot. *Oliveira Archives*.

Chapter 8: Development of the Natural Movements

Here we have again a subject where we cannot apply one system. Some horses are born with such natural broad movements, with such a natural cadence and good balance that, from the beginning of their training, they keep their balance and natural movement under the rider's weight.

Others also have very wide movements but do not have a good balance: under the rider, they start to weigh against the hand and put weight on their shoulders. Some others, by their conformation, lift their legs too high, bringing their weight towards the back and do not advance properly. Others have gaits without elevation and with short action, keeping their shoulders contracted.

In all these cases, we must first see how the back moves under the weight of the rider and try to find at the beginning of the work which attitude and rhythm/cadence to adopt. Some need to work with larger movements to be in a better balance, others require shorter movements which we will gradually increase as they get more cadenced. Finally, for some, it takes prolonged work in walk to obtain, in the calmness of this movement, a balance that we will be able to keep in trot and canter.

What I condemn is, in the name of "developing the gaits," one works in resistances which gives the horse the habit of weighing against the hand.

Lateral suppling exercises in tight figures, and the transition from one figure to another, bring the horses to balance themselves. Once they are balanced, we can then let them develop the gaits to their maximum potential.

The improperly named "Spanish walk," that we should call "suspended walk," has a role as a gymnastic exercise for the shoulders. I do not understand why the International Equestrian Federation calls it an "artifical air" and not a "classical movement." Go see how many horses in the whole world's paddocks are naturally doing suspended walk...

This movement gets developed with a horse in balance and a back that tolerates the weight of the rider, which is the connection between the hind legs and the front legs.

Nowadays we see abuse of the trot called "working trot." There are several different nuances of trot which suit a particular horse or a particular level of dressage. It is the task of the rider, who knows his horse, to recognize what are the good and bad sensations received, how to keep them or to change them. It is for him to decide how, and in which movement he must work.

The final result may be good for the rider and the horse, not always for the judge or spectator sitting on a chair.

Having a trained horse is not about having a collection of movements or having extended gaits, it is above all having a horse that is balanced, happy and without resistance.

Corsário in Spanish trot. Perform this exercise only with a horse that has strong, healthy legs. School of Quinta do Chafariz. *Photo by Pedro Villalva.*

Chapter 9:
The Running Reins

Incorrectly called "German reins," the running reins can have beneficial results on some horses if we do not overuse them, if we do not let the horse fight against them and if we do not use them on a systematic daily basis.

The great harm resulting from their use is that once the horse comes to the desired position through their action, the rider forgets to cede [yield]. The horse then gets used to force against the running reins and their action reinforces and develops the musculature of the lower neck the wrong way around.

If we instead use these reins from time to time on the horses that tend to carry their neck too high or lose their position during the transitions, they can be of great help in the training, as long as they are used with tact and delicacy, always "giving" immediately after the result.

Again nothing systematically.

They can be very harmful on some horses, and it belongs to the rider to decide upon their usefulness. If used, these reins can be attached either between the front legs of the horse or on either end of the girth on each side of the horse, about level with the knees of the rider.

They should not bring the head towards the back but instead, prevent the neck from standing too high. In the first case, they hollow the back; in the second case, and if the reins are released immediately, they prevent the back from becoming hollow.

We must not forget that the running reins were already used by the ancient riders to maintain the position of the horse before this position was

Two sets of reins prevent the horse from coming behind the vertical. [The lower set is a normal set of side reins, while the upper set is an overcheck which runs through a ring at the poll (to prevent coming behind the bit). This equipment used by the German cavalry is described in the next chapter. Editor's note.] *Illustration Jean-Louis Sauvat.*

confirmed. They used them preferentially on the cavesson.

Even later on, in the training of the horse they can be used, on a very temporary basis, for some movements in which the horse has difficulty in keeping his correct position. But as I said earlier, they should be used only briefly and with the constant concern to immediately give [yield] when the result is obtained.

Purist theorists, who are not able to train every kind of horse, tend to condemn the use of the draw reins. In the hands of a gentleman, a knife can cut meat into thin slices; in the hands of a boor, it can do strong damage.

Chapter 10: Work on the Lunge

In the appendix to the third edition of my book *Réflexions sur l'art Équestre*, I talked a little about the work on the lunge.

I insisted on the following point: when the rider uses the lunge to warm up or position his horse, it is *he* who should do it and *not* someone else.

Riding the horse afterwards will be conditioned by what we will have observed during the lungeing work: the attitude of the back, position of the neck, rhythm and the nerve impulses.

There are some horses that, when lunged with side reins, need to have the head lower, others higher.

At the beginning, avoid shortening the side reins too much, which makes the horse hold a head position that is not in harmony with the rest of his body. It is by acting this way that we hollow his back and keep his lower back from functioning.

Training accessories used by the German cavalry seem to me much better than just a pair of side reins. With the two pairs of reins, one pair on the side and the other passing through rings and attached close to the withers, we avoid the horse placing his neck too much behind the vertical. To know how to adjust them correctly, you should not only look at the head

The Spanish Rider is recommended for horses who lean too much on the fixed rein. *Illustration by Jean-Louis Sauvat.*

and the neck but also observe the whole body of the horse in movement. Later, as the horse gets rounder and maintains his balance, we can eventually shorten both reins and also the lower inside one, one or two holes, to bend him a little.

For horses that tend to lean on the reins, I advise using a "woodman" or "dumb jockey" with metal springs, making yielding easier. There is one drawing in the book just released about Commandant Guérin.[9]

Some horses need quite a long time on the lunge with accessories while for others, as soon as they take the correct

---

[9] *Dressage du cheval de guerre* by Alexandre Guérin, Jean Froissard, Éditions Crépin-Leblond, 1984 and also in *Nuno Oliveira* by Marion Scali, Éditions Belin, 2006. (- Translator's note.)

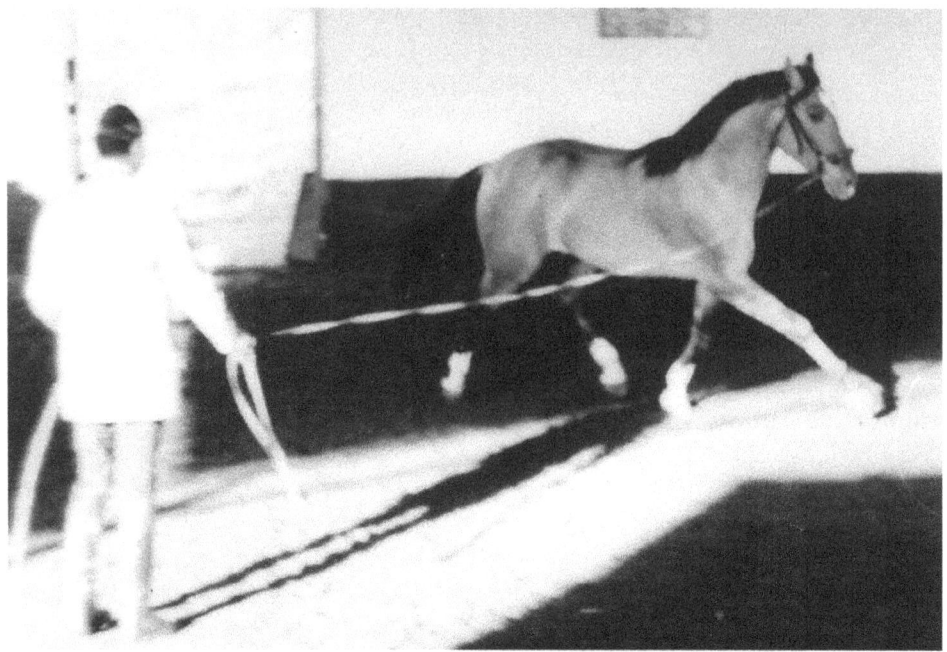

After several months of training, this young horse demonstrates improved freedom of movement and beginning self-carriage, shown here while being lunged by Nuno Oliveira without the aid of the side reins. *Photo courtesy of Stephanie Millham.*

position and keep it easily, there is no point to keep them working with accessories; lunge just for warming up when it is necessary.

When lungeing a horse, never forget that the lunge is the equivalent of the reins and the whip the equivalent of the legs. The circle that we ask for must be a geometric figure.

If you forget to adjust the action of sending forward with the whip and the elastic tension of the lunge, to keep the horse in a correct circle, allowing him to lean inside, it is a bad lesson for the horse.

The horse must learn to walk straight between each of the three circles we make in a rectangle, and when we work on the lunge, we must often change from one circle to another.

Here too, in lungeing with accessories it is very important to come back often to the walk, to let the horse cadence himself, to carry himself and to lighten himself before taking another gait.

The halt is also very important: it must be asked by the whip, which shows itself delicately behind, with small vibrations of the lunge and helped by the voice.

Do not forget that when you want to make the horse feel the cavesson on the bridge of his nose, it is not by pulling on the lunge that you will get a good result but by releasing the power to vibrate slightly.

The gestures of the hand holding the whip must be restrained and measured so the horse gets gradually used to seeing it without being afraid.

If the horse has the reins properly adjusted, the work on the lunge with a good cadence can be a precious aid and can be extremely beneficial. When mishandled, it can have harmful consequences, sometimes for the rest of the horse's life.

Chapter 11: Work in the Pillars

A horse that can piaffe between the pillars without a saddle or bridle is developing his muscles in the right way. Quinta do Brejo. *Oliveira Archives.*

In modern equitation, we can, of course, do without pillars. But we must not forget what the old masters used to say: "Pillars give spirit to the horses."

They can be a great way to help a horse in his piaffe (already learned outside the pillars).

The horse that, without a saddle and a bridle, can piaffe by himself in the pillars, rounds himself gradually, develops his muscles in the right way.

I do not agree at all in working in the pillars with side reins. This is too much constraint. The horse that can piaffe in the pillars unconstrained, without stepping backwards and without pulling the lead-rope, this horse is preparing and developing his balance for the collected gait.

The pillars give spirit to the horse. Quinta do Brejo. *Oliveira Archives.*

Here is how to start with a horse in the pillars:

An assistant holds the horse by the lead-rope attached to the cavesson, and before tying him he must lead the horse two or three times between the pillars.

When he goes quiet and straight through the pillars, then we attach him. The lead reins must have a length that allows the horse's shoulders to be a little bit ahead of the pillars. The assistant has some treats to give the horse when we ask him.

The master takes two long whips, approaches the horse, caresses, shows him one of the whips and moves it gently on the head, the neck, the croup, the hock-joint and the hind fetlock.

The horse who knows the ground work will not be scared. Reward with treats. Then the trainer stands behind the horse, a whip in each hand, equidistant from the flanks.

With the lunge, the assistant prevents the horse from going backwards or putting his head sideways. As did the ancients, the master begins to push the hindquarters to right and to left, using his voice saying, *"a dele, a dola."*

As the horse begins to understand this lesson, we repeat it one or several times, until he does it calmly without stepping backwards and without pulling the leads attaching him to the pillars.

Then we try the same thing without the assistant holding the lunge.

The third or fourth time that we take the horse to the pillars, the assistant holds the lunge attached to the cavesson, the master holds a whip in one hand and in the other a long whip that he will whistle or snap.

Then delicately, supporting the opposite side with the whip on the fat part of the thigh, the trainer will crack gently the long whip on the inside, not too close to the horse.

When the horse has moved a little bit without moving sideways, the master's voice stops him, the thong of the long whip on his loin. The assistant holding the lunge rewards the animal with a treat.

The movement will still be repeated three times and then one will proceed in the same way to the other side.

When the horse starts to move slightly, the teacher moves away a little backwards, he again takes up the two whips and alternately taps them on the ground rhythmically with the diagonal movement of the horse.

Caress and reward as soon as you get the result.

With the lunge, the assistant prevents the horse from stepping backwards, putting his head sideways or pulling too hard on the leads attaching him to the pillars, while performing subtle vibrations.

When the horse begins piaffe nearly correctly we remove the lunge and we ask for the same work.

We must caress and reward the horse frequently and he has to be able to stay in halt without moving for a long time. Ask each time for a little bit more precision.

When the horse will piaffe straight and quiet, without pulling on the leads and without stepping backwards, then, with the two whips behind him, the master takes again his long whip, each time a little further away from the horse and, by cracking the whip, will create more energy and brilliance. Always stop him with the whip's thong on his loin. For this, reassure and calm him with the voice when approaching him.

The meaning of this work is: when the master approaches the horse with the whip, this is for stopping him; later, when he will approach with the whips, he will be able to correct the engagement or suspension of the hindquarters by a light touch on the fat of the thigh or on the hind fetlocks or gently on the tail or on top of the croup.

To improve the raising of the front legs, it is better, instead of touching the breast, to give small touches on the withers with the whip.

At the end of each lesson, make the horse go through the pillars two or three times, very calm and straight. During the various phases of work, the horse can, of course, be attached higher or lower. It is for the trainer to observe, think and see what is the best for each horse.

Chapter 12: Work on Long Reins

Work on long reins may be a precious aid in the training of the horse, if done with attention, taking care of the cadence in which he works, and if you do not let the horse lean too much on the reins.

I do not mean the work on long reins as a presentation with a fully trained horse. For that, we first school the horse and when he is fully trained, we can then execute the movements that he knows on long reins. This can be a very beautiful show.

In *Haute École*, these presentations should be done with reins that go from the horse's mouth to the hands of the person on the ground without passing through the rings, the trainer staying connected to his horse.

In working on long reins, considered as an aid in the training, you should use the rings [of the surcingle] and know where to place them according to the height that you want to give to the horse's position.

The reins should frame and the trainer must stay away from the horse. For young horses, work on long reins is excellent on the straight center lines, geometric circles as well as in correct halt.

For very advanced horses, passage and piaffe on long reins, without the weight of the rider, can be very beneficial. You must constantly make

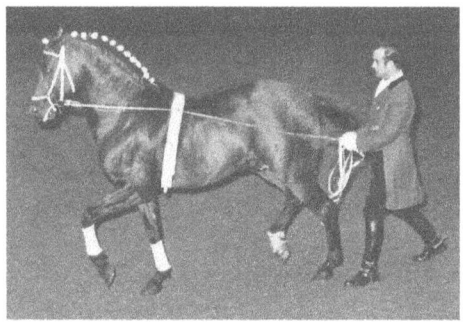

Corsário on the long reins.
Photo by Pedro Villalva.

sure that the horse does not put any weight on the reins.

If we allow a horse that pushes against the bit to piaffe or passage, he gets into the habit of putting weight on the shoulders and brings his front legs behind the vertical, and in passage, instead of engaging the hind legs, he will take the habit of leaving the hind legs behind the vertical line from the tip of the thigh to the hock. On the other hand, when the horse stays light in the reins while executing those movements without the weight of the rider, he can develop them harmoniously.

Although the work on long reins is generally an excellent exercise, with some horses it is better not to make use of it. It is up to the trainer to realize it. With some ultra-fine horses, with a very sensitive nervous system, I believe that the work on long reins is not recommended.

Chapter 13: The Mouth of the Horse: The Jaw and the Tongue

The horse's mouth is one of the most sensitive parts of his body. The current rider believes that one trains a horse only by the engagement of the hindquarters and that this is sufficient to obtain a soft mouth.

You must obviously engage and activate these hindquarters with clever and proper gymnastics, but you must be concerned at the same time by what happens relating to the mouth: observe the thickness of the bars, whether they are more or less fleshy, the length and the thickness of the mouth, to be able to choose the suitable bit. The current trend, that consists in putting a tight German noseband, without prior observation of the mouth, is a mistake.

Just as for humans, there are more or less talkative horses and others who are silent. We should know how long to let a horse chatter so that, thanks to the cadence and the impulsion, he calmly responds to the different demands and gradually stops clanking the bit in his mouth. If we want to prevent this too early, it can be done by tightening the German noseband, but what happens then? All the horse's head becomes contracted.[10] The parotids[11] cannot get out of their space, the neck muscles become rigid, and as a result, all other muscles become stiffer.

This is what one hears from most riders, who are unaware of what was written above: "Finally, the horse obeys! (and is compliant)…"

However, if we work with a mute horse, we arrive at the same result because a mute horse is a tense horse.

We must then ask for some wise and well-chosen exercises that relax the jaw. If he is in a double bridle, that can consist in dividing the tension on the reins (take and give) or flexions from the ground.

For the experienced rider, the spur has a lot to say in this case, but only for the experienced rider. When the horse is collected, with the weight on his hindquarters, he must let go of [deglutinate[12]] the bit upon a light demand of the rider. When we want a more extended gait, less sitting, his mouth must stay soft but less mobile. In the case of a tight mouth, many riders have difficulties in the piaffe or the pirouette. The horse stiffened in his jaw can of course still put weight on the hindquarters, but with constrained over-weight over his hind legs, without

---

[10] [The soft tissue structures become compressed between the jaw and the first cervical vertebra. - Editor's note]

[11] parotid gland is the largest salivary gland of the horse (Sisson 1975; Budras and Sack 1994) and is the salivary gland most commonly affected by disease. The gland is situated between the ramus of the mandible and the wing of the atlas. - Editor's note.

[12] deglutinate is to savor the bit. - Editor's note.

Some horses reach the peak of dressage training on the snaffle, others need the curb bit sooner or later. Quinta do Brejo. *Oliveira Archives.*

the ability to flex them as he can do when he is light in his jaw. Do not forget the correlation between all the muscles of the whole body of the horse.

Should we work the horse in a snaffle for long or should we put the double bridle earlier? It is a question that many riders ask. Again, no rule. Some horses can get to the top of their training in a simple snaffle. Others need the double bridle earlier or later.

A snaffle can be a very hard bit if the horse fights against it, and a double bridle a soft bit if it is used by an experienced hand and the horse responds to its action.

This is up to the rider to consider, to observe and to choose.

The hand that is not experienced but only good is often mistaken by receiving false sensations of lightness due to a tongue that is not quietly in its place, which goes back, curls up or goes over the snaffle.

In most cases, the wisdom of the requests, the right choice of exercises and an experienced hand can solve the problem. But with some horses which have a mania of moving the tongue, we must choose a bit with some space to make room for the tongue.

If the horse still opens his mouth a lot, a tighter German noseband can be useful, but only until the horse is calm in his mouth, at which point we will then return to the normal bits.

This is what more than fifty years of observation and study on the backs of horses taught me. Dressage is not only having a horse with the head placed and executing movements at the request of the rider, but also obtaining a flexible body that gives you pleasant sensations without any effort. And do not forget especially that, like his brain, the horse's mouth is part of his head.

Chapter 14: Some Exercises that the Old Masters Executed and which are Precious to Improve the Balance

I will quote two exercises among those that were used by the old masters to perfect the collection and the balance: the *foule au reculer* and the *passade*.

The *foule au reculer*: A horse able to rein back while keeping his lightness, with a relaxed jaw and ultra-light reins, can continue to rein back longer, and with the help of the rider's legs can make circles, change direction, make serpentines, without losing cadence or lightness. This exercise has the advantage of increasing the engagement by operating the loins and when going forward again, the balance is perfect. Do not forget that Baucher spoke of the advantage of prolonged rein backs.

In canter especially, after a good *foule au reculer*, the horse sits very well and is light, with engaged hindquarters. But, as I said above, this exercise is valid only with very light reins and a relaxed jaw. In case the exercise is requested by traction of the reins, instead of operating the loins, it contracts all the back.

The *passade* is also excellent for the improvement of balance: it can be done in two ways, with or without a flying change.

The horse already well-cadenced and light in his canter follows the long side in counter-canter. At about the middle of the long side, the rider uses his legs to send the horse inside the arena and makes him turn quickly towards the wall, without any action of the hand. The horse pivots on his inside hind leg and coming back to the track he continues his collected canter in a calm but more energetic canter, and the hindquarters sit down more. This exercise has the advantages of giving more brilliance in the collected canter, to keep the weight well backwards while releasing the shoulders. This exercise is recommended for horses who have short front movements and a canter lacking elevation.

For the *passade* with flying change, you follow the long side on the right canter, you take the horse off the wall, not more than his size, then without using the hands, only by using the legs, you turn toward the wall while asking a flying change. I find that this form of *passade* is less useful to improve the canter, it is more a movement for a finished horse, whilst I consider that the *passade* without the flying change is an excellent exercise. [See photo next page.]

A precious exercise of the old masters is the passade, shown by Invencível.
Photo by Francine Halkin.

Chapter 15: The Degree of *"Ramener"* Appropriate for Work

Bettina Drummond with Soante: the appropriate degree of flexion of the poll and position in hand for the particular horse in a particular exercise. *Oliveira Archives.*

Theorists say: *"The poll should be the highest point."* This is, of course, true, at the end of the training, on a rounded, straight horse whose whole body stays harmonious. But during the training, it is up to the rider to observe how the back, the loin, work and in which position the horse feels most comfortable. The verticality of the head is not mandatory. It may be a little in front or a little behind the vertical.

On some horses that tend to hollow their back by putting the neck too high and having a ewe neck, working with the head a little behind the vertical during a certain period of training makes his position come to normal instead of being too high, as the horse progressively grows. For other horses that tend to be placed behind the vertical, we must work a little beyond this vertical. What is necessary is that the neck is rounded.

I hardly dare to speak to current riders about the *"ramener outré"* where the horse, by the action of the combined effect, brings the lower jaw closer to the neck, and he savors the bit more actively. I have practiced it often on horses that needed it. This is not a system, it is a way which, in the hands of a skilled rider, can help solve certain problems. Beudant spoke about the *ramener outré.*

Chapter 16:
How to Hold the Reins

The International Equestrian Federation [F.E.I.] established, since the beginning of this [20th] century, that the classic way to hold the reins for dressage shows was to hold them separately. In the past, that was the way to work the young horses.

I will not argue about this because, by habit and fashion, I do use that separate way to hold the reins. However, there is always a moment, beyond a certain degree of schooling, where, in the lesson, I hold my reins in the left hand and check the collection and straightness asking the horse to move in that manner, including in half-passes and zig-zags with a correct bend. You must not forget that every human tends to use more force on one side than the other.

This [riding with reins in one hand] seems to be out of bygone riding practices from the past that do not interest the contemporary riders.

However, during a freestyle performance in a fairly recent international dressage competition, a Russian rider, holding his hat in his right hand, executed the exercises of the Grand Prix level. The audience clearly enjoyed it and applauded warmly.

I repeat, in the old school, holding the reins separately was for breaking-in and

Take all the reins into the left hand and ask the horse to do all exercises like this, the whip standing up as a sign of its mere redundancy. Bunker in canter pirouette. Quinta do Brejo.
Photo courtesy of Lucy Jackson.

work with the young horses. On the trained horse, riders used to hold the reins in the left hand, the whip platonically in the air with their right hand.

Note: Tie the reins to the wall, interpose a dynamometer,[13] hold them separately as we do today and measure the tension: see for yourself....

---

[13] an instrument which measures the power output of an engine. - Editor's note.

Chapter 17: Lateral Flexions

A trained horse should have the neck neither too rigid nor too soft. Riders, when they feel resistance on one side, tend to push in that direction and bring the head inside by traction of the rein, convinced that they can solve the problem in this manner. Obviously, the horse turns his head due to the traction and gives for a really short moment, only to resume resisting immediately. It is a bad process since you have to apply it for the whole life of the horse.

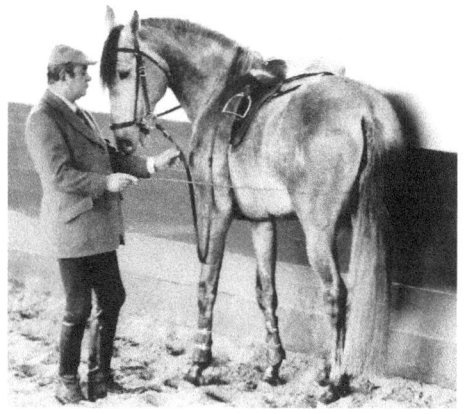

A young stallion showing the lateral flexions, 1984. *Courtesy of Kathy Cleaver.*

The practice of the lateral flexion, first at the halt and afterwards in movement, that we call *"placer fléchi droit"*[14] is requested mainly by the leg and the spur and brings the head more or less laterally depending on the case, the rider knowing at which degree of bending the horse surrenders the best.

The inside rein, of course, gives the position but should not be tenser than the other. This lateral flexion must be requested after direct flexion, with a relaxed jaw and only with that condition.

Once the horse brings his head to the desired point of flexion, without tilting it and without putting more weight on one or the other shoulder, he must relax more his jaw and we must give the reins. If we demand often this flexion in halt, we can then ask either on a straight line or in half-pass on the circle around the shoulders or around the hips.

Modern equitation has somewhat left aside all those things because it is not based on a permanent search of lightness. Yet it is that equitation of lightness that allows the rider to enjoy an agreeable horse, a horse that is not traumatized in his body or his head.

While writing these lines I am thinking about some of my old horses who looked so young and an over twenty years old Anglo-Arab that is still in my stables.

---

[14] When practicing the lateral flexion, the horse must keep his head straight in the curve; this is easily verified by observing the horse's ears which are to remain on the same line parallel to the ground. - Editor's note

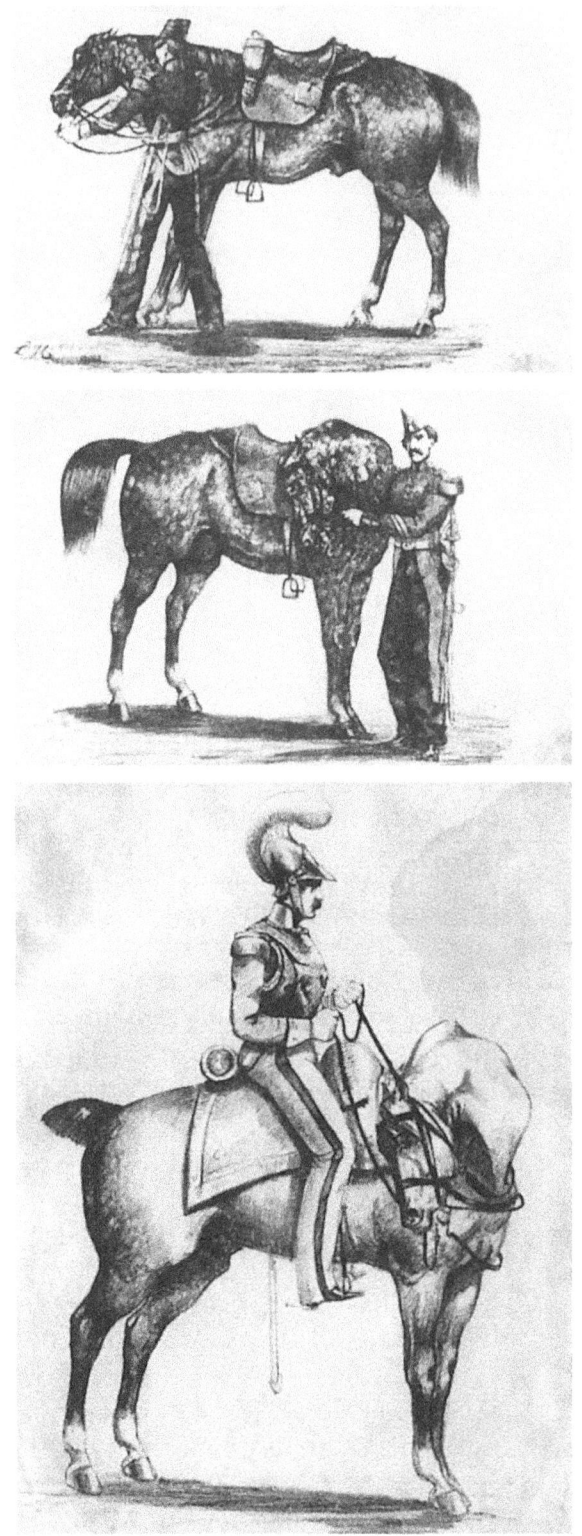

Lateral flexion and letting the horse release the poll and jaw.
From François Baucher, *Méthode d'équitation*, 1842.

Chapter 18: The Center Line

When working in an indoor or outdoor arena, do not forget to take the center line often in all three gaits, with a straight horse.

In the middle of the short side, you must turn with the help of the inside leg so the horse begins the center line really straight.

An exercise I often practice is, while staying on the center line, to go and come back, executing some half pirouettes around the haunches at both ends, one to left, the other to right. It is good to halt at X, very straight, rein back two or three steps and go forward very straight.

Make this exercise in one direction and the other.

If the horse keeps his cadence and his lightness in a rigorously straight position, this center line can be even more useful than the wall to begin the first steps of piaffe: the rider is more careful to keep his horse really straight on the center line than along the wall. And it is this attention to straightness that makes the horse himself more attentive and receptive.

Two years ago, in a clinic in Belgium, I was asked to work a very inattentive horse that ignored the rider at any pretext. For ten days, I worked him almost exclusively on the center line,

Developing straightness on the centerline. *Courtesy of Stephanie Millham.*

with good results. Thanks to my concern to keep him really straight, the horse was attentive, and even allowed me to ask him for some steps of piaffe on the center line.

If we work the horse well on the center line, trying to keep him straight, light and collected, we can then give the reins and he will stretch his neck, maintaining the line, straight, at any gait. It is an exercise that riders forget yet it is extremely important in horse training.

Chapter 19: In what Canter to Ask the First Flying Changes

This is a subject of enormous importance and with no rules either.

With some horses, we must ask for the flying change in a shorter and "sitting" canter; with others, in a bigger canter a little less collected and more swinging. Not to know which canter to ask the horse for the first flying change derives from a fault of observation and reflection.

Some horses are more comfortable in a large canter, where they are naturally balanced and calm, and it is in that canter that one should ask, and thereafter confirm, his first flying changes.

One should even begin to bring the changes closer in this canter and once they are confirmed we will then begin to reduce the canter, but knowing well at which point. The rider who has tact knows how far he can reduce the canter so the flying changes stay flowing.

Other horses that are not naturally balanced in a large canter, where they need the intervention of the rider's aids (for whom we might think the collected canter to be even harder), must first be put into a well-confirmed and quiet "sitting" canter.

It is in this canter that we will ask for his first flying changes, without letting him lose that canter after each flying change. It is only—and in this case, it takes longer than in the first case—when the horse will keep a "sitting"

The change of canter lead starts with the lift-off of the outer hind leg and ends with its landing. *Oliveira Archives.*

canter (more collected) and will quietly do a few flying changes in this canter that we may consider extending it slightly. If he stays comfortable in this canter, we can ask for a few isolated flying changes, with the constant concern to obtain them with calm and ease. In this case, bringing the flying changes closer together will only be demanded much later.

One must often return to a collected canter to ask again the flying changes.

Finally, a flying change is a departure to canter made from the canter. The *Écuyer* knows how he must request the departure from the walk with this or that horse. There are, here, some subtle nuances regarding each horse.

Euclides in right lead canter. *Oliveira Archives.*

Chapter 20:
Horses that Swish Their Tails

Many horses swish their tails. This is because of the incorrect action of the rider's legs, or hands, or the way he sits on his horse. Others swish the tail because of physical distress. In the first case, the accord of the legs and hands must be correct and the isolated action, either of the hand or the leg, should neither surprise nor scare the horse.

Riders forget that the leg begins in the hip and finishes at the endpoint of the spur, which is the strongest part to touch the horse. But between the two, there also are some light touches and subtle pressures that have a calming effect and that put the horse between the legs.

There are also subtle touches of the upper or lower part of the calf from back to front, and not from the front to the back as we see often. Finally, there is the combined effect that calms and immobilizes the whole body of the horse.

I have seen horses execute many movements that we could qualify as classical if the horse had stayed calm, without swishing the tail, and if the eye had not lost all expression of happiness; those are not high school airs, just some forced sort of activity.

For the horse that swishes the tail because of physical distress, this is, first, the case for the veterinary, then for the rider whose requests will be delicate.

Concerning the legs of the rider, I would like to remind you again: they push, they reassure, they square the horse between them, they relax...

Chapter 21: Neck Extension

It must be done softly and gradually without the horse stretching his neck by throwing it down brutally; doing so softly is proof of a relaxed and round back. If a horse is not capable of giving a correct neck extension at the three gaits and staying cadenced, without hollowing his back, it is because the work has not been good.

We should, for example, be able to execute a good pirouette at the canter and then reward one's horse by a neck extension, with him taking a larger canter but staying calm. Yet, if you give the reins and the horse does not give a good neck extension, we can be sure that the horse has not been worked in the correct collection but that he was clumsily compressed between the hand and the legs. When I give lessons to less advanced riders I often ask, when they feel the horses stable in their position, to let the horse stretch his neck, without weight in the hands, without losing the cadence, in a medium pace. If the horse tugs the reins and dives his neck brutally to the ground, it is because his back, instead of getting rounder, becomes flat, which then gives you a hollow horse. Even at the halt, after proper demand, in direct flexion, the rider who has

The lowering of the neck is proof of a relaxed and rounded back. Lucy Jackson riding Baritone. *Photo courtesy of Jane Turley.*

worked his horse well may request a neck extension. His legs still, the horse stays square, staying there for as long as the rider wants, and comes back to the *ramener* and the direct flexion, still without moving.

All those small details that I spoke of since the beginning of this book are very important. Equitation is an art composed of thousands of details, and if the rider forgets one of those, then the following work is not correct.

Chapter 22: Knowing How to Establish and Confirm Good Balance

Michel Henriquet, passage on Miguelista showing superior balance in *descente de main*. From Michel Henriquet's *30 Years with Master Nuno Oliveira*.

The horse must learn to balance himself, to move in the three gaits, in the variations inside the gaits and the transitions between these gaits. The rider must know which exercises suit this or that particular horse so he keeps his balance. The request for the classical movements must also be chosen in the sequence that is best for each horse.

Some horses need to piaffe before doing flying changes; for others, the piaffe will cause difficulties in flying change. We should also know in which particular attitude to request each movement. Throughout the training of the horse, we must request without losing the balance.

The development of the movement and the brilliancy comes later, once the horse has understood the movement and balances himself easily in the execution of that chosen movement.

The mark of good schooling is not an over-gesticulation, it is the calmness. It is the maximum of energy within calmness, without exceeding what each horse is capable to give.

When lightness is lost and cadence is broken it is because the rider, instead of making himself one with his horse, did everything to please the gallery, unfortunately turning his horse into a pedestal.

Postscript

More than half a century spent on the backs of horses, more than forty years spent providing serious teaching to riders, allows me to write the above lines, and that is the fruit of a whole lifetime of practice and love of the horses.

When I was young, I had the chance to have a real Master. We learned before anything else to improve the balance of any horse. And very often, a horse that seemed without qualities became unrecognizable, thanks to the patient work, a progression based on the reflection of the rider, his tact and his observation.

Today, we look with contempt and rejection at some, at first sight, less talented horses in their conformation, their gaits or their balance. We know a system; we want to apply it to the horse that seems to combine the "essential" qualities.

But if a rider can love his horse and evaluate his possibilities, if he examines everything that true master trainers have written for centuries, resulting from their experience, he will see that many of these horses that we think are bad can improve a lot, becoming sometimes really good.

In all arts, the artist learns the technique and all of its small details and, afterwards, he accomplishes his work, sublimating the technique through Love.

Australia
Geelong, Victoria
1st January 1986

Last photo of Nuno Oliveira, taken in Australia 1989. *Oliveira Archives*.

Memorandum

Canter backwards is achieved with a very light seat and leg action, never with the hand. *Photo by Pedro Villalva.*

Intended for the riders already well-advanced in the art, with a perfect seat and a perfectly developed equestrian tact.

Of course, it is not necessary to teach a horse to trot or canter backwards. If he is strong, with strong hocks, and manages to piaffe or canter in place very lightly, he will then go to the rear imperceptibly, not as a consequence of the traction of the reins but with them half loose.

Book 5
Reminiscences of a Portuguese Rider

Nuno Oliveira and Ansioso, passage. *Oliveira Archives*.

"I love in the arts all that is beautiful; I don't believe at all in what they call "The School," and I love what is cheerful, what is serious, what is terrible, what is big, what is small, etc. ... I love everything on condition that what is small is small, what is big is big, what is cheerful is cheerful ... in short, that everything be as it should be: "true."

– From a letter by Giuseppe Verdi
to the Painter Domenico Morelli

Dedication

This book is dedicated to all those who have helped me in my Equestrian career, and to my students around the world.

Contents

Foreword...170

Introduction..179

Horses and Horsemen of Portugal...................................180

Breaking-in Young Horses..182

The Study of Sensations...185

An Intelligent Lesson to Give the Horse.........................187

Pronounced Asymmetries in the Incurvation of Certain Horses.........188

How Man's Interactions Influence the Horse.................189

Remarks of an Almost-forgotten Art: Haute École in Sidesaddle........190

French Equitation, Equitation of Latin Expression........192

Equitation in General...193

A Few Reflections on the Future.....................................194

My Childood and Teenage Years......................................195

The Following Years..197

The Coliseu Dos Recreios...198

How I Met Colonel [Alois] Podhajsky.............................199

The Decades of 1950-1960..200

The Riding School of Quinta Do Chafariz......................201

Quinta Do Brejo 1973..210

Foreword

Nuno Oliveira asks me to prologue his memoirs. Who am I to deserve such a great honor?

Certainly not for my equestrian level, because as a dressage rider I was forced to give up just when I was beginning to reach a sufferable level, due to a serious car accident. The friendship that such an honor reflects comes, in part, from the prestige my father achieved in the national equestrian milieu as a scholar, as a promoter of horsemanship, as a scientist and researcher of the Iberian horse, as the savior of the Alter Stud Farm, and as a zootechnician horse breeder. Maybe it also comes from the fact that I was one of Master Oliveira's enthusiastic supporters and a frequent visitor of his riding school at Quinta do Chafariz, in Póvoa de Santo Adrião for many years.

My friendship with the Master comes from the time he started riding for the bullfighting rider José Rosa Rodrigues the horse, Yankee, that I bred. The sporadic visits at the beginning soon evolved into a daily and prolonged interaction for several years (until I became disabled), riding my own horses and watching the Master's work and the lessons he gave to his students. This acquaintance brought me an intimacy that gives me the privilege of having been chosen to preface his work.

Nuno Oliveira trusts my friendship but knows that I will not spare him any criticism. I have never spared him, as a matter of fact. Since the beginning of our contacts, either because I have a different equestrian mentality from the majority of the Portuguese, and especially from the High School followers; either because I never paid for lessons from the Master, as I used to ride in the school at lunchtime and had my horses in their own stables; perhaps also because I am older, and somewhat raw [*e bruto* in Portuguese], I have never been in the position of an unconditional admirer of the Master, and for that reason, I have never refrained from criticizing him. This fact brought me many fights that were solved with a lot of fuss, it's true, and some momentary breaks in relations; but the friendship was always strong enough and based on a sincere admiration to overcome the crises. Nuno Oliveira, like all of us, has positive and negative sides. Personalities of a very marked character have very marked qualities that distinguish them, and defects as well.

Nuno Oliveira's memoirs would be incomplete without the narration of some of these particularities. It would not be good for him to boast about his virtues, even though they may appear in his writings, nor would it be appropriate to expect him to be aware of some of his defects nor include them in his memoirs.

I will take it upon myself to fill this gap by, as in the past, fencing against himself about his defects, or against his detractors concerning his sometimes misunderstood virtues.

Yes, do not think that Nuno Oliveira was born, as a rider that is, in a bed of roses. His beginnings were hard, even painful!

As he says, he was born to Equitation in Master Miranda's riding school, his great cousin, when he was about five years old. The Riding School of Master Miranda, former Riding Master of the Royal House, was the last teaching establishment where the equestrian tradition and the rules of civility and courtesy were kept, already in times of the Republic.

The revolutionary spirit of the time was still being felt when Nuno Oliveira decided to follow in his cousin and Master's footsteps, dedicating his life to horsemanship, replacing his beloved Master, who passed away in 1940. He was about seventeen years old and in his last year of high school when he gave up his studies to dedicate himself to his passion. His family took it badly. They cut off or cooled their relationship with him. Nuno was left alone with his passion. He had no riding school, no stables, no money. Some officials and former students of Master Miranda gave him a hand, and soon he began to have to deal with the horses that the other riders couldn't handle. Nuno began to make a name for himself in the Portuguese equestrian scene, a bit ungenerous everywhere in the world, especially in Portugal.

Portugal is proud to be the cradle, along with Andalusia, of Equitation, *Equitação à Gineta*[15], the basis of all modern Equitation, whose roots go back to the highest antiquity (four or five thousand years before our era). The Portuguese, rich or poor, noblemen or commoners, military or civilian, come from descendants of horsemen and are therefore born horsemen, as we can see in the fairs where stable boys, *campinos*[16], bullfighters, military, farmers, industrialists, capitalists, doctors, people of all ages and social levels, men or women, all ride horses trying to perform exercises that have to do with the High School.

The *Equitação à Gineta* is typical of the peoples of the southern Iberian Peninsula and its Central and South American derivatives, but its "High School" facet is the appanage of the Portuguese people. This is to say that every self-respecting Portuguese is a horseman, or at least is (or at least thinks he is) an equitation expert. "Presumption and holy water, each one takes what he wants," goes the popular saying. When Nuno Oliveira emerges in the equestrian world, envy and spite explode from all sides. A few praise the young rider, but most seek to denigrate his work. With no one to defend and praise him, feeling master of his art, needing to impose himself for economic subsistence even, takes attitudes that are not pleasant to the eyes and feelings of the "experts," and begins his systematic demolition behind the scenes of Equestrian Art.

It is a struggle that lasts... and persists until our days.

---

[15] From *Zenet*, a tribe at the time the south of the Iberian peninsula was invaded by Muslims; a way of riding with shorter stirrups and more agile and malleable horses opposed to the style with heavy military horses ridden by men in armor, their legs descended in long stirrups [*Equitação à brida*]. (- Translator's note)

[16] Wild bull keeper (- Translator's note)

Nuno has to impose himself through courage and hard work. A few friends and disciples, few but good, help him in this battle. The official Portuguese equestrian scene only begins to have the courage to recognize some of Master Oliveira's virtues when he asserts himself abroad and the specialized magazines and publications welcome him as one of the "greats" of world equitation.

"Nobody is a prophet in his own country" is by now an old saying, and Nuno is a good demonstration of that. Proof of this is the enormous number of foreign students that annually attended him, the schools from Australia, Peru, the United States and Europe that claim his teachings, and the very small number of Portuguese who take advantage of his knowledge. He created a School, spread forgotten principles, has Portuguese disciples who are apostles and are spreading his concepts and methods, but practically no one goes directly to the source to "drink" from the Master.

It is true that the Master's character, always unstable and unpredictable, has become more difficult every day, but I don't think this is a reason to waste his knowledge for the benefit of Portuguese riders.

Forged in the dens of those who are incapable and envious, the prejudices against him continue to play. Nuno, a young man of nineteen or twenty, appeared at that time in the equitation milieu, very slender and all in black, wearing tight pants, a short jacket, fedora hat, and black gloves, a costume faithfully copied from his old Master Miranda, with his black hair lacquered with brilliantine, and his equally black thick eyebrows. Only what shone on him was the black marble of the eyes drowned in a huge white lake that targeted strangely when he widened them. Nuno worked at that time in Azeitão. He was an emulator of Baucher and Fillis. They gave him the malicious nickname of "Fillis de Azeite."[17]

Henri de Chatelanaz was the friend who helped him in his first steps outside his father's house, allowing him to ride his horses and his daughter's horses on his farm in Marvila. Around this time Nuno had the opportunity to ride an Anglo-Arabian horse named Bruno, French in origin, ridden by the distinguished and long-lived rider Rodrigo de Castro Pereira. Bruno was a great machine, but somewhat difficult. The way he solved some of the problems Bruno presented was one of the great pillars of his affirmation as a rider. His first students were Júlio and Guilherme Borba, Diogo de Bragança, and Pureza de Mello.

In Guilherme and Diogo, the Master had not only two of his best friends but also the best apostles of his art/science: Guilherme as the Master of notable riders and mentor of the Andalusian School of Equestrian Art in Jerez de la Frontera, Spain, and Diogo as a writer, with the publication of the beautiful book *L'Équitation de tradition française* [*Dressage in the French Tradition*, Dom Diogo de Bragança, Xenophon Press 2011].

Nuno had another great triumph with Pureza de Mello. A French horse came to Portugal, Vauclerc by name, of

---

[17] A joke that plays with the similitude of the words Fillis and fio, and Azeitão (a place) and Azeite (olive oil); A "fio de azeite" is a thin drip of olive oil and Nuno Oliveira was at the time very thin. (- Translator's note)

Anglo-Arabian breed, an excellent horse but of an inflexibility and nervousness that made his training a great problem. He was handed over to the care of a well-known and distinguished officer and riding teacher that put on him a dumb jockey with side reins and a bit with strong shanks. The horse defended himself with desperation and the bridle crushed his bars, and he was reported unfit.

On Nuno's advice, Pureza's parents bought the horse and Nuno undertook to train him. Ridden by Master Nuno and Pureza (under the Master's indications) Vauclerc eventually became remarkable. To the astonishment of those who knew the horse and his background, Pureza showed up one morning at a fox hunt with the Santo Humberto Team, where he went several times, did jumping shows, and finally exhibited in High School presentations in which Vauclerc did everything you wanted: all the low school, passage, piaffe, flying changes every stride, canter in place and to the rear, pirouette, ballotade, Spanish walk and trot, canter on three legs, *révérence*, etc.

A fact occurred around this time that deeply marked the pride of the Master and determined the deep hatred he has for the dressage competitions: urged by some friends he condescended to present himself in a dressage competition on the occasion of an official horse show. He showed up, as he always did, wearing black... and was not allowed to participate. Vexed, he swore he would never show again.

After a few years, however, he would compete again, then dressed properly. They ranked him last, behind some riders whose horses rebelled inside the enclosure or were always fighting the bit. They were all military and so was the jury. After this, Nuno not only never entered again, he didn't take any of his students to competitions and, what is worse, he created in his students a mentality of horror towards dressage competitions. We have had many fights due to this mentality because I believe that it is here, albeit with reservations, that one can well judge what each one is worth. It is not the same to perform a brilliant exercise when one can do it, or to have a horse that performs it when one wants. "I know that routine," etc., but between the two extremes lies virtue, and it is in the frequency with which the school students are judged that the true caliber of the training given to the horses and riders is affirmed.

Otherwise, it is always easy to say "I am good" or "my horse is trained," but always refusing the comparison that only the predetermined exercises and in the designated places show that the horse obeys and is ready to perform the exercises when you want; that statement will never pass from a personal opinion, from bravado, without consistency worthy of credit. To appease, I will narrate a fact that illustrates the self-promotion phase of the young Nuno Oliveira:

"The one who praises the bride is the father that wants her to marry," but as Nuno had no one to compliment him, he was forced to make, sometimes, his own self-praise. We were at the Fair of São Martinho in Golegã. Colonel Jara de Carvalho, a distinguished horseman, and Rosa Rodrigues, a bullfighting rider, a disciple of the Colonel—who was already retired—and I were watching the riders go by in the promenade path [*manga* in Portuguese] surrounding the arena. Nuno was riding the little Almonda, a Veiga horse, and executed an endless and extremely correct series of flying changes every stride. He passed by, pretending not to have seen us. On his way back, expressing a studied surprise, he raised his inclined head, arched his black eyebrow in that characteristic gesture of his, widened the eyes showing plenty of white, and came over to greet us courteously.

Master Jara boasted about the excellence of the work. "He's not at his best today" [*"Hoje não está de boa maré"* in Portuguese], he replied. "I only got a series of 215 flying changes every stride without mistakes." Then he dashed off. Jara, a man of few words, merely grunted between his teeth: "Jerk; too bad, because he's a good rider."

And since I am talking about series of flying changes on Almonda, an exercise in which the Master is an expert, I would like to take this opportunity to narrate another great exhibition of the Master that I will never forget. Nuno Oliveira, at the time, went three times a week to ride the old horses in his care, Gentil and Garoto, horses that he had trained when he had few clients and therefore time to dedicate to training the horses that were given to him. Having a great *afición* [enthusiastic avocation - Editor's note], and a great capacity for work, he strove to bring those two animals to the maximum of their performance capabilities.

Garoto was a beautiful Lusitano horse, bred by Luís Ervideira, snow-white, with a long mane that reached the tip of his shoulder and a thick tail that brushed the ground. The mane and tail were the delight of the owner and the horseman and earned the great aficionado and rider Faustino da Gama a sarcasm that became famous, given the exorbitant price for the time at which the horse was purchased: "mane and tail for thirty thousand escudos." In reality, Garoto had nothing more than a mane and tail, but he possessed a character, a learning ability, and an energy that surpassed the physical and motor difficulties that were allotted to him. He had no walk, trot, or canter. He would excessively tuck up his forelegs and paddle. At the canter, he would bang his shoes against the rider's stirrups. A horror!

Having nothing else to ride and having several years to train him, Nuno devoted all his enthusiasm and knowledge to accumulating equestrian gems on that poor horse: He was an expert in piaffe, passage, flying changes every stride, pirouettes, levade, *révérence*[18], Spanish walk, Spanish trot, canter on three legs, canter in place and to the rear... what do I know!

One day I had a visit from a Spaniard, Miguel Cuchet, a knowledgeable horseman who had been a disciple of Baucher. An old fox or naked-tail monkey knowing many tricks, he was not impressed by equestrian fantasies. He was looking for bullfighting horses for his young daughter, a *rejoneadora* of merit.

I arranged with Nuno to show him Garoto's work. We went to Azeitão. Nuno rode Garoto and presented him with his entire repertoire. D. Miguel liked it but was not surprised. "Horses that are too routinized end up doing things by heart; they no longer have equestrian merit," he said. I was at the gallery next to D. Miguel, and I took it personally. I told him that it wasn't about tricks, but good horsemanship, that the horse was obedient, balanced, and relaxed and, within his possibilities, did what he was asked to do, and when he was asked to do it. It wasn't a

---

[18] bowing - Editor's note.

training of ropes and sugar like in the circus. There was no routine!

To illustrate my statement I told Nuno to execute flying changes with asymmetrical strides, for instance, three strides to one side and two or four to the other. Nuno did so, at our command, in various combinations. The madness went to our heads, and I began to command various exercises, as I thought of them:

"Nuno, see if you can execute the canter by making flying changes every stride until you reach the canter in place without losing the flying changes." Nuno executed.

"Nuno, try the pirouette in flying changes at every stride." Nuno executed.

"Nuno, strike off at the canter immediately in flying changes at every stride." And Nuno left without missing a single canter leap.

"Nuno, half-pass at the canter with flying changes at every stride." And Nuno did it.

"Nuno, piaffe, do a complete rotation in piaffe, transition into passage, do half-pass in passage, stop and...and so on..."

Nuno tried everything and Garoto performed everything, exercises linked together as he had never been asked to do before, and without hesitation, without mistakes, without rebellion, without nervousness, calmly and without the need for spurs or whip. He did everything commanded only by the seat of the rider.

D. Miguel Cuchet was amazed and I, who knew and hated the horse, surrendered to the evidence: those who want, go further than those who can! There is no doubt about it.

Nuno never again had the time to deepen the training of any horse to the limit of obedience to which he took Garoto. He has never again had a horse with such a complete range of exercises as Garoto, but one of the qualities of Master Nuno's School, which makes it attractive for students to attend, is the quality of training of the lesson horses and the number of trained horses he has. Of course, this is the fruit of much knowledge and work of Master Nuno, and one of his great merits, a merit that not all riding masters—even those of great international renown—can boast of.

I know a German Master of great international renown who has an academy where I have admired several trained horses, out of the fifty-four he has. This rider came to Portugal and I took him to the riding school of Quinta do Brejo, in Avessada.

I had warned Master Nuno about our trip, and he was waiting for us with a class of men, about seven or eight on horseback, in the open arena under the command of his son João, and another class of a dozen ladies in the covered arena, under his direction. About twenty horses in all, mounted.

Master Nuno does not have the virtue of humility! The Master ordered his class to execute several movements and one by one the ladies, according to their degree of advancement, displayed what they could do. After a while, the German couldn't refrain from saying: "I am amazed at the number of horses that tackle the difficult dressage exercises. I only have a few that do the difficult exercises like piaffe, passage, flying changes at every stride, or the pirouette. How many horses capable of this does Mr. Oliveira have?"

I asked: "Master, how many horses do you have doing flying changes at every stride?"

"Twelve," he replied.

"And piaffe?"

"About fifteen."

"And passage?"

"*All*," he said abruptly.

My German was dumbfounded, having proof *"de visu"* that it was not bravado. He was not an admirer of Nuno Oliveira, quite the contrary because he saw him mainly from the angle of the extensions and the correctness of movements. This, to tell the truth, is neither the prerogative of our horses nor the dominant (or sufficient) concern of our School riders. But he couldn't help but whisper to me: "There is no doubt that I have to review my concepts of Equestrian Art because I have never had the facility for training that I see that you have." I would add that it is not only our art, but also that of our horses, which lend themselves like no other breed to concentrated airs, exercises for which they have been selected for millennia, whereas German horses have been selected for "pulling cars" at the trot and being open behind, and the racehorses or the Arabians for the wide course, in which collection has never been selected either. Neither the psychology of the bridle, nor the suffering spirit, nor the ability to collect themselves by the use of the spur's point, has ever been selected. These means irritate non-peninsular horses and cause them to open and contract by rebelling and fleeing punishment instead of submitting and obeying.

I have referred to Master Oliveira's working capacity, but few will know how to give him his due. I can testify by the contact I had for years daily, almost all day long, that Nuno Oliveira's work schedule was, in Póvoa de Santo Adrião, as follows: At five-thirty or six o'clock Nuno was already on horseback, and he invariably rode ten to twelve horses daily, until eleven o'clock. Nuno would ride each horse for about half an hour, quietly, without great demands each time. His secret lies in the sequence of exercises, in the dosage of demands that never exceed the horse's perception and response capacities, so as never to unnerve or force him. This is called breaking tact. It is also based on a perfect knowledge of the horse's psychology and his physical ability to respond to the rider's demands. At eleven o'clock the students began to show up for individual lessons. At one o'clock, lunch. A very copious lunch. Nuno ate too much and only indigestible food, ending with cognac to help digestion. He drank little and I never saw him drunk.

At two o'clock came the boys from the schools, collective classes, and the Master slept his digestive nap in the wicker armchair, collapsed to the side while his employee Abel directed the maneuvers. Around three o'clock arrived the individual students or short classes. Nuno kept teaching until 9 or 9:30 at night. In the afternoon, a few aficionados would appear, such as Father Borba, Aníbal Neto, Visconde da Corte, and many others. From Ventura's tavern came coffee, cognacs, an orangeade for me; the classical or opera recordings would come out (this is one of the Master's things), and the work would be to the sound of good music. I can't forget another of the Master's fancies: it was the "Taxi." Nuno abhorred mechanics. He never wanted to have a car or a motorcycle. He preferred the taxi, the taxi around the corner from his house in Odivelas. For everything and for nothing he used Mr. Xico's taxi. He forgot his handkerchief. A phone call: "Mr. Xico, go to my house and bring me a handkerchief." There were handkerchiefs for sale next door that cost twenty-five cents, and the taxi cost twenty escudos, even then. And when customers appeared, mostly foreigners, wanting to buy a horse, or just to look around, the taxi would come. Nuno would leave everything and accompany them all day, and sometimes more than one day; he would cover the Ribatejo and the Alentejo, showed the stud farms, paid for lunches, paid for the taxi, and didn't always sell or help sell the desired horse.

Portuguese horse breeding owes Nuno Oliveira a gratitude that very few people realize. It was Nuno who opened the doors to exporting Portuguese horses and propagated our equestrian art, and all tourism owes him a lot as well. Nuno was the herald, the flag, the ambassador of Portugal throughout the world: Italy, Switzerland, France, Belgium, Holland, England, Spain, Canada, United States of America, Peru, Venezuela, Philippines, and Australia.[19] To these countries, he sold several horses more or less trained. For much less, João Núncio and Simão da Veiga and others were decorated. When will there be justice?[20]

In my enthusiasm, I have already gone on too long. I apologize. Nuno Oliveira is, without the shadow of a serious and loyal contest, the Portuguese rider with the greatest international projection. He has a less spectacular sector of action than the Olympic intervention or international dressage competitions or even *rejoneio*, but he has the honor of going further to take the "good news" that Portugal has kept of the Equestrian Art, based on the lightness, the relaxation of the horse, the study of the psychology and nature of the horse, which allows making riding an intellectual sport discipline, therefore of superior nature and not just a physical exercise in which the rider is the irrational executioner who, by "painful methods," leads the horse to be the rational partner who, in order to get rid of the abuse, has to guess and adapt to what the rider often does not even know he wants, much less knows how to get the horse to execute his desire…

Nuno Oliveira is the only rider who has been requested from abroad to teach his method in internationally renowned riding schools such as Saumur, and national schools even from other continents.

As a rider, as a horse breeder, and as a Portuguese, I owe Nuno Oliveira a great deal of gratitude, not only for the many hours so pleasantly spent in the riding school at Quinta do Chafariz, hours that these memories have revived in my fading memory.

Fernando Sommer d'Andrade
Lisbon, February 8, 1981

---

[19] And also Colombia, Thailand and New Zealand. (- Translator's note)

[20] He was later decorated with the degree of Official of the Order of Infante D. Henrique by the President of the Portuguese Republic, General António Ramalho Eanes.
(- Translator's note)

República Portuguesa

O Presidente da República

Grão-Mestre das Ordens Portuguesas

Confere a *Nuno de Oliveira*

o grau de *Oficial*

da Ordem do Infante Dom Henrique.

Nos termos do Regulamento da mesma Ordem são-lhe concedidos as honras e o direito ao uso das insígnias que lhe correspondem.

Dado em Lisboa e Paços do Governo da República, aos 4 de Outubro de 1984.

O Chanceler da Ordem,

Official of the Order of Infante D. Henrique.

Introduction

I had written these lines with the intention that they be read only by my friends and students in Portugal. Some friends who understand Portuguese, however, have encouraged me to add some notes written during the last years, and to have them translated into English and French. These memories are those of many years devoted to the study of the horse, that noble animal which, for centuries, has aided man in making the history of nations. Today, replaced by the machine, the horse is the companion of thousands of people who are interested in him; he helps them to endure all that the routine of life brings and to give that life a little more charm. I hope that this little book will be pleasant for horse lovers all over the world.

Nuno Oliveira[21]

---

[21] Written in Portuguese and finished in Brisbane on December 31, 1981, published in Portugal in 1981, and published in French in 1982 by Crépin Leblond.

Horses and Horsemen of Portugal

Our horses are wonderful!

It is a pity though that the breeders in most of our farms want to create black, chestnut, or striped blue horses while paying no attention to the gaits or other qualities.

I am hoping that little by little, those in charge of breeding horses in Portugal will become true connoisseurs; aware of what is going on abroad and focusing on preserving the purity of our breeds and creating intelligent crossbreeding to obtain horses that can be used in all equestrian disciplines.

Unfortunately, in Portugal, people still believe that the horse and horse riding are only for the rich. This is simply not true! When I go to France, I see many riders who work all day long, who do not earn big salaries and who drive several kilometers to ride one hour after their work.

In the US, there are many men and women that are happy to groom and ride their horses after work. In the USSR and other eastern countries, there is a strong love for the horse. Go and visit the state riding schools where, to ride, one does not need to be rich, but love for horses and talent is all that is required.

Look at the riding lessons for handicapped children that are provided in certain countries of Europe, which is to be admired. Why are we in Portugal, a country with an equestrian heritage and marvelous horses, so far behind? We are behind in the education of pupils and behind because riding goes on being the prerogative of a certain social class. The wealthy are not always those with more sensitivity or more inclined to consider the horse a marvelous animal. They frequently use him as a pedestal to satisfy personal vanity. In Portugal, it is mainly certain officers who ride, because they have the necessary facilities to own and keep horses just as the wealthy do. There are also some horse-dealers who torment the horses—convinced that riding is about pricking with the spurs and pulling on the reins to have the horse in an attitude that they take as full of brilliance—thus enabling them to ask for some more thousands of Escudos[22] from the fools who buy from them.

There are of course the tauromachy riders. This is a centuries-old tradition and, while I am shocked by the vision of the poor bull being tormented and stabbed, bleeding in front of the people's frenetic applause for centuries, I think highly of some of the riders. I cannot forget a great number of extraordinary riders who performed in the arenas, in particular João Núncio.

A long time has passed since I last watched a bullfight and, recently, I had to attend one. Experts claim that there has been an enormous evolution in

---

[22] Portuguese currency prior to conversion to euros in 1999. - Editor's note

tauromachy but I thought that the horsemen were riding infinitely worse than their ancestors were; rarely do you see a horse whose sides are not bleeding. I have often bitterly noticed people in my gallery smiling ironically as I give a sugar cube to my horse after riding him; they must think this is an unmanly gesture! Likewise, some people happen to mockingly watch me work my horses while listening to music that appeals to my sensibility. They have never understood that the duty of man, the very reason for his existence, is the quest for that which is beautiful, not for that which is ordinary. I hope that future generations in Portugal want to belong to a more advanced group of nations that will think and act differently. It is a question of education.

Breaking-in Young Horses

In our country, as well as in others, there is a tendency to break in young horses too quickly and too roughly. The worst is that this hasty breaking is a compression into a prematurely forced attitude and doing so leads to frequent irregularities in the movements of the hind legs and therefore to concave backs. Naturally, this affects the horse's longevity. Why does one see thirty-year-old horses still working in the Spanish Riding School of Vienna? Definitely because their breaking-in was methodical, rational and gradual.

As a rider, you will not be able to obtain good results by wanting to transform your horses that naturally have rather short gaits, with a rounded gesture, to resemble those of some European breeds. One can obtain a more extended gesture of the front legs but the hind legs will not follow; the back becomes concave and the swinging movement of the canter is affected by the premature overuse of the extended trot. In case the horse possesses a balanced and natural extended trot, I see no disadvantage in practicing this pace rather early. In case he does not possess that trot, one will not obtain good results by forcing him prematurely.

To obtain this, one must have the horse well-balanced and with a certain degree of roundness so that he can extend the gesture of the forehand through the action of the hind legs.

Riders forget that when they extend a movement, they should start it having in mind the return to a shorter movement, not through the force of the reins but rather by lowering the haunches. Similarly, one must also have in mind that in this stage of work the degree of the *ramener*[23] is proportional to the speed and the extension of the movement.

Certain horses become nervous and insensitive to the impulsive action of the legs resulting from the premature use of the spurs, while in other horses it can provoke muscular contractions that may remain throughout their entire life.

It should be noted that the use of side reins should be the subject of careful consideration. It is of extreme importance to know how to adjust them. Their length is determined by the horse's back, the shape of his loins, the way his neck is built and how it is attached, and also the pace at which he is to be worked. You will do well to remember that the side reins correspond to the rider's hands and the lunge whip to the rider's legs.

To engage someone's attention in a conversation, one must know the dosage of relaxation or nervous influx that is required. If the amount of relaxation is excessive the listener falls asleep; if the amount of nervous influx is too strong the person will become nervous or angry. So, it is not dissimilar with the

---

[23] [the horse being flexed longitudinally at the poll with the head raised. - Editor's note]

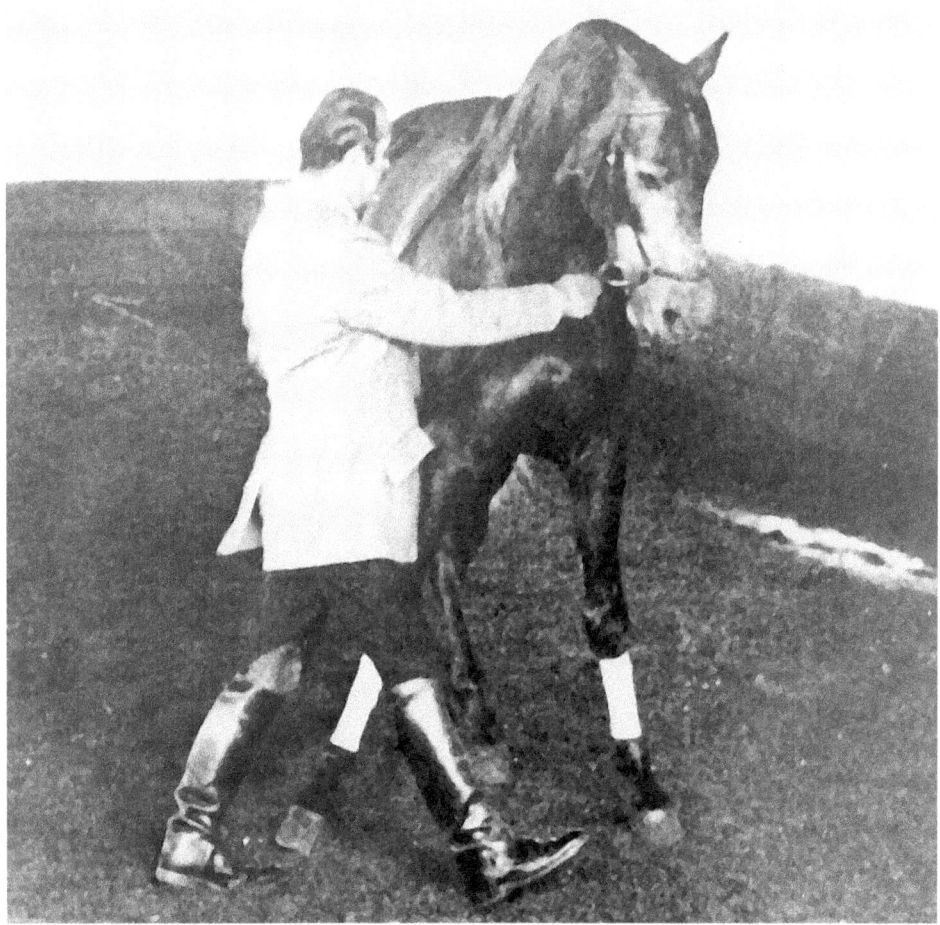
Vizir learning the lateral movements from the ground. *Oliveira Archives.*

horse, for it is precisely this dosage that should be the basis of his entire education. So many riders forget to watch the horse's eyes and expression! Yet that is how you become aware of his happiness or its absence.

When working a young horse, it is important to know how long to stay in rising trot, when to return to sitting trot, when to have a deep seat and when to elevate the seat. The sitting trot should be asked at the moment the rider feels the horse is well-balanced, free from resistance due to weight displacement. The rider's seat is deeper when he wishes to push the horse on and lighter when he simply wishes to remain passive.

The duration of the lesson will depend on the physical capacity of the horse, his temperament and the state of his morale. One should finish the lesson bearing in mind the next day so that the horse starts it with progress in the attitude and execution of the movements and also accepts it in relaxation.

Methodical, rational and gradual training affects the horse's longevity. Nuno Oliveira develops self-carriage in the collected trot of a young Andalusian in America.
Photo by Carol Sostman, courtesy of Sally Cleaver.

The Study of Sensations

When a rider is unable to feel whether in a given day his horse is more relaxed or stiffer, he is not practicing equitation as an art. There is no point or value in forcing a horse to execute this or that movement. It only demonstrates the imbecility, the foolishness and the vanity of the rider. To give a lesson to a horse, in the first place it should be a lesson of rational gymnastics with the purpose of making his body more supple and apt to execute such or such movement effortlessly. Any system that is not based on the impeccable rider's seat, and on the influence the impulsive or relaxed action of his upper body has on the balance of the horse, is an empiric [24] system.

If the action of the hand is not preceded by an adjustment of the upper body to the sensations received from the back of the horse and his hind legs, the hand works badly and cannot communicate well with the head and the neck. On the other hand, when its action is preceded by the adjustment of the upper body to the sensations received, the upper body functions like the beam of a scale and the hand collaborates with it, then its use is judicious.

It is good to remember that the fingers of the rider close and open: he closes them at the moment of resistance, and only at that moment, and opens them exactly at the moment the horse yields his resistance. Therefore, the hand of the rider works like a filter.

There is much talk about the lightness of the hand of the rider but one forgets the lightness of the legs. If the legs are contracted and tight against the flanks of the horse, they compress him and do not communicate impulsion. What is even more concerning is that if they are pressing against his body, the rider's back, loins and waist are contracted. Obviously, if the horse steps sideways suddenly or jumps, one presses the knees against the sides of the saddle, but normally the whole leg must be relaxed.

It is evident that the rider's body, seated correctly in the saddle, must be straight. Many horsemen adopt this position to be more majestic on horseback. Now beauty, for the one who looks, is to be able to forget the rider and have the impression that the horse moves freely and effortlessly. I remember a few years ago congratulating a Belgian friend and pupil (with one of the best *assiettes* [seats] that I know of) and saying, "My dear friend, I congratulate you, for I find you less magnificent on the horse, and more relaxed."

---

[24] empiric: based on experience and observation rather than on systematic logic. - Editor's note.

Euclides, Geneva 1962. Only a good rider's seat allows the horse to work correctly. *Oliveira Archives.*

An Intelligent Lesson to Give the Horse

I have very often started the lesson with a well-established work program in mind. However, one needs to feel the horse's mood at that moment, to feel the sensations that he communicates to us, and eventually, it will be necessary to give a very different lesson from the one we had planned. It is not necessary to make him execute every day the whole repertoire of the exercises and movements that he knows. By doing so, by neglecting perception, the horse is mechanized. When, for example, one wishes to complete a lesson with a more difficult exercise, or begin to teach that exercise, the preceding movements should prepare him physically and morally for it. What is very important is that the degree of demand is not excessive and that the horse finishes the lesson with the desire to go on performing a little longer than what was asked.

Obviously, occasionally you have to run the entire repertoire. At that time, the rigorous correction of a less well-executed exercise is left for the next day.

The constant use of force with the rider's arms can never bring the horse to perform gracefully and with fluidity. Firmness (which, of course, requires a certain amount of force) must occur for only a fraction of a second. As soon as the *cession* [25] is obtained, this firmness is immediately followed by the relaxation of the body and the hands of the rider. If the arms are placed correctly, that is to say, the elbows close to the body and not with reins too short or too long, it is the waist and the fingers that relax. This resistance and this *cession* are simultaneous.

It is not the clock that determines the length of a lesson. It is the intelligence of the rider, who must determine when and how this lesson should end. It can be very long or a few minutes. The training of a horse requires a certain amount of reflection on the part of the rider, reflection followed by rigorous observation of the physical and mental state of the horse to determine where some resistances come from. Resistances are overcome not by the opposition on the part of the rider but by appropriate gymnastics. Indeed, all that I have just said about the lesson to be given to a horse does not exclude—quite to the contrary—the necessity of respecting a certain discipline in the geometrical execution of figures. The consequences of a bad lesson given without thinking are paid at a high cost. Some horses as a result are affected for their entire lives.

---

[25] [yielding of the resistance - Editor's note.]

Pronounced Asymmetries in the Incurvations of Certain Horses

All horses have an easy side and a difficult side. There are, however, some who present this asymmetry in a more pronounced way. They resist strongly on one side and do not accept the contact of the rein on the other. Most riders tend to persist on the side of the resistance until they get a bend on that side. This is a huge mistake. In this way, the horse becomes accustomed more and more to lose contact and not to accept it, respectively, on his concave side. The way to avoid this is to try to bend the convex side by yielding in that side and to try to maintain contact on the side where the horse does not want to accept it. Again, it is necessary to determine whether the horse refuses to bend on one side because of a physical resistance on that side or a physical resistance of the other side.

It took me many years to understand what I have just explained: we must think carefully and ask ourselves whether the resistance comes from the difficult side or the easy side. The muscle masses can develop badly on one side to the detriment of the muscles on the other side. It is also important to check that the weight of the horse does not fall on the outside shoulder; if this happens, the work that is being done is not correct.

How Man's Interactions Influence the Horse

The groom who takes care of the horse in the box (when this work is not done by the rider himself) may have an adverse effect on the horse's character if he is not calm and has no affection for him. Whether by his gestures, abrupt or nervous, by the way he saddles him, puts the girth or the bridle on, he will influence the relaxation of the horse when he returns to the arena.

The blacksmith also has a good or bad influence, not only when he is calm or abrupt when shoeing the horse, but also by his way of shoeing and respecting each limb's conformation. Most blacksmiths look only at the hoof without taking care of the obliquity [26] of the fetlocks or tendons.

The horse is an animal that has an enormous sensibility and faster reflexes than those of man. It is important to seek to capture his attention and to keep him interested. The horse also tries to understand his rider and immediately perceives his state of mind.

I remember one day, about 5:30 a.m., when I was riding my horse, Xévora, I felt at one point that he became tense, stretching the neck and pointing the ears. I was working him at the walk and heard no outside noise. A few minutes later, there was an earthquake. I felt it only at that moment; the horse had already sensed it.

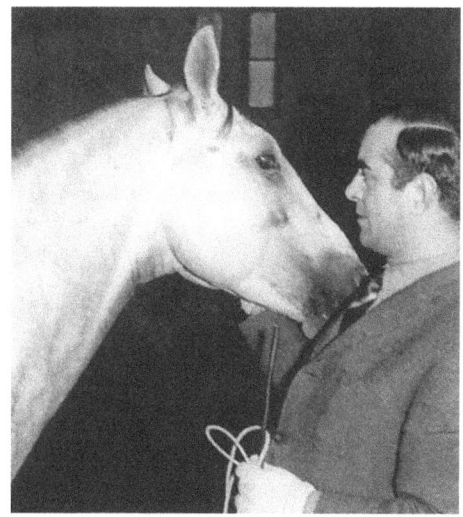

Patience and affection: to know how to use such valuable tools is a sign of a rider's sense. *Oliveira Archives.*

On the day of my father's funeral in the afternoon—dressed exactly as usual—I began to work Corsário on the lunge, the way I always did. At one point, I saw Corsário stop, raising his ears and looking at me. This extremely sensitive horse felt that my state of mind was not as usual, despite appearances.

In the early morning, I often notice that the horses Harpalo Prince and Levante, who are in the boxes from where one can see the path that overlooks my farm, look up this path as soon as the day dawns, with their ears pointed. I do not see anything, but a few minutes later, I see on this road the two grooms coming to work.

---

[26] obliquity: an inclination or a degree of inclination. - Editor's note.

Remarks of an Almost-forgotten Art: *Haute École* in Sidesaddle

In my youth, the majority of ladies rode sidesaddle in Portugal, one hand on the reins, the other holding the whip near the flanks of the horse as if it were a leg. In the past, I have trained many horses both for jumping and for *Haute École* in sidesaddle, placing a blanket on my legs to simulate the long skirt that the ladies wore. The left boot had a special device in which the spur was inserted low on the heel to be able to touch the horse in the right place.

I have always found it more beautiful to see the horses trained by my master or by me ridden in sidesaddle rather than astride. I thought it might be interesting to give some details on how to ride in this manner.

First of all, the horse has to be a sturdy individual, with a beautiful and strong neckline coming out in front of the saddle like that of a swan. He must be entirely dominated and have been trained by a master to do the airs of *Haute École*. In my school I have several horses who are capable of doing flying changes every two strides, with a lady alternately using the leg on one side and the whip on the other, as well as doing piaffe and passage. One performs levades, the other ballotades. Of course, they also perform the *Basse École* movements: shoulder-in, half-pass, etc.

On horseback, the lady must take the curb rein in the left hand, allowing the snaffle to hang loosely, grasped between the thumb and the index finger. The right hand holds the whip gracefully down by her side.

Ideally, the saddle should be built up on the left side enabling the rider to sit squarely with her shoulders parallel to those of the horse.

The lady learns to turn the horse by the weight of the body and by a slight indication of the fingers on the reins, and then she learns to do half-pass easily, even to the left.

The master must stand in the arena to assist the rider in piaffe, if necessary, by placing himself behind the horse and, initially, touching the horse with another whip for the airs above the ground. A delightful spectacle has nothing to do with the way amazons [27] ride in hunting which requires them to use both hands and thus do without the right arm to replace the right leg. It is only recently that one rides in sidesaddle holding the reins in both hands. It was ill-considered not to have a horse trained well enough to be able to perform all the movements with the reins in one hand and the whip in the other (as can be seen on historic engravings). The old school way is safer once the *assiette* (seat) is solid and the *Haute École* airs are easier to ask for than when riding astride.

I have already been asked whether a lady could train her horse without

---

[27] amazons: amazon is an admiring term for a statuesque, athletic woman rider. - Editor's note.

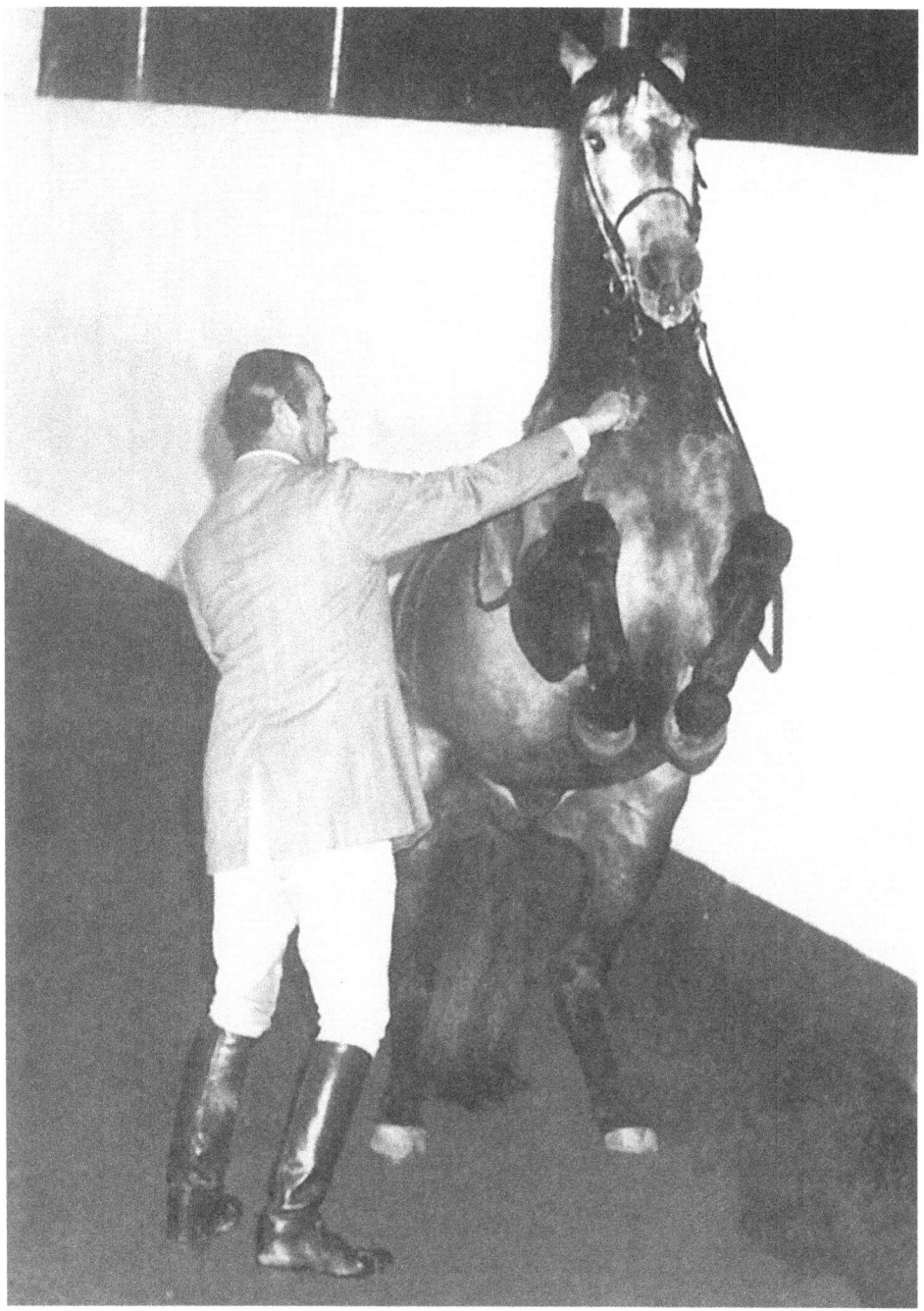

Jabute, school levade in hand. *Oliveira Archives*.

riding him astride. The answer must be negative, although a lady friend of Baucher is supposed to have succeeded. But I suspect Baucher to have been behind this...

French Equitation, Equitation of Latin Expression

Spanish walk and Spanish trot, shown here by Corsario, remain part of the Latin tradition of Portuguese equestrian art. *Oliveira Archives.*

The Germans currently impose their criteria of models and gaits and also of equitation, given the number of their dressage riders and their horses. It is therefore on these criteria that the competitions of dressage are judged. It seems to me difficult at this moment to change the judges' approach to the matter, as the influence of Germanic riding and the Nordic countries that copy it is very strong.

The French equitation—an equitation of Latin expression—is characterized by the lightness and grace of a perfectly relaxed horse giving the impression of handling himself without the help of his rider. Let us try, we Latins, to preserve this lightness and grace in the work of our horses, a work that can thus be described as equestrian art.

The Cadre Noir of Saumur, which is the conservatory of this art of Latin expression, must and endeavors to keep this mark in its *Reprise des Écuyers*. I want to pay tribute to its [then] current *Écuyer* en Chef, my friend Lieutenant-Colonel Pierre Durand, whose sharp mind always has the concern for truth in riding.

Equitation in General

Corsário executing a passage ridden only with a piece of string [without a bridle]. *Oliveira Archives.*

All that I have just written applies to any rider, even if he has completely different demands. It is unfortunate, however, that the desire to win often means losing the notion of progression. How many riders attach more importance to the performance itself of an exercise or jump rather than its form! In Equestrian Art, it is not a question of impressing the observers, but rather of establishing with the horse such harmony and understanding that when the rider dismounts, he feels that there have been moments of profound beauty and that his spirit could rise above vulgarity and mediocrity.

Art is the sublimation of a thorough technique. Art is only possible if the human being, stripped of all his vanities, really tries to love the beauty of what he is doing. Riding is neither different from other arts nor free from the influences of other artists. Art is knowing how to love deeply.

A Few Reflections on the Future

With age, the rider gains a healthy philosophy, arriving at a valid result without vanity. Nuno Oliveira rides half-pass on Bunker. *Oliveira Archives.*

Having spent more than half a century riding and traveling around the world, I often ask myself whether it has been worthwhile to give so much of myself, so much effort and so much time to riding!

In today's world, where there are so many social differences and so many miseries, the horse is sometimes the symbol and the pedestal of wealth. During one of my trips to a third world country, I travelled along a pathway to work and upon arriving at a clearing I witnessed a scene that deeply shocked and saddened me: a native woman, under a scorching sun, digging the ground with a baby tied on her back.

On another occasion, in a tropical country where I was giving lessons, I was staying in a house with air conditioning and all the comforts. A wall was being raised around the garden and some barbed wire had been laid there. Behind this wall lived people in barracks. They grew rice watered with the sewage water of the house where I was staying.

Riding is an art that is part of the culture of the peoples who have practiced it for centuries. We must try to level the social differences, develop and facilitate education so that different forms of culture become accessible to everyone, so that riding can be practiced by those who are really interested and who are actually talented.

I believe that it is not possible to arrive at a valid result without getting rid of one's vanity and superiority complexes. If, with age, the rider loses some of his physical capabilities, he gains a healthier philosophy as well.

My Childhood and Teenage Years

How often I think back to the time when I began my equestrian initiation at the riding school of my Master and cousin, Joaquim Gonçalves de Miranda! I remember learning to ride with a small Portuguese saddle, without stirrups, on a horse called Bright, an English Thoroughbred that Master Miranda had schooled in dressage as a young horse.

My father used to bring me to the riding school on Saturday afternoons, and during the week I impatiently counted the days until the following Saturday.

It was around the age of twelve that I started to really become interested in equitation. Any moment that I had free after school, I walked to the riding school because I did not have a penny. In this school, where one could make real pragmatic studies, I learned that riding is an art full of subtleties and that the one who practices it must refine all his feelings.

Master Miranda had been an *Écuyer* of the Royal House and had habits from there, which he kept until his death. I remember two small facts: one day someone entered the school wearing a hat. One cannot imagine the fury of Mr. Miranda and the way he reprimanded this man; he immediately took off his hat, put himself in a corner and for the rest of the time no longer dared to say a word. Another time, a friend of mine who was a pupil at the riding school, a farmer and son of the Minister of Agriculture, expressed the desire to take part in a walk that Master Miranda was doing with his students, as he did every Sunday. As this rider used to ride in the school in Spanish style boots and breeches, Master Miranda sent him to his home to try on a pair of his own trousers, a bit like jodhpurs. This rider went on horseback on a Sunday afternoon with pants borrowed from the master, because it was unthinkable that he would wear his usual outfit.

The last months of his life, I often went out on horseback with the master, he on Guerrita, I on Chiquito, to his house at Rua do Meio à Lapa, and I then returned to the riding school, with Chiquito in hand, by Travessa das Almas. I would then go to dine with my parents—on foot and as fast as possible—and after dinner, I would go back to Rua do Meio à Lapa—always on foot and as fast as possible—to hear the master talk about horses! He was there with his wife, cousin Leopoldina, whose legs were paralyzed, and their maid Olímpia.

I remember the day when the coffin containing the remains of King Dom Manuel II arrived in Portugal. Master Miranda put on his coat with his decorations, his top hat, ordered the most beautiful bridle be put on Gentil and told me to get dressed as well as possible, and we left under the torrential rain of a winter morning to Avenida 24th of July, where Mr. Miranda stood with impressive dignity, hat in hand, to pay the last homage to his king whose coffin passed slowly along towards the Royal Pantheon.

As for the master's equitation, I remember perfectly his great discipline, the calmness of his horses and their perfect submission, his insistence on getting correct halts from which all his horses performed any high school air. The canter had an extraordinary fluidity, the flying changes were full of brilliance, very large, and the passage was executed with the longest suspension times I have ever seen. He died in November 1944 and still today, more than 40 years later, I remember very often my beloved master.

The Following Years

After Master Miranda's death, I was able to continue riding. In fact, at that time, cavalry and artillery officers had the right to have a horse, which they could then sell for their profit. Two officers entrusted me with their horses to work. I rode them on the street and rarely had permission to work at the military riding school. I continued like that, still without a penny in my pocket, until the day when a horse dealer asked me to ride several horses. That was when I started to earn some money. Little by little, I began to be entrusted with a few horses to work, which meant a lot of work for little pay. One day, a former client of Master Miranda, Mr. Chatelanaz, made me come to his house and asked me to ride his horses regularly. This is where, for the first time, I was able to work in decent conditions. Then, I trained Diestro, one of the horses that taught me the most and that I presented a few years later at the Coliseu dos Recreios. There too I trained Almonda who performed impeccable passage–piaffe and piaffe–passage transitions and a very long, flowing series of flying changes every stride. Later, when I had my riding school, Almonda helped teach many students.

A year after I began working for Mr. Chatelanaz, I was approached by Manuel de Barros, who later became a pupil and friend. He asked me to take

Listao, piaffe. *Oliveira Archives.*

care of the training of some mares at the Quinta dos Arcos in Azeitão, a property that belonged to his father-in-law, Carlos Ribeiro Ferreira. There, I had the opportunity to deepen my knowledge of Equitation in the excellent riding school that was built there, thanks to the horses that I calmly trained there for years. Moreover, Manuel de Barros bought and brought all of the equestrian literature from France that could be found. Then, I trained Gentil, Garoto, Germinal, Fidalgo, Horizonte, Quiçá and so many others… but I will specifically point out Gentil and Garoto. I presented Gentil at Coliseu dos Recreios in 1952 and Garoto several times. Both were presented often at my students' shows.

The Coliseu Dos Recreios

When I hear some riders, who believe they are imbued with great classicism, and despise the circus, it makes me laugh. I presented Diestro and Gentil in the performance of an international circus company for eighteen days at Coliseu dos Recreios. Once, I repeated with an orchestra and they paid me 350 escudos per session which, at the time, was a substantial sum for me. The brave horses behaved as well as possible. I presented work on two tracks, passage, Spanish walk, flying changes every two strides, pirouettes at the canter, and Gentil executed the levade and the *reverence* [bow] with only a ribbon in the mouth.

I remember one Thursday afternoon Admiral Gago Coutinho was there in the front row. I stopped in front of him with Gentil bowing and the Admiral, smiling, thanked me by taking off his navy-blue beret.

I have a rather funny memory of that time. Every night, a skinny middle-aged man, dressed in dark grey and looking like a connoisseur of the subject, applauded me with enthusiasm. After a few days, I decided to go and thank him for his respect for my work. You could not imagine my astonishment when he told me he knew nothing about riding: he was paid to applaud!

Behind the curtain, before my turn, I listened to Baby Mistin[28] play the

Curioso, passage. *Oliveira Archives.*

xylophone. He was a child and his last piece was the opening of Franz Von Suppé's "Poet and Peasant." Even today, when I hear this music, I feel a certain nostalgia for this time that was so difficult for me.

It was then that I trained the Anglo-Arab mare Silène, which later I showed at the International Jumping Show in Lisbon, where she performed around 500 flying changes every stride along various figures.

Around the same time, I trained Listão, Yankee, Vauclerc and so many others. I also worked an extremely difficult French Anglo-Arab, Bruno; he was so dangerous to get on, because he attacked the rider, that I had to jump on his back from the lower half of the school's gate.

---

[28] Baby Mistin is an actor, known for "The Colgate Comedy Hour" (1950). https://www.youtube.com/watch?v=Q2Ot80bXsdA

How I Met Colonel [Alois] Podhajsky [29]

After its visit to Spain, The College S. João de Brito brought the Spanish Riding School of Vienna to Portugal for a charity presentation at the bullring of Campo Pequeno. At the same time, two bull-fighting riders, José Rosa Rodrigues and David Ribeiro Telles, took part in a bullfight and it was thought that the Colonel could do the "cortesias," [30] with the Portuguese rider, on the Colonel's horse Pluto Theodorosta. David Ribeiro Telles had a white horse but Rosa Rodrigues did not. I was asked to bring my white horse Garoto. As he had never entered a bullfighting arena, I went to ride him before lending him to Rosa Rodrigues. Colonel Podhajsky was then in the arena and he signaled me to enter. From the corner of my eye, I observed the movements he was performing on his horse and I performed the same with Garoto. After a good half-hour spent executing with Garoto everything that Colonel Podhajsky did with his horse,

Garoto in passage. *Oliveira Archives.*

we dismounted and my friend Fernando Sommer d'Andrade introduced me to the Colonel. I told him it had been an honor to see him work and that I had enjoyed his riding; he replied that it was mutual. We have since become friends and when, five years later, I went to Vienna, he received me with great hospitality.

---

[29] Alois Podhajsky was the director of the Spanish Riding School in Vienna, Austria as well as an Olympic medal-winner in dressage, riding instructor, and writer. He competed at the 1936 Summer Olympics and the 1948 Summer Olympics.

[30] The "Cortesias" (courtesies) mark the beginning of the Portuguese bullfight. At the beginning of the bullfight all the participants enter the arena and greet the public, the direction of the bullfight and eminent figures present in the venue. - Translator's note.

The Decades of 1950-1960

November 27, 1954 issue of *Vida Rural* with Nuno Oliveira's article entitled: "Feet at a Funeral," from *Equestrian Art: The Early Writings of Master Nuno Oliveira,* Xenophon Press 2022.

At that time, I was writing a few articles on equitation and on various events that had happened during the week, both with horses and with students. I was paid one hundred escudos to write each article, and they appeared every Saturday in a periodical called *Vida Rural*. I took the photos that illustrated the articles with the first Polaroid model that an American student had offered me. A few years later, students suggested that I collect these articles, give them some order and publish a book, so I did. A small edition of 500 copies appeared under the title: *Breves notas sobre uma arte apaixonante*.[31] Later it was translated into French and English with great success.

During these years, I met and taught outstanding Portuguese riders including Maria da Pureza de Mello, Maria José Lupi, Dr. Guilherme Borba, Dom Diogo de Bragança [*Dressage in the French Tradition*, Xenophon Press 2011], Manuel Veiga, Dr. Carlos Veiga, the brothers João, José and Francisco Núncio, Dom Luiz and Dom José de Athayde, Miguel Abrantes and also a charming American woman, Sally Robbins, who spent a year in Portugal learning equitation.

---

[31] Translated as: *Short Notes on a Fascinating Art*. This book was published under the name of *Réflexions sur l'art équestre*, which was a revised version made with the collaboration of Mr. René Bacharach and later translated into English under the name *Reflections on Equestrian Art*, translated by Mrs. Phillis Field [J. A. Allen] now Crowood Press. 62 articles written by Nuno Oliveira in the 1950s will be published in one volume in 2022 by Xenophon Press entitled: *Equestrian Art: The Collected Early Writings (1951-1956) by Master Nuno Oliveira*. Translated by Pureza Oliveira.

The Riding School of Quinta Do Chafariz

In 1956, with the help of a group of friends, I opened the riding school of Quinta do Chafariz in Póvoa de Santo Adrião. I stayed there until 1973, when I built my current riding school in my property of Quinta do Brejo, in Avessada. I worked hard for 17 years and hundreds of students and horses have attended this school. For eleven years I organized in December a charity festival to benefit the poor of the parish. These festivals consisted of fifteen to sixteen numbers and were very successful; there were always two sessions, one on Saturday, one on Sunday. I remember the efforts of all the ladies who took care of the decorations; the improvised bar under the shed next to the arena, the presenters, the lighting technicians and the help of my great friend, Dr. Guilherme Borba. We lived in an extraordinary atmosphere during the rehearsals, which often ended at two o'clock in the morning. The day of the show arrived and everything worked perfectly.

During that time, I remember giving over a hundred lessons on Saturday afternoons. The riders came to take lessons from all over the world, and I trained many horses who went abroad where I showed them: Euclides, Beau Geste, Ulisses, Maestoso Stornella, Ansioso, Farsista, Saturno, Ousado and Odeleite.

During my first years in this riding school, my friend and student Cabral Valente had the idea of organizing a televised program on the training of the horses, from the breaking-in of young horses to the execution of the more complicated exercises of *Haute École*. This series of broadcasts was filmed entirely in my school with horses at various stages of training.

Also at that time, the Portuguese Horse Society organized a show at the bullfighting ring in Campo Pequeno during the Lisbon festivities. The officers of Mafra performed a show led by Colonel Fernando Pais. I showed Almonda with my distinguished student D. José de Athayde riding Garoto. I remember having executed various figures in flying changes every stride and in front of the place where they released the bulls, eventually transitioning the canter to canter in place while doing flying changes every stride. After the show, I was congratulated by several riders and one of them told me that it was a pity that the horse Almonda lost his impulsion in flying changes every stride....

During the summer of 1958, a French businessman who lived in Geneva came to Portugal. His name was Auguste Baumeister. He had been to the horse show in Cascais where he had met my friend Dr. Ruy d'Andrade. He came to the riding school to see and buy Euclides who was then in training and belonged to the Andrade Stud. For two and a half years I continued to train this horse and gave advice to Mr. Baumeister, who frequently came to Portugal for his business. Shortly after buying Euclides, he sent me a Lipizzaner horse from Switzerland, Maestoso Stornella, who had been bought as a colt in Austria. In 1961 the two horses left for Geneva and I showed them both at Meyrin's riding school in front of a large audience. Everything went fine and the horses worked well.

In this occasion, I met Mr. Araldo Mastrangelo in Geneva, a world-renowned veterinarian who, after seeing Euclides' performance, was enchanted by the Portuguese horses. Subsequently, I sold some horses in Switzerland thanks to his enthusiasm. On the occasion of the transport of some of these horses, I sent him Beau Geste as a gift. It is with Beau Geste and also with Maestoso Stornella in long reins that in 1962 I made a presentation in the Parc des Eaux Vives which was a very beautiful site with the lake in the background. That same year, I showed Euclides and Beau Geste on the day of the Grand Prix of the International Horse Show in Lucerne which was filmed for Eurovision.

From this show, I have two memories: the day before I had been presenting these two horses and Tesouro at the Harras d'Avenches. A truck with an attendant was supposed to take the horses to Lucerne afterward. At the last minute, neither the groom nor the truck arrived. I had to ride Euclides followed by Beau Geste ridden by an employee of the Stud until Faoug, twenty kilometers away from where the horses spent the night while I was staying in a small hotel belonging to Von Gunten who had purchased Tesouro from me. The next morning at five o'clock, a special wagon for the horses was attached to the Lucerne train. On arrival, I had to go across Lucerne with Euclides in hand, followed by Beau Geste, held by a

Euclides in Milan. *Edmond Reynaud Archives.*

man who knew nothing about horses. I remember this was at the greatest morning traffic hour. My God! Finally, I put them in a stable owned by Mr. Kaufman, went to the hotel and, exhausted, had to be interviewed for radio, press and television. When at the end of the meal my wife and some friends arrived, I remember their apprehension on seeing me coming out of the restaurant room doing a serpentine. I took a cold shower and at four o'clock I entered the arena on Beau Geste, to the sound of the March of the Consular Guard to Napoleon in Marengo. I remember the beautiful levade he performed while I counted slowly until 12.

In the summer of 1962, Mr. Casthelaz inaugurated his riding school. I showed Euclides; my son João, who was 14 years old, showed Maestoso Stornella. Next, I performed a *pas de deux* on Maestoso with Mrs. Marie-Louise Firminich on Zafer, that Mr. Casthelaz had bought from me, and I finally worked Beau Geste on horseback and long reins. Everything went very well and I remember, when I went to sit in the front row to see my son's presentation, that my friends noticed my nervousness and calmed me down with a smile. He worked with impressive calmness, and I still remember the brilliant work of Maestoso Stornella in transitions passage-piaffe and piaffe-passage. So, thanks to these presentations, people started to talk about the Portuguese horse in Europe.

A year and a half later, I was invited to show Euclides in Paris, at the Cirque d'Hiver, on the occasion of the Gala de la Piste, a show given for the benefit of disabled circus performers.

Having never worked on a circus arena before and after only two rehearsals, Euclides made a remarkable exhibition. Among other movements, he performed expertly executing flying changes every stride and canter pirouettes. I had the pleasure of having Euclides' breeder with his wife in the audience. After that, I had to fulfill some social duties for much of the evening and then accept a dinner offered by a group of friends. It was already early morning when I returned to the hotel. I was still sleeping when, at 8 o'clock in the morning, the phone rang. Captain Pierre Durand was calling me on behalf of Colonel Chevalier who was putting a van at my disposal to drive Euclides to Fontainebleau, where I was to show him in the presence of the officers who were there. I told him that it was impossible given my other obligations in the afternoon, but I made an appointment for him to come and see Euclides working at the Cirque d'Hiver. When I got there, a platform had already been laid and a juggler was training, leaving only a quite small space free. Euclides was bridled, and after riding a little, I invited Captain Durand and Lieutenant de Croute, who was accompanying him, to mount the horse. Durand rode him brilliantly and said to me as he dismounted, "What a *mise en main!* It is the right horse for the Chief *Écuyer* of the Cadre Noir to have." We became friends and corresponded regularly, and in 1978 he asked me to come to Saumur to watch his *écuyers* working and share with them part of my extensive experience. I was pleased to go there several times for a few days.

The shows that I performed at that time in Europe were highly commented on by the specialized press, both in France and Switzerland, and brought an influx of students to my school. Two horses from Switzerland were sent to Portugal for me to train, the German mare Anglette, and the French Anglo-Arab À l'Affût. At that time, I had trained among others Zurito, the French Thoroughbred Talar, and Ulisses.

The Cadre Noir *écuyers* who came to participate in the jumping show in Lisbon came to visit me. At the jumping shows of Lisbon and Porto, I had some students of mine who performed and I rode the horses Listão, Ulisses, Valioso, Violáceo, Silène, and Saturno. My best students at the time were Christiane Farnir, Teresa de Santa Iría and Michel Henriquet [*30 Years with Master Nuno Oliveira*, Xenophon Press 2011]. René Bacharach translated my book *Refléctions sur l'art équestre* into French and I published a collection of photographs entitled *Haute École* [all of which are included in the companion volume to this work, *Equestrian Art: The Early Writings of Master Nuno Oliveira.*] Around 1965, I bought an Alter horse called Cursista, which I later named Curioso. Shortly afterwards, the director of the National Stud of Alter, my friend Dr. Manuel Leitão, sold me Corsário and Ansioso. The following year, I presented Curioso and Ansioso in England, at Wembley, in the Horse of the Year Show. Curioso worked impeccably and Ansioso, who had only been shown twice, performed a brilliant piaffe on the center line with a spotlight on him. I remember that thousands of spectators applauded to the cadence of his piaffe steps.

The stables at Wembley were home to nearly 700 horses. Every day when returning to the boxes to see my horses after lunch, I noticed that a lovely girl of eight or ten years spent hours in front of Ansioso's box and gave him carrots, caressing him. The morning of my last presentation, I went to see the horses before leaving for Ireland and the little girl was still there, in front of Ansioso. So I had the horse tacked up and put her on him, made him walk a few meters, turned him around, let him go and the brave Ansioso stopped in a brilliant piaffe with the little girl on his back. Quite a few years later, already a woman, she happened to live near a student of mine and showed her one of my photos with Ansioso that she had hung on the wall of her living room.

It was during my stay in Wembley that the English edition of my *Haute École* album was released.

I remember that before the second to last session something tragicomic happened. The day before, my friend John Paget had informed me that the Portuguese ambassador would be present. The next day, after the performance, I was preparing to go and greet His Excellency when, to my astonishment, John Paget took me to a place quite different from where our ambassador should have been. He was seated at a table in the first row of a restaurant overlooking the arena, accompanied by his wife, my wife and an English couple from the organization. I went to see His Excellency, who was rather confused and offended not to be in the Royal Box with the other ambassadors. At the end of the show, furious, I went to find Dorian Williams, Secretary of the Horse of the Year Show, and told him in a rather unpleasant tone that I would not ride the following days and return to Portugal as soon as possible because I did not allow my country to be insulted in the presence of its ambassador. Dorian Williams, very red, finally managed to calm my very "Latin" anger and explained to me that an invitation in due form was sent to His Excellency four months previously and remained unanswered. When the ambassador arrived at the last minute, they had to politely ask an English family who had reserved a table seven or eight months in advance to give it to His Excellency.

The following month, I made a presentation in Paris for a television program with Euclides and Beau Geste, again at the Gala de la Piste. They worked well; however, Euclides was less brilliant than the first time because he was not in excellent condition. My friends, the Laurenty family, and their father-in-law Lambert came from Belgium on this occasion. I went back to Liège with them and stayed a few days at their property in Xhoris. Since this visit, I regularly go to Belgium to give clinics.

At the beginning of the following year, Portugal's frontier was closed to the export of horses because there was fear of an epidemic. As I had been asked to perform some presentations in Liège, Ostend and Brussels, I consequently rode Dragon, a Portuguese horse that I had sold to my friend Jean Persin and that he had trained. During this time there were floods in Lisbon and its surroundings and four horses drowned in the stables of the Quinta do Chafariz riding school. Against my will, since I needed to earn this money, I had to finish my presentations in Belgium. When I returned to Portugal, I remember that my son João (who at the time was seventeen years old) told me as he presented the blank checks that I left him: "Father, a hundred escudos is missing because I could not go on the road with my motorbike and I had to take a taxi to go to the school."

At the end of that same year, I had to make a presentation again in Belgium at the inauguration of a riding school in Brussels and at the Agriculture Show. Euclides was not in shape, so we had Beau Geste, Ulisses, and Saturno, whom I had not seen for years, brought from Switzerland. They all worked wonderfully and Beau Geste was presented twice by Christiane Farnir, who rode him brilliantly.

This year Curioso was sold to Bilbao, and around the same time Dr. Manuel Leitão asked me to organize something to help the Alter Stud, which was then going through a difficult period. I had an idea to decorate the riding school of the Necessidades Palace and to organize a performance on riding in Portugal. We showcased at the entrance an exhibition on Portuguese equestrian themes and organized a two-week performance, which was received warmly by the audience. We showed Corsário, Ansioso and Brioso as well as the colt Sinal, who was presented in hand by a groom from Alter, and also Aljezur, a Portuguese Anglo-Arab who was in one week ridden by Christiane Farnir and the other by Mrs. Maria da Pureza de Mello, all of which helped the Alter Stud to recuperate a bit.

I recall two facts during these shows. The first is this one:

At the entrance of the exhibition that I had organized was a large photograph of King Dom Carlos I, riding Machaquito, an Alter ancestor of the horses shown, and two flags of the Restoration were hanging on the pillars. I was summoned to the National Secretariat of Tourism where a senior official told me he found it all very monarchist, which he did not think appropriate. I replied that I had no problem putting a photo of Dr. Bernardino Machado riding an Alter horse if he could find me one, and also adorn the arena with a green and red flag as long as there could be found a historical affinity with the Royal Alter Stud… on the other hand, I had asked that a quartet or sextet of chamber music (which I thought I would install on the small galleries at the top of the arena) accompany the work of the horses. They found the idea fanciful and laughable. All I could get was the Cavalry Band of the Republican National Guard, which opened the show; then my own records of Mozart and Beethoven were played during the presentations. Thanks to these efforts to help them, I got the opportunity to buy Farsista at the Alter Stud, who was a very tall colt already at the age of three.

The next year, on the occasion of the International Horse Show of Geneva, I presented Euclides and Beau Geste in long reins. It was always a success but I remember with sadness that one evening, after being warmly congratulated by the commander of the School of Bern and some of his *écuyers*, I met some Portuguese former students of mine, sent by the Portuguese Federation, who asked me if I was not ashamed to present Portuguese horses abroad!

When I returned to Lisbon, many students continued to come from all over the world, and I devoted myself to training Farsista, which was quite difficult because of his enormous mass.

In 1968 my pupil Albert Moyersen, who lives in Italy near Milan at a beautiful property and has a riding school in Carpiano, organized an equestrian party with a Louis XV parade [carrousel] executed by his students whom I had taught and prepared and also a horse-drawn carriage parade. For this occasion, I presented Euclides, Beau Geste and Ulisses and again Beau Geste in long reins.

The Italian temperament and the beautiful sun made these presentations have an extraordinary impact. My wife told me that a lady sitting next to her during the show claimed that I was talking with the horses, although my mouth was closed. Throughout the presentation and despite my wife's efforts to dissuade her, she continued to say *"Parla con i cavalli."*[32] I never stayed as long on horseback as that day. In the evening after dinner, before taking us back to the airport, a group of students surrounded the car and fired a few revolver shots in a spontaneous display of enthusiasm and friendship. This was the swan song of the presentations of Euclides and Beau Geste.

The following year their owner, Monsieur Baumeister, who was ill, sent me Euclides and Beau Geste from Switzerland. Euclides came limping and with emphysema that made him cough constantly. Two or three days later he went to Alentejo to the stud farm where he was born; he died there a few years later, having served as a stallion. Before leaving, I wanted to ride him just for a moment. After my day's work, having given my last lesson to five or six students, I had Euclides saddled. I put on a record I had recorded in Switzerland with various music and which served me for years for my presentations and I headed to the stable, preparing myself to take a turn on a lame and coughing horse. Much to my surprise, having mounted him behind the door, I saw Euclides point his ears, enter the school neither lame nor coughing, and without having me even approach my legs, perform all his repertoire. The record stopped, I let go of the reins, and Euclides limped and coughed like an old horse.

I dismounted and I remember that my eyes were full of tears. The few students present were witnesses to this and Thelma Granpré Molière, my Dutch student, still talks about it. How to explain this fact? Simply because horses have a lot more sensitivity than we can imagine.

That summer, with the school full of students from abroad, I continued to work Farsista and train Corsário in long reins in an outside ring full of jumping obstacles, which was not easy with the temperament he had. At the end of the year, I presented Corsário in long reins for the International Jumping Show of Brussels and improvised a pas de deux with Farsista and my son João on Corsário. I remember a funny thing. The first day, while I was warming up Farsista on the track, already dressed and in top hat, I saw my friend Michel Henriquet and his wife who had come from Paris for my presentation. Wishing to salute Madame Henriquet with a broad and chivalrous gesture, I took off my top hat and Farsista violently turned 180 degrees. During my preparation in Portugal, I had inexplicably forgotten to accustom Farsista to stay in place when I took off my hat. Immediately after this scene I had to enter the arena and for the whole week I took off my hat on the center line with great care, in a very slow gesture, by putting it in front of my stomach, and all went well.

---

[32] He is talking to the horses.

Book 5 Reminiscences of a Portuguese Rider

I also remember that one evening, before the show began, one of the organizers approached me saying with a rather pretentious air, "Maître Oliveira, as you come from a republican country, I want to teach you to greet the Queen." His pedantic look annoyed me, and I replied that in my life I had already seen some kings, princes, queens and princesses and I turned my back. I was behind the curtain on Corsário, ready to enter, while the speaker, Jose Hofman of the Belgian Equestrian Federation, said: "Majesty, the master Nuno Oliveira will present you two horses of the old Portuguese royal race" and gave a summary of what I told him about the Alter horse and the Portuguese horse. The curtain opened and, at the sound of Beethoven's 9th symphony, the spotlight in his eyes, the brave Corsário entered the arena, charging in at a gallop then halting, ears pointed, seven or eight meters from the Queen. I bowed and respectfully took off my top hat. I then worked in a circle about 15 meters in diameter.

These presentations have further helped the Portuguese horse's reputation.

In December of the same year, I was invited by Colonel Kirkpatrick O'Donnel, President of the Spanish Equestrian Federation, to present a horse for the inauguration of the huge Club Del Campo riding school in Madrid. I asked the owner of Curioso to lend him to me and he was sent to me from Bilbao to Madrid.

I showed him for two days, after refusing to do so until the last minute. Indeed, when I arrived in this monumental riding school, I saw at the entrance a large Spanish flag beside a Portuguese flag—fortunately, having explained the cause of my refusal, we hoisted a Portuguese flag of the same size as the Spanish flag.... On the second day, the Prince of Asturias and current King of Spain attended my presentation and was very kind to me. That day, having started my work to the sound of a Mozart concerto, the audience was not silent. I stopped at the corner of the track and was preparing to go out when the prince got up and with a gesture asked for silence; the silence having been observed, I was able to finish my work. Curioso worked really well, in a very light manner, and he was very correct in everything he did. One day, my dear friend and distinguished student, Dr. Guilherme Borba, returning from a visit to the Spanish Riding School of Vienna and from Germany, went through Bilbao where he mounted Curioso. On returning to Póvoa de Santo Adrião, he told me that Curioso was the best trained horse he had seen on his entire trip. I shrugged, moved; I hugged him and told him that I had never managed to obtain a good cadence in the piaffe with Curioso.

In early 1969, I started to train new horses. Farsista had remained in Belgium, Ansioso had been sold to a pupil and Corsário began to be used in student lessons.

In the spring, I was asked to go to Lima, Peru, to give lessons in the Huachipa Equestrian Club to a group of dressage riders. Peru is a really exciting country. I have been involved for years in the evolution of this country, and I have personal friends among the military who led it and revolutionized it. The following year, I had the honor of giving a one-month course to the officers of the Military Riding School who had come with their horses to the equestrian club of Huachipa. Two Portuguese horses went to Lima: first Ousado, for my friend Dr. Manoel Pablo Olaechea, and a year later, Odeleite, for Isabel Arias Sanders.

I was giving a lesson when I saw a van arrive with Ousado after an 18-day boat trip. On stepping out of the van,

Ousado did not seem tired, even wanted to play. I asked for a bridle and saddle. I mounted and entered the dressage rectangle. It looked like he had been ridden the day before. I worked for 15 minutes while performing with him all his repertoire: it is a testament to the marvelous character of the Iberian horse. I presented him in public at the end of the month and for a few years, I showed him at the same time as Odeleite. The last time I did so was with my son João who was giving lessons in San José, Costa Rica. I had phoned him proposing for him to come to Lima after his work. We repeated a *pas de deux* two or three times with a similar layout of the Prix St. Georges, and then we presented ourselves one evening in front of a very large public audience. It was the night of the dressage championship.

After finishing the sequence, we left in extended trot, circling the track around the rectangle; the two horses really had an extraordinary gesture. We separated and I asked Ousado for more than 100 flying changes every stride. Then, pausing under a tree, I waited for João who, with Odeleite, performed a canter pirouette and flying changes every two strides. He put his horse in passage, approached me, and together we went around the outside of the rectangle in passage. We went back into the rectangle again, stopped at the center and greeted the enthusiastic audience, who applauded for a long time. We had worked to the sound of Verdi's Te Deum. I think this was the best presentation I have ever made. On loose reins, we were heading towards the stables when a pretentious young Frenchman, a professional rider at the time being in Lima, said to me with a snobbish air: "Sir, very successful." I turned to João: "I'll jump right off my horse and wring the neck of this guy." João managed to calm me down and we went back to the stables. I, unfortunately,

Ousado: only those who love, understand and feel the horse can develop a true horseman's feeling. *Private collection.*

do not have the film of this presentation because it has been damaged.

At the reception that followed, His Excellency the Ambassador of Germany came to congratulate me, saying that it was unfortunate that such a beautiful presentation was not accompanied by other music. I told him that what he liked was precisely inspired by the music that made me really resonate.

That year I trained several horses, and I remember those I made the most progress with: Impostor, Invencível and Harpalo Prince. Among my students, at that time, I had Princess Thérèse de Mérode and Patricia Findlay, who today gives lessons in England, and Filipe Graciosa.

In 1972, I went to the United States for the first time to give lessons in Maryland and Massachusetts. One month later I went to the Philippines, Manila, to give some advice to the riding instructors. Corsário had then been in the Philippines for quite some time since he had been sold to Mitus Sison, a student who has been coming for years to spend a month in my school. I showed Corsário at the annual Polo Club Show in Manila,

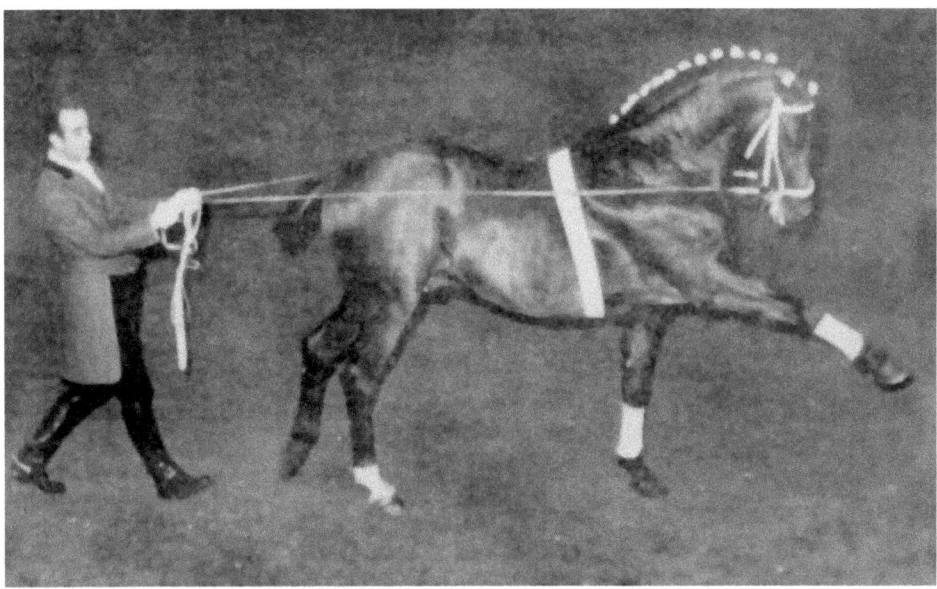

Corsario on the long reins in Spanish walk. *Oliveira Archives.*

both ridden and in long reins. It was another moment of intense emotion in distant Asia. Of all the horses I have trained, Corsário has been one of those I have cherished the most: he was hypersensitive and extraordinarily beautiful. I showed him in the evening under the spotlight to the sound of Verdi's Te Deum, and in long reins with the "Va Pensiero" chorus of the opera *Nabucco*, also from Verdi. During the rehearsals, I prepared him to perform the Spanish trot in long reins which he had only previously done mounted.

I remember a little tragicomic incident. His Excellency the Ambassador of Portugal was invited; he obviously did not accept the invitation, due to—I do not know how many—excuses. He was asked for a record with the national anthem and the only existing one was a 78 RPM vinyl recording done in 1942 by the Police Band. At the opening of the show, which consisted of a Horse Championship, a Junior Dressage Championship and my presentation, I was in front of the flags of the Philippines and Portugal, and after hearing a beautiful interpretation of the Filipino anthem, I felt a contraction in the stomach when I heard the first notes of the "Heroes of the sea, noble people..."[33] in this old and horrible record.

During that year, I received two groups of English people interested in dressage. The trips were organized by Captain Mora who lived in England. We performed shows with students and I presented Impostor who had not yet left for Belgium.

Although quiet 17 years earlier, the huge expansion of the suburbs and the increasing traffic around the Quinta do Chafariz made this place become impossible to have horses. So, I started the construction of the riding school and stables at Quinta do Brejo where the horses moved in March 1973. The following year, to my great joy, my son João returned to Portugal to work with me.

---

[33] Known as "*A Portuguesa*," the national anthem of Portugal. - Editor's note.

Quinta Do Brejo 1973

I started giving lessons at the riding school on the last day of April; it was planned to open on the first days of May. On April 30, I returned from Belgium by plane and arriving at Quinta do Brejo to put everything in order, I found my student and colleague, Alain Godeau, in riding gear. He was the first student to inaugurate the Quinta do Brejo riding school.

Obviously, the Portuguese students found this school too far from Lisbon. In recent years, few of them have attended. But from all over the world, from Asia, Africa, Australia, North and South America, students, many students have come. And those who had passed through Póvoa de Santo Adrião prefer the tranquility of the countryside a thousand times more for taking lessons.

Ten days later, I flew to Lima to perform with Ousado and Odeleite on the birthday of my friend, the former club president, Manoel Pablo Olaechea, to whom the club members wanted to pay tribute and make a surprise. So, I sent my students to swim for three days at the beach of Ericeira and I left on a Thursday in the afternoon to arrive in Venezuela in the middle of the night. At eleven o'clock in the evening, in Caracas, I rode the Thoroughbred horses of my friends and former ambassadors of France in Peru who, at the time, were ambassadors in Venezuela, had dinner with them and flew at 5 a.m. I arrived in Lima around noon at the airport where my friends

Ousado in half-pass at the trot.
Oliveira Archives.

were waiting for me. They had taken Manoel Pablo Olaechea there on the pretext that somebody of interest to the club was arriving from Caracas. He was completely astonished to see me! After a hearty creole meal, I went to change and ride the horses in the afternoon.

The next day, I worked on the gallop track and presented them in the evening before a large audience. After a supper followed by a ball, I was taken to the airport where I took a plane back to Caracas. In the tropical heat, I waited eight hours for the plane to Portugal, arrived the next morning, shaved, took a bath and gave my lesson at 10:30 to the students, rode my horses in the afternoon and gave the students a lesson again. When I got home, I was exhausted.

At the end of the year, I returned to Peru to give lessons, then to Costa Rica, in a riding school that was inaugurated and which belonged to Arturo Aguero Pallacios. He had come the previous year to take classes in Portugal. During his stay, he and a Dutch friend who lived in Costa Rica were received several times at my home and became friends of the family. In tribute to my wife, Arturo decided to call his arena "Branca Oliveira Riding School."

My wife arrived in Costa Rica a day after I arrived from Peru. The inauguration of the school was very moving; my wife, who had received a huge quantity of roses, gave one to each student in the school, to those who were on horseback as well as those in the gallery.

After a week of lessons we returned to Portugal, and after a long ten-hour flight we arrived in Lisbon in the morning. As usual, I shaved, took my bath and went straight to Quinta do Brejo, where we did not live yet.

I rode a few horses all day and at the end of the afternoon the Anglo-Arab, Il Trovatore. This one had perhaps been insufficiently lunged; he violently threw me on the ground. I mounted him again and only managed to calm and relax him at 9:30 in the evening. Once again, I came home completely exhausted.

In the years that followed, I continued to receive countless foreign students and four times a year spent two weeks in the United States teaching lessons in a riding school that my great friend Phyllis Field had built in Maryland for that purpose. I went to Belgium, France and Luxembourg to give clinics in May and October, for some years in Peru and twice in Costa Rica.

I also want to mention that for four years Susan Cromarty, today, Mrs. Miguel Oliveira, was my secretary and student, and has helped me a lot to maintain the pleasant atmosphere that all foreign students have appreciated at Quinta do Brejo.

During my first visit to Saumur, the Chief *Écuyer* asked me to ride his horse Myosotis and try piaffe. As soon as I was on him, I realized that it would be difficult given his morphology[34] and the school work, but I also realized, from the way he resisted with his neck and mouth when asked for a greater degree of *rassembler*, that several *écuyers* had unsuccessfully attempted the piaffe. We closed the doors of the Bossut Riding School and in the presence of the Chief *Écuyer*, Lieutenant-Colonel Durand, the former Chief *Écuyer*, Colonel Saint-André, my son João and Captain Rémiat I worked Myosotis. At the end of six sessions, the horse did some steps of brilliant piaffe. My son João came to me and told me, very moved… or rather he did not tell me anything. Late at night, while we were walking in Saumur, he told me that that had been a historical moment in Equitation.

At that moment, I remembered that a few years before, a French general had asked one of my French pupils: *"And your Portuguese master?"* in a demeaning tone.

In 1976, a troubled period of Portuguese political life, Mr. João, the barber of Malveira, my son João and Colonel Matias, then commander of the Military Center of Physical Education, Riding and Sports of Mafra, organized the horse show of Malveira. They asked me to make a presentation and, since I refused, Jorge Matias

---

[34] the general aspects of biological form and arrangement of the parts of a plant or an animal.

threatened me laughingly that he would bomb my riding school. So, I went there, in black pants and jacket, a dark-colored tie and without a hat. My old friends, *so-called fascists*[35], were there. I showed Junco under the spotlights, to the sound of the opening of Verdi's *Traviata* and, in the end, I went out to the sound of "Va Pensiero" of the opera *Nabucco*, also by Verdi.

The next day the newspapers reported that Master Nuno Oliveira had made a presentation to the sound of Strauss's waltzes! In the end, João and the man who regularly cuts my hair gave me a cockade[36] that I keep in my office with pride.

In 1979, I went to Canada, a wonderful country, to give a week of lessons in intense cold. On my way back and after stopping in the United States, I gave a week of lessons in Costa Rica, where I informally showed Gabrielle Adorno whom I had sold to D. Silvya de Pozuello. Once I arrived in Portugal after a very long trip—having travelled to Costa Rica, Miami, New York, Lisbon—I came back in the morning to Quinta do Brejo, shaved, took my bath and, in the afternoon, I rode my horses.

As I was riding, Va Pensiero, who had not been shod for a long time and whose hooves were too long, stumbled while cantering and I, with my 80 kg, was sent over his neck, a feat that made me have horrible pain for several months.

On the occasion of the Salon du Cheval in Paris, a book compiled by

Ingemisco, young Luso-Arab, beginning piaffe. *Photo courtesy of Stephanie Millham.*

Jeanne Boisseau, based on the notes taken by my students, and especially those taken by my excellent friend Antoine de Coux, who has been attending my classes for 14 years, was put on sale. This book is entitled: *Notes sur l'enseignement de Nuno Oliveira.*[37]

During all these years I have, as usual, received many students from all over the world. Among them, I would like to mention Jean Magnan de Bornier and Bettina Drummond.

In 1980, I received Jean-Marie Donard, Maître de Manège of the Cadre Noir, for a week. He is a high-class rider, one of the best I have known.

I also trained several horses, including Rigoletto, Fra Melitone,

---

[35] In the context of the 1974 April revolution, people owning horses were considered fascist by some extreme leftist factions. - Translator's note.
[36] cockade is a knot of ribbons, or other circular or oval-shaped symbol of distinctive colors which is usually worn on a hat.
[37] The English translation of this work is entitled: *The Wisdom of Master Nuno Oliveira* by Antoine de Coux.

Levante, Nabucco, Jabute, Junco, Va Pensiero, Gabrielle Adorno and especially Ingemisco.

The officers who follow the Instructors Riding Course or the Equestrian Improvement Course in Mafra have also, in the last six years at the end of their course, come to spend an afternoon with their instructors in my school. My son João and I ride some horses, show them a student's lesson and then invite one or two to ride one of our horses.

These friendly relations have allowed groups of foreign students to be invited to go for a horse ride in the Tapada de Mafra.[38]

Since my school is relatively near to them, in my very little free time I also visit them occasionally and I am always received with a lot of friendship.

In 1976, Phyllis Field translated my book into English under the title *Reflections on Equestrian Art* [published by J.A. Allen, now Crowood Press].

At the beginning of 1980, I had the pleasure of being approached by one of my former students, a great Portuguese show jumping rider, asking me to ride his horse with which he had collection problems in order to enter more important events. I worked him a little and it seems that the result was not bad. It was his rider who said this.

I have written these lines on the other side of the world, in Brisbane, Australia—where I spent two months giving lessons and riding horses—not out of vanity, but to talk about horses and especially the Iberian horse. With age, the physical possibilities of the rider diminish, but when one really intends to deepen one's art, the mind, thought and reflection take a higher degree.

Seeing the progress of my students here, two girls and a 19-year-old boy working with young horses, I think I did not waste my time. All these years spent trying to pass on to others what, with much effort and hard work, one has acquired and learned is good, and it is part of a vast world called Love.

Nuno Oliveira, Brisbane, December 31, 1980

"Ho procurato con anelito di perfezione d'elevarmi al di sopra della materialità circostante."

"I have endeavored with a longing for perfection to rise above the surrounding materiality."

– Giacomo Lauri Volpi

---

[38] Royal hunting grounds and forest park of the Convent of Mafra.

Appendix: Conference on Descente de Main

Nuno Oliveira on Florido, Lusitano, *mise en main* from *30 Years with Master Nuno Oliveira*, Xenophon Press 2011.

---

[39] Written part of the conference held by Nuno Oliveira in the Centro Militar de Educação Física, Desportos e Equitação, in Mafra, Portugal, on the 24th of July 1981.

Appendix

Ladies and Gentlemen,

Who am I to talk to you about Equitation, the horse? The only merit I may have is to understand that the horse has been for countless centuries the most important conquest of mankind.

And today, in the century[40] of the machine of ultra-perfect technology, in which the human being puts his feet on the moon, the horse, that wonderful companion of man, gives us a bit of poetry in a life that is also becoming a bit mechanical by force of the circumstances of the time in which we live.

Ladies and Gentlemen, we are gathered here to pay homage to the horse, man's most beautiful conquest, as the wise Buffon[41] so aptly put it:

"Riding is the art of utilizing the horse, of teaching him to be the collaborator of man."

And I believe that the great writings on Equitation, those who made law in their time, were those who advised rational systems, without brutality, and not those who used force or resistance.

It is evident that the horse, through the centuries, has been selected according to fashions or the way of employing him, but his spirit remains a mystery.

The Equestrian Art has been the concern of certain men of spirit who created it to precisely succeed in using the horse without transforming that spirit, that mind, in a spirit of revolt.

I will start by quoting Xenophon, the Greek:

"The horse will accept the bridle better if each time he accepts it he shall be given a good treatment."

So, four hundred years before Christ, people were already thinking about rewarding, what was later pompously called the *Descente de Main*.

I quote here from Xenophon precisely the part of rewarding for the fact that the horse accepts the contact of the bridle, of a piece of metal that is placed in his mouth.

Over the centuries, much has been said about the horse's mouth and bits, and many changes have been made to these bits, inventing dozens and dozens of models whose inventors wanted, on the one hand, to make people believe that they were the secret to obtaining yielding and, on the other, the way to dominate him.

Of course, depending on the shape of the horse's mouth, the size of his mouth, whether it is more or less fleshy at the bars, one must choose the bit, but this is a secondary question.

What I want to talk to you about today, what I want to make you think

---

[40] [20th century - Editor's note.]
[41] Georges-Louis Leclerc, count de Buffon (1707-1788), French naturalist, remembered for his comprehensive work on natural history, *Histoire naturelle, générale et particulière*. - Editor's note.

about with me, Ladies and Gentlemen, is not to forget that the horse's mouth is in his head, the head where the brain is also located. The horse is, no doubt, provided with a form of reasoning, of course to a much lesser degree than that of the human being, but which is clearly a reasoning mind with anxiety, fear, and I don't know how many other things. Not long ago, while I was in Australia, I read in a newspaper article describing that the Americans had done experiments to check the intelligence of animals with monkeys and dogs and had correctly concluded that animals reasoned, and reasoned in their own way. I dare not say, but I dare to think, perhaps better than certain humans.

Well, Ladies and Gentlemen, you realize by now that what I want to talk to you about is the horse's mouth and the hands yielding to his acceptance of the piece or pieces of iron or steel that were put into his mouth.

I have already quoted Xenophon, so, let's go to the Middle Ages and look through the writings of that time for someone who was concerned about the horse's mouth. I quote Lorenzo Rusio, marshal [*marescallus de Urbe*] in Rome, an *attaché* to the house of a nephew of Pope Nicholas II around 1288. Here is the citation:

"To train a horse it is necessary at first to put a light bridle on him and as sweet and gentle as possible, and when you put it on him at first you should rub it with honey or other sweet materials because when he feels the sweetness he will accept it better."

And let's go into the Italian Renaissance and here I'll quote Federico Grisone from his *Gli Ordini di Cavalcare*, about the horse's mouth and feeling that he doesn't force or is heavy on the hand:

"When the horse is too heavy on the bridle, and when walking he forces the rider's hand, it will be necessary each time to make him rein back a few steps so that he is straight and light."

Let us continue then in the study of the classics, of those who, for centuries, obsessed with the same passion that, Ladies and Gentlemen, brings us together here, have been concerned with the horse's mouth and with the precaution that his mouth is molested as little as possible.

I will now quote Salomon de la Broue[42], *Écuyer d'Écurie du Roy de France* and of Monseigneur the Duke of Spain, and whom the Count de Lanscome-Brèves called the "Restorer of French Equitation":

---

[42] Salomon de La Broue (1530 – 1610) was a French riding master. His treatise on riding, *Preceptes Principaux* published in 1593, was the first to have been written in French. Like Antoine de Pluvinel, he was a pupil of Gianbattista Pignatelli. De La Broue was *écuyer* to Jean Louis de Nogaret de La Valette, the first Duke of Épernon, and *écuyer* ordinaire of the Grande Écurie du Roi in the reign of Henri IV. [Editor's note from Wikipedia]

De La Broue, like Pluvinel, was one of the founders of the old French *haute école*. His methods centred on calmness in hand, freedom and lightness in order to obtain the best results from the horse; he rejected the use of force or constraint in training.

"And when the horse is young, it is necessary to pay attention that the mouthpiece does not rest in a bad place in the mouth."[43]

Let us enter the seventeenth century and here I quote Samuel Fouquet de Beaurepère, a gentleman native of Anjou and *Écuyer de la Grande Écurie du Roy*:

"For if it is true to say that the horse is guided and driven by the bridle or that the bridle subjects him to the rider's will, it is necessary to draw from this infallible consequence that the driving of any horse cannot depend on more than two things, namely, the good bridle and the rider's knowledgeable hand, obviously working together."

Let us go and plunge into the night of the past, when the absence of the automobile, the train, the airplane, the motorbike or motor scooter, and even the helicopter, certainly made man more knowledgeable about the horse than us. Ladies and Gentlemen, I quote now from the Duke of Newcastle[44], Lord of Cavendish, Bothel and Hipel, Baron of Bolsover and Ogle, Viscount Mansfield:

"It should be noted that all the rules of our Art are to make a horse sensitive in the mouth, an essential condition for him to become sensitive in the flanks!"

We come to the eighteenth century and in the Tuileries Riding School [Paris], let us listen to François Robichon de la Guérinière:

"We have mentioned that a good hand combines three qualities: lightness, gentleness, and firmness.

"The light hand is that which does not feel any contact at all of the bit on the bars. The gentle hand is that which feels a little of the effect of the bit without giving too much contact.

"The firm hand is one that holds the horse in full contact with the bit. It is indeed a great art to know how and when to use these three different effects of the hand. Their use depends on the nature of the mouth of each particular horse. The effects must be applied without constraining the animal and without suddenly abandoning contact with its mouth. Stated another way, after yielding, which is the action of a light hand, the rider must gently take in the reins, looking for the feeling little by little, the contact with the bit in his hand. This is followed by the firm hand that resists more and more and keeps the horse in stronger contact. After this, contact with the bit is gently and gradually diminished before passing back to the light hand, for the gentle hand must always precede and follow the firm hand. The hand should never suddenly yield or resist. This can ruin a horse's mouth and cause head tossing.

"There are two ways to yield the hand. The first, which is the most common, is to lower the bridle hand in the manner already mentioned. The second is to take hold of the reins in the right hand above the left and, by loosening the left hand, to gradually transfer contact with the bit to the right hand. Then the left hand is removed. After this, the right hand is lowered until it rests on the horse's neck. Then the horse is completely free and without bridle. This last method of

---

[43] The actual quote is: "And when the horse is young, and his adult teeth are not yet grown, it is necessary to take care that the mouthpiece does not press on it." ("Et quand le cheval sera jeune, qu'il n'eut encore poussé l'escaillon: il faut bien prendre garde que l'embouchure n'appuie dessus." - Translator's note by Gérard Dufresne in *Nuno Oliveira, Oeuvres Complètes*, Belin, 2006.)

[44] *The New Method of Dressing Horses*: also known as *"A General System of Horsemanship,"* an updated facsimile of the London edition of 1743, by William Cavendish, Xenophon Press 2020 - Editor's note.

yielding the hand is called the "descente de main." It also may be performed by holding the end of the reins in the right hand at the same height as the horse's head with the right arm straight out and forward. The rider should, however, be very sure of his horse's mouth and of its obedience before he attempts to try this last method.

"The rider should guard against using the yeilding hand or performing the "descente de main" when his horse is on its shoulders. The correct time to perform either of these movements is after indicating the half-halt. When the rider feels that his horse is on its haunches, then is to time to subtly yield the bridle hand or even to perform the "descent de main." As the rider abandons contact with the bit at the same time the horse is on his haunches, the horse has to become light in hand since he has nothing at all on which to support his head. This is one of the subtlest and most useful of all the aids in horsemanship. It is also one of the most difficult to know how to correctly time and perform.

"There is still another way to use the reins, one that is not seen very often. This is to attach each rein to the curve of the banquet so that the curb will not have any effect. This method is known as "working with false reins." It is sometimes used with young horses in order to accustom them to the feel of a bit when they are just beginning to be put in a bridle." [45]

The Duke of Newcastle wrote a dissertation on the reins of the bridle, which appears to have some plausibility in the speculation, but which, in my opinion, is destroyed in the execution. He says that *"on whichever side the reins are pulled, the mouthpiece always goes on the side opposite the branch: that when the branch comes in, the mouthpiece goes out,"* so that, he continues, *"the reins being separated, when the right rein is pulled, the mouthpiece goes out on the other side and obligates the horse to look out of the volte and the curb chain is also pressed on the outside."* This principle is destroyed by usage, which proves to us that the horse is determined to obey the movement of the hand on the side on which the rein is pulled. By pulling, for example, the right rein, the horse is obliged to yield to this movement and to bring the head to that side. I agree that by simply pulling the rein, without bringing the rein close to oneself at the same time, as one should, the contact (*appui* in French) will be stronger on the opposite side; but this will not prevent the horse from obeying the hand and carrying the head on this side, because he is obliged to follow the strongest impression, which does not only come from the contact (*appui* in French) which is made on the exterior side, but from the rein which acts on the mouthpiece, pulls it, and consequently the head of the horse also, on the side where one wants to go. Moreover, by using one's hand at the right time, one shortens the inside rein a little and then the bit presses on the part that one wants to influence.

"It should be noted again that when using the outside rein by carrying the outside hand toward the inside, that this action moves the horse's outside shoulder toward the inside. This causes the outside leg to pass over the inside leg. When the inside rein is used by carrying the hand to the

---

[45] English translation from *Ecole de Cavalerie, The Expanded Complete Part II*, Xenophon Press 2015. See the bridle diagram on page 150. The entire citation of M. de la Guérinière in the original text of the conference is in French. - Editor's note.

Appendix: *Descente de Main*

outside, the movement will extend the inside shoulder. This is to say, make the inside leg cross over the outside leg. The reader can see the way the bridle hand is carried and that they are able to move the forehand of the horse. The rider who does not understand how to use the reins works without the aid of rules and basic principles."[46]

Let us continue and now listen to Montfaucon de Rogles who for thirty years was *Écuyer de la Grande Écurie du Roi*:

"One yields the hand to the horse to freshen the bars and remove the pressure of the mouthpiece, [pressure] which was produced by the action of the hand."

Also around the same time let us quote Count de Drummond de Melfort, born in 1722 to a family originally from Scotland:

"The simplest and most gentle bits are those that best serve Cavalry."

Now I will quote the Marquis Ducroc de Chabannes, who was appointed *Écuyer* at the School of Saumur in 1815, in his book *"Cours Élémentaire et Analytique d'Équitation"*:

"The mouth retaining all its sensitivity will obey the slightest impression of the bit."

We come to François Baucher and here I will quote him, omitting to say that he was… not omitting, perhaps the greatest genius of Equitation of all times; I quote [from a *New Method of Horsemanship* published as *François Baucher: The Man and his method*, Baucher/ Nelson Xenophon Press 2013] in the chapter entitled *"Succinct exposition of my method by questions and answers"*:

"Question: What kind of bit suits the Horse?

"Answer: The gentle bit.

"Question: Why is a gentle bit necessary for all horses, whatever their resistance?

"Answer: Because a hard bit always has the effect of holding the horse back and surprising him when what is needed is to stop him from doing wrong and to get him to do well. Now, these results can only be obtained with the help of a gentle bit and above all with the help of a wise hand."

I quote a German author of the same time, Gustav Steinbrecht, who on page 28 of his book *"Gymnasium of the Horse"* [Xenophon Press 1994] says:

"These small actions of give and take of the reins that are so necessary to keep the horse's mouth constantly sensitive are operated with subtlety, by repeated relaxation and closing of the fingers."

Now, let's enter our century. At the very beginning of the century, we read General de L'Hotte, who was a disciple of Baucher and later *Écuyer en Chef* in Saumur; well, let's go to page 36 of his book *Questions Équestres* [*Equestrian Questions*, Xenophon Press 2021]:

"Lightness finds first of all its manifestation in the submission of the jaw, which is the first joint [ressort in French] to receive the effect of the hand, and its submission is made evident when it responds with relaxation to the soliciting action of its play. The mobility of the jaw is not only verified by its submission; the flexibility of this region goes further by causing that of the neck and then of the other joints [ressorts in French] through the correlation instinctively existing between all the muscular masses."

---

[46] English translation from *Ecole de Cavalerie, The Expanded Complete Part II*, Xenophon Press 2015. The entire citation of M. de la Guérinière in the original text of the conference is in French. - Editor's note.

Here I conclude my quotations from great horsemen and authors who, Ladies and Gentlemen, have dealt with the mouth of the horse.

I do not want to forget my memories of the Portuguese masters that I saw in my youth and among them I want to mention: Mestre Joaquim Gonçalves de Miranda, D. José Manuel da Cunha Menezes, the Captains António Correia and Caeiro Vieira, the last of whom I accidentally saw, already at an old age, riding a horse for two or three days. They had the principle that riding could only be qualified as art if the horse worked with a light mouth and completely relaxed.

I apologize for telling you only about the past up to now. Well, my dear friends: let us dive deeply into the Equestrian present and of what is happening in the world.

High School is now called "Dressage" all over the world—it means teaching—now, the term is incorrect because teaching is necessary to do in any horse discipline, teaching to jump, teaching to run on a racetrack properly, and teaching to pull a cart or a plow.

In the seventeenth century men dressed in a jacket and wore a wig. Now, Ladies and Gentlemen, thank God we have short-sleeved shirts, we go around without a tie, and I even think it's becoming fashionable to go to someone else's house for dinner like this.

Such is fashion.

In the seventeenth century, horses were ridden with the reins in the left hand and the right hand platonically held a whip in a graceful position. Now two reins are used in each hand.

In his treatise on horsemanship, the Count D'Aure[47] said that in Versailles, the great academy of Europe at the time, the extended trot was considered detrimental to the *rassembler* of horses that were very much upon the haunches and were intended for piaffe and school jumps upon the haunches. Then came the racing Thoroughbred that invaded Europe as a sport horse, a hunting horse, a horse with low and wide gaits, and here all the current world that practices equitation is in debt to Baucher. Baucher with his love of the High School, which he was able to transpose from his observations as a poor young man, observations that he made behind the gates of Versailles watching D'Abzac, and other masters wearing the tricorn [hat], evolve on Navarra horses, Spanish horses, in short, on round horses.

Therefore all of us riders around the world, including the Germans, owe a debt of gratitude to the one who, moments before his death, holding the hand of his beloved disciple General Alexis L'Hotte, said to him: "Always like this (immobilizing his hand), and never like this (withdrawing his hand towards his stomach)."

Equitation changed, though, because the model of horses used was different.

The gaits became wider and with more suspension but also less elevation. The same is true for the piaffe.

We began to practice the extended trot with the horse placed and in the

---

[47] Viscount Antoine Henri Philippe Léon Cartier d'Aure was a French riding-master, and author of important treatises on dressage. He was *écuyer en chef* of the Cadre Noir of Saumur, and later to the Emperor of France, Napoléon III. He was made an officer of the Légion d'Honneur in 1849. - Wikipedia. - Editor's note.

hand because the [new] model of horse was suitable for this.

When we think that the German, Ridinger,[48] advocated horses that paddled outward for the practice of High School and school jumps, because he claimed that the paddling motion threw weight on the haunches, whereas today, a horse that moves like that, no one wants him... I repeat, fashions.

And fashions are also related to the type of horse that each nation has.

There is a tendency in the world today to breed and use a standard type of horse that is close to the German horse with English blood.

Riding is no longer an art, but a sport that is difficult to perform. It requires—and I speak of dressage because it is the discipline to which I have dedicated myself and which I have observed throughout the world—horses with wide movements, naturally well-balanced, of good temperament, not too fine in order to be able to withstand aids that are not fine, and a dose of physical strength in the arms and waist that have nothing in common with the concern of the gentle and relaxed mouth that was the preoccupation of all of these authors that I have quoted.

Performing Grand Prix Dressage today is a very difficult task, but the artistic aspect has been replaced by the precision of the machine, the spirit of the times, and above all the spirit of discipline of the Germans, influenced by their powerful, heavier horses that make up the majority and that get first places by their work discipline. To win, what is needed above all is to have the exact notion of describing geometrically perfect figures at the exact time and moment. It is very difficult, but the artistic expression of the horse has been lost.

Not long ago at one of my training clinics in Saumur, the *Écuyer en Chef* played different films that we watched together with the *écuyers* of the Cadre: The first was Colonel Lesage riding [the Thoroughbred] Taine at the [1932] Los Angeles Olympic Games: His aids were impeccable and discreet, the tension of his reins much lighter than is now used. He walked less quickly than present day competitors.

The other was a film of Filatov[49] in Rome: less finesse of aids but still infinitely more than the current riders.

And the last film was of a winning Olympic horse of the late twentieth century with his rider. The aids, the tension of the reins were much more visible and infinitely stronger. And above all everything takes place at a different, much greater speed. The classic airs are less beautiful, have less artistic expression.

It is the fashion. Dressage becomes a sport.

Let's keep calling High School to the Art.

But what is more serious is the fact I am going to tell you, Ladies and Gentlemen: in the screening of the last movie we saw the horse mounted by his rider coming from the stable to the warm-up ring and to my astonishment I saw the horse do a terrible tête-à-queue[50], and despite the opening reins

---

[48] Johann Elias Ridinger (1698-1767) - Editor's note.

[49] Individual dressage Gold Medalist Sergei Filatov rode Absent in the Olympic Games, Rome 1960. - Editor's note.

[50] literally: head to tail, meaning turned around 180 degrees. - Editor's note.

and the futile efforts of his rider, he escaped to the stable! I also saw in that film the horse's return to the ring; he was mounted by his rider with her private trainer behind, with a whip in his hand.

Ladies and Gentlemen: admiring the cadence of this horse on his half-passes when he is in the twenty by sixty arena, performing, as they say in circus jargon, "his number," but knowing that outside the rectangle he cannot be dominated, I feel confused, knowing that the World and Olympic Champion of Dressage, as it is called in current fashion, is that which has replaced the *Haute École* of Monsieur de la Guérinère, who wrote in his book *École de Cavalerie*[51] *La Grâce est un si bel ornement de l'Art.*[52]

And this is how it is judged, and most of the time by ignorant people who do not know what a horse is.

In this regard, with your permission, I will tell you three anecdotal cases. Years ago my dear friend Fernando Sommer de Andrade sold me a horse that he had bred, a horse of pure Portuguese breed that I trained to perform all the exercises of Grand Prix Dressage. I sold him to a client of mine living near Germany, a disciplined man in everything; if he weighs a few grams more he goes on a diet, eats vegetables, drinks water, walks for hours on foot, what we around here think of as a bore! He repeats the Dressage tests on foot in the arena before competing. He is a lame rider; he pinches with his spurs all the time, he pulls at the poor horse's mouth, but he does the exercises at the spot, at the moment, by heart. It's horrible.

About two years ago, Filipe Graciosa, Captain Martins Abrantes, and, I believe, Lieutenant Colonel Pombeiro, went from here to a dressage competition that took place at the Salon du Cheval in Versailles. They are, without the slightest doubt, infinitely superior as riders to our man, water drinker, diet practitioner, and I don't know of how many other sacrifices.

I have sometimes had the pleasure of sitting at the table with the above-mentioned riders and I believe that they are all lovers of good food, they are not boring, in short, they are Latin people. I hope, Ladies and Gentlemen, that you take a certain philosophy from this.

The second anecdotal fact that I can tell you is the following: I have a Belgian student who competes with her mare in dressage tests. Every time I go to Belgium she shows me her classification from the different competitions and the judges' comments for each movement. What amazes me is when I read the considerations of a certain judge and I see on a half-pass at the canter the following comment: "Lack of crossing," followed by the respective low score. My God!

And the third is this: I was in Saumur a year and a half ago giving a clinic at the same time that a course for French dressage judges was being held. The judges were staying at the Hotel Budan where I also had a room. One day, late in the afternoon, I went down to the lounge and sat in an armchair waiting for Commander Carde[53] to come and get me for dinner at his place. The judges

---

[51] [*École de Cavalerie*, Xenophon Press 2015]

[52] "Grace is such a beautiful ornament of art."

[53] Christian Carde won the 1979 French dressage championships. He was the French national dressage team trainer from 1985-1989, the *Écuyer en chef* of the Cadre Noir from 1991 until his retirement in 1999 after which he judged a short time internationally.

came down and, in the same salon, sat drinking, without seeing me because I was in a chair at the end of the lobby and had my back to them. I listened to the plethora of considerations and nonsense they said about dressage. They were quite amazed when they saw me getting up to meet Commander Carde at the appointed time.

I have been able to ride some dressage horses around the world trained by experts. I have also been allowed to ride some of the expert jumping horses of great world riders. What is curious is that the latter, by the need to collect the horse in the turns, have a *rassembler* and a lightness that the former have lost. Despite considering themselves the best riders in the world, the former are certainly much lower than a Frédy Knie[54], and their work is, as I have mentioned, a number made not in a difficult round arena of twelve or thirteen meters' diameter but one of twenty by sixty meters.

It is not my intention to destroy the dressage competitions in my conversation with you. What I regret is that the way of judging the competitions, the fashion that has been put in the execution of classical equitation, has nothing to do with Equestrian Art. I don't think I can classify the absence of grace as Art.

Notice the passage and the piaffe of most horses, notice how it goes from being a graceful and harmonious exercise to becoming a grotesque spectacle. Notice the pirouettes with the horses raising and lowering their necks. Why? Because in force and compression none of these airs can be executed correctly.

Evidently, if we Portuguese want to start entering world dressage competitions again, we must, above all, learn with the Germans a discipline that we do not have, we must play the game of the other countries: buying horses that are in fashion and riding in the fashionable way, but do not forget that fashions change.

There is already a slight tendency to return to a less strong and more discreet riding in certain countries. Notice the Russians, for example.

I have just been given a book by a former *Écuyer-en-Chef* of the Cadre Noir, Colonel de Saint-André, and by the present Lieutenant-Colonel Durand about the Cadre Noir which is very interesting; I would like to quote two passages written by Lieutenant-Colonel Durand:

"Le sommet de l'Art est atteint lorsque des chevaux brillants réagissent avec impulsion à des aides invisibles." [55]

And also: *"C'est la sobriété qui marque la manière française."* [56]

I also quote a passage from Colonel de Saint-André:

"Si enfin le dresseur pousse ses exigences jusqu'à obtenir la légèreté, il connaitra les satisfactions de l'Art Équestre: porté par un cheval rassemblé, qui le couvre de son encolure soutenue, la bouche moelleuse, ils frôlent tous les deux le sol, dans la descente de mains et de jambes." [57]

Ladies and Gentlemen: Here in this house where we are gathered by the same enthusiasm, the Horse, Equitation, in a country of equestrian tradition, cradle of great riders of the past and wonderful

---

[54] Frédy Knie (1920-2003), born in Geneva, was trained in all fundamental circus disciplines and at an early age was soon billed as "Europe's youngest high school rider," and became one of the greatest circus horse trainers of his generation.

[55] "The pinnacle of Art is reached when brilliant horses react with impulsion to invisible aids."

[56] "It is sobriety that marks the French way."

horses, and where unfortunately everything has tended to drop in level, together let us make an effort so that the Equestrian Art is not lost.

As you have just seen, everything I have said above has a regionalist stamp, from a western and southern European that is accustomed to looking at France as a model, ignoring everything that happens in the north or beyond the Rhine.

Well, let's analyze German Equitation, and let's analyze the Spanish Riding School of Vienna. The Germans are hard-working and disciplined people. I was in the United States watching a television program where a German citizen was interviewed and asked several questions about life in Germany. One of the questions was: "Why are you Germans the richest people in Europe?" The answer from the German citizen was: "Because we work harder than others, and in a team spirit."

The Nordics are a bit like that too, and we Latin people are totally different. We Latin people and southern Europeans have much more of a tendency towards individualism and much less of a team spirit.

The Germans with their Trakehners and Hanoverians, less hot-blooded than the Thoroughbreds or the French Anglo-Arabians, practiced on those horses an equitation where the tension of the reins and the action of the legs are much more visible because those horses allow it.

One *Maître de Manège* of the Cadre Noir returned to Saumur after a clinic in Warendorf, Germany, and he wanted to apply to the French horses what he saw this particular clinician do every morning, which was to beat the horses to bring them to the boil so that then the collected airs were easier; the French horses that did not have the same balance and had more blood did not permit this, defending themselves.

Now, also because of the mass of German horses, the rider's back has extraordinary importance.

If we read the German classics, for example, Gustav Steinbrecht and Waldemar Seunig, and if we watch the teaching of riders in Germany, we notice that the torso of the rider is the first concern: it acts as the fulcrum of the scale and the action of the hands is always preceded by an adjustment of the torso to the sensations received from the horse's back.

Cadence is of the utmost importance. And the horses stand at attention even before the rider mounts.

I even remember four or five years ago riding at Karlsruhe [Germany] a Portuguese horse of Andrade breeding and trained by Egon Von Neindorff, a flexible horse by breed and nature, and being amazed by his rigidity.

Of course, these German-trained horses are precise in their work. It doesn't matter if they are strong or not, what matters is that the horses execute the movements or exercises with precision, but the form, the fineness, the spirit of the horse, do not matter.

As these horses have large gaits, their riders need to sit deep in the saddle, and if they do not have strength in their waist and back, they are not able to dominate them.

---

[57] "If, finally, the trainer pushes his requirements to the point of obtaining lightness, he will know the satisfactions of the Equestrian Art: carried by a collected horse, which covers him with its sustained neck, with a soft mouth, they both graze the ground, in *descente de mains et de jambes*."

Appendix: *Descente de Main*

The Spanish Riding School of Vienna, supplied with horses descending from the Iberian ones but crossed with Northern European (Danish) type mares, in a marvelous setting that is the arena designed by Fischer von Erlach, and also due to the Austrian temperament that the Eastern Latins have, has a lighter and more subtle stamp than the German equitation but does not prevent, however, that in most cases we find horses working completely contracted, by the use of force and a lot of spur.

Let's not forget that the perfection we see in most of the execution of the exercises is because these are horses that have had years and years of training and sometimes more than one or two dozen years of training.

Due to the type of horse, they have much shorter gaits than German horses and are criticized for this.

Their airs above the ground are executed well upon the haunches and the Saumur horses, which are on the one hand less beautiful and on the other hand more difficult, were the preference of the French riders of the beginning of this century, and in particular of General de L'Hotte, to show that with less rounded horses one could perform school jumps without being as collected, that is, not as loaded on the haunches.

They created jumps that are executed more in a horizontal balance than in collection.

Ladies and Gentlemen, I think I have already bored you too much.

I would like to end by asking you to pay homage to the horse, that wonderful companion, by trying, every time we ride him, to do it with the soul of an artist.

The artist is the one who knows how to love.

If I dare to show you a film of some horses that I have worked with during my already long equestrian career, horses on which I have eagerly sought lightness and relaxation, allow me to quote, to counterbalance the current trend in teaching students, Titus Livius [58]:

"Id cum majore vi equorum facietes si effrenatos in hostes equos inimittitis quod soepe romanos equites cum laude fecisse sua, memoriae proditum est. De tractisque frenis bis ultro citroque cum magna strage hostium infractis omnibus hastis transcurrerunt."

"You will turn their clash more impetuous if you unbridle your horses to hurl them against their enemies. It is a maneuver that has worked for Roman cavalry and does them honor. Unbridling their horses, they attacked the enemy hosts, turned on their footsteps, and further pierced them breaking all their spears and doing the greatest carnage." (Translation from *Nuno Oliveira*, Portuguese edition.)

Let us not unbridle ours but let our hands work gently so that the horse understands his rider and works relaxed and willingly and not as a slave.

Thank you very much.

---

[58] Livy, Roman, in full Titus Livius, (born 59/64 BC—died AD 17), along with Sallust and Tacitus, is one of the three great Roman historians. His history of Rome became a classic in his own life-time and exercised a profound influence on the style and philosophy of historical writing up to the 18th century.

Telegram sent to Branca Lory Oliveira [widow of Nuno Oliveira], on the 15th of February, 1989, by the President of the Portuguese Republic, Mário Soares.

"I extend my deepest condolences on the death of your husband, Master Nuno Oliveira, whose disappearance is an enormous loss to the world of equestrian art. In this time of mourning, I want to remember his remarkable action at the service of an art of such ancient and noble traditions in our country and pay tribute to the master who gave so much prestige to the name of Portugal in the world."

Xenophon Press Library

www.XenophonPress.com
Xenophon Press is dedicated to the preservation
of classical equestrian literature.
We bring both new and old works to
English-speaking riders.

30 Years with Master Nuno Oliveira, Henriquet 2011

A Journey Through the Horse's Body, Fritz 2012

A Rider's Survival from Tyranny, de Kunffy 2012

Another Horsemanship, Racinet 1994

Austrian Art of Riding, Poscharnigg 2015

Broken or Beautiful: The Struggle of Modern Dressage, Barbier/Conrod 2020

Classic Show Jumping: the de Nemethy Method, de Nemethy 2016

Classical Dressage with Anja Beran, Beran 2021

Divide and Conquer Book 1, Lemaire de Ruffieu 2016

Divide and Conquer Book 2, Lemaire de Ruffieu 2017

Dressage for the 21st Century, Belasik 2001

Dressage in the French Tradition, Diogo de Bragança 2011

Dressage Principles and Techniques: A Blueprint for the Serious Rider, Tavora 2018

Dressage Principles Illuminated, Expanded Edition, de Kunffy 2021

École de Cavalerie Part II, Robichon de la Guérinière 2015

Elements of Dressage, von Ziegner 2022

Equestrian Art: The Collected Early Writings (1951-1956), Nuno Oliveira 2022

Equestrian Art: The Collected Later Works, Nuno Oliveira 2022

Equine Osteopathy: What the Horses Have Told Me, Giniaux 2014

Federico Grisone's "The Rules of Riding," Grisone/Tobey 2023

Fragments from the Writings of Max Ritter von Weyrother, Fane 2017

François Baucher: The Man and His Method, Baucher/Nelson 2013

French Equitation: a Baucherist in America, 1922 & Hand-book for Horsewomen, Bussigny 2023

General Chamberlin: America's Equestrian Genius, Matha 2020

Great Horsewomen of the 19th Century in the Circus, Nelson 2015

Gymnastic Exercises for Horses Volume II, Eleanor Russell 2013

H. Dv. 12 German Cavalry Manual of Horsemanship, Reinhold 2014

Handbook of Jumping Essentials, Lemaire de Ruffieu 2015

Handbook of Riding Essentials, Lemaire de Ruffieu 2015

Healing Hands, Giniaux, DVM 1998

Horse Training: Outdoors and High School, Beudant 2014

Horsemanship & Horsemastership Volume 1, US Cavalry 2021

Horsemanship Training Films 3 DVD set, US Cavalry 2021

I, Siglavy, Asay 2018

Journey Through the Horse's Body, Dr. Christina Fritz 2022

Learning to Ride, Santini 2016

Legacy of Master Nuno Oliveira, Millham 2013

Lessons in Lightness: Expanded Edition, Mark Russell 2019

Mark of Clover, Barczy Kelly, 2022

Methodical Dressage of the Riding Horse, Faverot de Kerbrech 2010

Military Equitation or, A Method of Breaking Horses, and Teaching Soldiers to Ride, Pembroke, and *A Treatise on Military Equitation*, Tyndale 2018

My Horses Have Something to Say, de Wispelaere 2021

Principles of Dressage and Equitation, a.k.a. Breaking and Riding, Fillis 2017

Racinet Explains Baucher, Racinet 1997

Releasing the Jaw, Poll, and Neck DVD, Mark Russell 2021

Riding and Schooling Horses, Chamberlin 2020

Riding by Torchlight, Cord 2019

Riding in Rhyme, Davies 2021

Schooling Exercises In-Hand, Hilberger 2009

Science and Art of Riding in Lightness, Stodulka 2015

Sketches of the Equestrian Art, Barbier/Sauvat 2022

The Art of Riding a Horse, D'Eisenberg 2015

The Art of Traditional Dressage, Volume 1 DVD, de Kunffy 2013

The Chamberlin Reader, Chamberlin/Matha, 2020

The de Nemethy Method: A training seminar, 8 DVD set, de Nemethy 2019

The Ethics and Passions of Dressage Expanded Edition, de Kunffy 2013

The Forward Impulse, Santini 2016

The Gymnasium of the Horse, Steinbrecht 2018

The Horses, a novel, Walker 2015

The Italian Tradition of Equestrian Art, Tomassini 2014

The Maneige Royal, de Pluvinel 2010, 2015

The New Method of Dressing Horses a.k.a. A General System of Horsemanship, Cavendish 2020

The Portuguese School of Equestrian Art, de Oliveira/da Costa 2012

The Quest for Lightness in Equitation and Equestrian Questions, Nelson/L'Hotte 2021
The Rules of Riding" Gli Ordini di Cavalcare, Grisone/Tobey 2023
The Spanish Riding School & Piaffe and Passage, Decarpentry 2013
The Spanish Riding School: The Miracle of the White Horse DVD,
    US Lipizzan Association 2021
To Amaze the People with Pleasure and Delight, Walker 2015
Total Horsemanship, Racinet 1999
Training Hunters, Jumpers, and Hacks, Chamberlin 2019
Training Your Foal, Ettl 2022
Training with Master Nuno Oliveira, 2 DVD set, Eleanor Russell 2016
Truth in the Teaching of Master Nuno Oliveira, Eleanor Russell 2015
Wisdom of Master Nuno Oliveira, de Coux 2012

www.ingramcontent.com/pod-product-compliance
Lightning Source LLC
Chambersburg PA
CBHW051355110526
44592CB00024B/2997